Indiot

ANA SPOKE

Published by Ana Spoke, Melbourne, Australia
www.anaspoke.com

ISBN-13: 978-0-9944312-3-3
ISBN-10: 0-9944312-3-6

For Josh

Table of Contents

THAT'S JUST TOO MANY GRAND!

"Hey, is that you?"

I paused digging in my backpack and looked up at the woman in front of me. I tend to defy most rules, but not the waiting-line etiquette, which requires you to stare straight ahead and pretend not to notice people around you, let alone point fingers or address them directly.

I shook my head and returned to my bottomless backpack. I was already pissed off and far from excited to sign autographs. If it turned out I forgot my passport, my adventure of a lifetime was going to end right here, at Los Angeles International Airport.

Friggin' shitbucket.

I paused for a moment, closed my eyes, and sucked in a big, relaxing breath of air that consisted, for the most part, of body odor, fries, and cheap coffee. All those wankers who claim they love traveling had to be lying—so far traveling smelled like shit.

"You're that girl," the woman said.

I looked up again. Judging by her velour sweatpants and vinyl Louis Vuitton ensemble, she wasn't the kind who gave up easily.

"No," I said, trying hard to contain the internal combustion. "I'm not. I just look like her."

"Yes, you are," Velour Sweatpants said and snapped her fingers, as if to a beat only she could hear. "You're ... what's your name?"

"Isabella," I said on autopilot and inwardly cursed myself. "I'm not her."

1

"That's right." Velour Sweatpants elbowed her run-of-the-mill husband, who was engrossed in his phone. "It's Isabella."

"That's nice," he said without looking up or pausing his rapid thumb movements.

Velour Sweatpants elbowed harder. "Hon, she's that billionaire girl."

The man looked up and brightened instantly. "Hey, you're that billionaire girl!"

"I'm not a billionaire," I said. "I mean, Isabella Maxwell isn't a billionaire. She just worked for Mr. Hue, who is a billionaire, but that's all. And those rumors about her being pregnant with his baby are *not* true."

"How do you know that?" Velour Sweatpants said. "You must be her, then." She was pretty perceptive for someone unable to distinguish between a luxury bag and a cheap Chinese knockoff.

"Everyone knows that, it was in all the tabloids," I said. "Look, I get this all the time, it must be the blond hair, but I'm not her."

"Yeah?" Generic Husband said and held up his phone for me to see the photo from my graduation, the one in which Mr. Hue had just hoisted me up in his arms. "Tell me this is not you."

"Good one, hon." Velour Sweatpants slapped him on the shoulder, and he beamed at her. They were a team, however obnoxious, and I felt a sharp pang of jealousy.

"It's not me," I hissed and returned to exploring the cavernous insides of my backpack. My passport seemed to have vanished. At least my ticket was there, safe in the travel agency's mini folio.

The couple left me alone for the moment, but I could see from the corner of my eye that they were taking selfies with me in the background. I turned my back to them, only to find that people behind me were also taking photos.

"I'm not her." I looked around. The Manchester Airlines check-in line snaked and looped this way and that, surrounding me on all sides by the sea of waiting passengers. They were all staring at me as if I were a talking gorilla in the zoo.

"I think you're awesome," a businessman in a suit and flip-flops said breathlessly. "Mr. Hue was a fool for letting you go."

"Thanks," I said. "I mean, he didn't. Cause I never met him."

"I see," Flip-Flops said and swallowed nervously. "Can I take a quick pic with you?"

"Please don't," I said. My plea had the opposite effect. Flip-Flops tried to put his arm around my shoulders while everyone else held up their phones, excited about their Facebook or Twitter updates, or whatever. It would've made a dramatic update for my own Twitter feed—something about struggling through economy check-in on my way to a philanthropic journey. I might have made it as a celebrity, but I was still close to my people. Like, super uncomfortably close.

I was trying to push Flip-Flops away with one hand and cover my face with the other when my suitcase bumped me in the shin. I looked down just in time to see an opportunistic teenager tearing off the address tag.

"Hey!" I yelled and reached to snatch the tag from him, but just then, my backpack strap dug into my shoulder. I turned and slapped a hand reaching into its open depths. "No! Cut it out!"

There was another tug at my suitcase. I bent down, ready to grab the teenager by his sticky-fingered hand, but it was some new guy, pulling on the zipper.

"What are you doing?" I said, incredulous. It was one thing to take pictures, but this mob looked hell-bent on taking a souvenir, too. Flip-Flops pushed the newcomer aside, and I was about to thank him when he hunched down, trying to push the zipper past the tiny combination lock.

I kept shouting "No!" and "Stop!" but nobody listened. People at the back were shoving to get a better look or a chance at something they could sell on eBay, and for a moment, it seemed that the crowd was going to pummel me as if I were a quarterback in possession. I was preparing to take a knee and make a dash on all fours between legs and suitcases, when security finally showed up, in the form of two cops in bulletproof vests. One of them, a scrawny man, started talking on his shoulder radio and asking people for their IDs. Instantly, everybody was back to starting positions, claiming to be unsure of what had just happened.

"What's going on here?" the other cop said, a stout woman with a no-bullshit attitude and equally stern hair. She looked me up and down. "Are you that girl?"

"Yes," I said. I wasn't about to lie to the po-po. I heard "Told you" whispered behind my back. "I'm Isabella Maxwell. I haven't done anything wrong. I'm just waiting for check-in."

"We'll see about that," the female cop said and unsnapped the tape used to corral the waiting herd into something resembling order, then ushered me and my belongings out of the waiting line. For a few terrifying seconds, I was sure I was being arrested. Maybe Sandra reported me for breaking our contract, or it was illegal for someone to pretend to be pregnant and then leave the country. I was preparing to plead the Fifth, when the cop stopped in front of the first-class counter.

"Got a situation here," she said to the attendant, an angelic young thing in a tiny pillbox hat. "The general public got a bit too excited about a celebrity sighting."

I felt a flash of relief from not being arrested, followed by an even hotter wave of pride at getting some long-overdue respect from a uniformed officer.

"I see," the attendant said in a voice I would have expected from a third-generation blueblood. I wondered if "classy" was a mandatory subject in Manchester Airlines flight attendant school. She looked my way. "And you are?"

"Isabella Maxwell," I said.

"Of course." The attendant smiled. It boggled my mind to think that such an exquisite creature was serving at a counter and not working in the "industry," or at least married to one of her first-class clients. There was no hope for the rest of us, educationally and genetically inept. "May I please have your tickets and passport, Miss Maxwell?"

I handed her the ticket. "I can't find my passport. I've checked my backpack at least a hundred times, and all I can find is my driver's license. Is that okay?"

"I'm afraid it has to be a passport with a valid visa," she said apologetically, as if it was she who did such a poor job packing for my trip. "Have you checked your pockets?"

I patted the sides of my brand-new rain jacket. It cost a fortune, but I had to be prepared for anything India was going to throw at me, and, according to Dad, at least one of those things was going to be constant rain. It seemed hopeless until I felt the hard edge of the passport in the chest pocket and the overwhelming sense of relief in roughly the same area.

"Oh my God," I mumbled, trying to fish it out. "Thank you! So embarrassing … I always put things in special places, so I don't forget them, but then I can't remember the special place and end up losing them anyway."

The attendant studied my ticket, my crispy-fresh passport, and a printout of my electronic tourist visa. The cop's radio came to life in a burst of static, and she mumbled something into her shoulder.

"Are you traveling in economy today?" The attendant looked up, puzzled.

"Yes," I said, resisting the urge to tell her that calling a two-thousand-dollar ticket "economy" made about as much sense as calling a regular cup of coffee "Grande."

"So, would you like an upgrade to business or first class?" the attendant said, still puzzled.

Wow. I remembered stories of people getting upgraded, although I couldn't remember how they'd managed to accomplish that miracle. Being mobbed by economy passengers seemed as good a reason as any.

"Yes, I would," I said. "Thank you!"

The attendant nodded and returned to her keyboard. "That will be eight thousand, three hundred, seventy-eight dollars and ninety-eight cents. How would you like to pay?"

The world went dark for a moment while my brain struggled to add this new number to the original cost of the ticket. I wanted to ask her in which universe would anyone *like* to pay that much money for anything, except maybe a house, but seemed unable to get enough air in my lungs to do so. I grabbed my chest and had a flashback to Dad doing the same just a few months prior.

That seemed to get the cop's attention. "What's the problem?" she said and moved in closer, towering over the counter with her radio and attitude.

I pointed at the attendant, who in turn pointed at her screen. "That's the upgrade price."

I couldn't see the screen, not that it mattered. "So the total price is eleven grand?" I'd finally found my voice and my basic math skills. "That's just too many grand!"

The attendant looked at the cop for support. "It's, you know. The oil prices?"

"That's just bullshit," I said authoritatively. "I can buy an oil rig for that much." I had no idea what the asking price of an oil rig was, but I knew that eleven grand could buy me a car. Could probably buy a boat, too—I'd rather sail to India than get tricked by a business.

"What's the problem?" the cop asked again. It sounded like she was asking me what *my* problem was.

"It's too much," I said. "Don't you think eleven grand for a plane ticket is too much?"

"It's insane," she said, and I brightened up. "But *you* can afford it."

I bit my tongue. The cop wasn't only scary—she was right. My definition of "affordable" took a giant leap in the months after Sandra sold my tell-all book. Still, I couldn't bring myself to think of the money as my own.

"It's for the poor," I said. "The money, I mean. I'm only going to India to help this prince get back his fortune and convince him to spend it on helping the poor."

"Right," the cop said, giving the attendant a "something's wrong with this girl" look. Her radio came back on. She conversed with it in abbreviated gibberish, then turned back to me. "I have to go. Are you going back to economy then?"

I turned to look at the economy crowd, which seemed to have grown even larger in the last few minutes. People were still snapping photos of me, only slightly more discreetly.

"Are you sure you can't upgrade me for free?" I begged the attendant. "On account of me being a celebrity in danger?"

"There's no danger," the cop said. "Jessica Alba flies economy all the time."

"Yeah, but she's adorable, and everyone likes her," I snapped. "I can't imagine anyone trying to take her stuff when she's not looking!"

The cop's radio buzzed again. "I've gotta go," she said, and left.

The attendant and I stared at each other in silence.

"You've got to help me out here," I said finally.

"I can't." She was apologetic but unmovable, like a beautiful stone wall.

"I can't go back to economy," I said, heaving the suitcase up onto the belt, where she could see it. "Look—they tore off my address tag! If I go back, they'll tear me to pieces."

She shook her head. "I can't."

It seemed that my Puss-in-Boots sad pleas were not going to melt her defenses. I had to think fast.

"Okay," I said, pretending to drag the suitcase away. "I guess I'll have to let the millions of my Twitter followers know about this injustice. Hard to believe Manchester Airlines can be so cruel to its customers."

"Millions?" Her voice changed. Perhaps there was a secret gate in that stone wall after all.

"Yeah." It wasn't exactly millions, but it was close to *a* million, which was still a lot, even if most of those were porn accounts. "My Klout score is, like, ten thousand. Do you know what that means?"

She shook her head. To be honest, I didn't know either. I just remembered that funny word mentioned in some article on social media. I strained every available neuron to remember what it said. "It means that I'm a social media influencer. That's right. If I tweet about Manchester Airlines trying to steal eight grand out of the mouths of malnourished

Indian babes, while ignoring the bullying of a celebrity, it goes viral just like that." I snapped my fingers to indicate the speed with which I expected every bit of crap I posted on Twitter to become a social media sensation.

"Could you wait just a moment?" the attendant said and dialed a number. She whispered a name and a desperate-sounding request into the phone while I pretended not to care about the outcome.

Within a few moments a male manager appeared, once again confirming gender inequality in the workplace. He listened patiently to my complaints, as impressed with my social media presence as the girl attendant. More importantly, he had the right access codes to alleviate "this unfortunate inconvenience" and assure that I would "have a nice flight" with Manchester Airlines.

I checked my Twitter-follower count on the way to the first-class lounge. It was up by at least a couple thousand in just the last hour. *We can do anything.*

Me and this army.

I CAN'T! DO THIS! SOBER!

The thin line between love and hate is nothing compared to the one between envy and guilt.

To think that just a few months ago, I barely had enough to eat and spent most of my time longing for the simple luxuries of everyday celebrity life. Now I was overwhelmed with guilt at letting others carry my luggage, serve my drinks, and do everything I was perfectly capable of doing myself. The first-class lounge was nearly empty, so the staff almost fell over each other asking if I needed any help in sitting down and flipping magazine pages. The constant catering was suffocating rather than relaxing—after all, I wasn't a baby or a quadriplegic. I kept saying "No, thank you" to everything and didn't even go to the bathroom, afraid that someone would follow me, offering to wipe my butt.

Worst of all, I had nothing to post on Twitter. I couldn't bring myself to brag about the upgrade or to post a picture of my champagne glass. I was finally "young money" with "rubber band banks" in my bra, but I just didn't feel like rapping about it to my peeps, who were probably at work, suffering in the name of mortgages and tuition. Lucky for me, it was less than an hour before the first-class passengers were asked to board and I escaped, bypassing the waiting line on my way to the plane.

This is a temporary setback, I thought, following a flight attendant to my seat. *I'll be immersed in poverty in no time.*

Yet somehow, those thoughts were replaced by giddy exhilaration as soon as I settled into a velvety-soft seat inside my very own little cabin. *Okay, so maybe this is worth the money,* I told myself, eyeing every lavish

9

detail. It looked almost like an office cubicle, only obviously an exceedingly expensive one. Instead of a computer monitor, my own impressive TV promised to occupy the endless hours. Curvy walls hid me from other passengers, so I kicked off my shoes and curled my legs under me.

Maybe this could be fun.

The flight attendant returned and offered me a warm and moist towel with a pair of silver tongs. I was about to tuck it into the front of my tank top when I saw her raise her eyebrows just so. *Oh, right,* I thought, and instead used the towel to wipe my hands and gingerly touch it to my neck. She gave me a gracious smile and left. *Get a grip*, I said to myself, silently thanking the cubicle walls for shielding my faux pas.

The walls not only provided privacy, they also promised to guard me against chatty old men and screaming kids. I mean, seriously, who can afford to buy first-class tickets for their children? *Millionaires, that's who. Millionaires with spoiled, bratty kids.* I listened to the sounds of hushed voices and thanked God—it seemed I was lucky that day and the millionaires left their spawn at home.

Just one last bit of unexpected luxury before I get to Delhi, check in to a reasonably priced three-star motel, and start working on my plan. I took out my journal and paused with my pen over a blank page. This kind of monumental event required a profound journal entry, but nothing suitable came to mind. Instead, a tiny and tired voice inside me said I deserved a break after all I'd been through during the last year. That recharging batteries could help me come up with a new idea, a sequel to my book, perhaps this time with actual literary value. If the first one sold for a million, the second one was sure to sell for two or three, which would come in handy—there would never be enough millions to help all the needy of the world. It's a big place.

I put the journal down, closed my eyes, and draped the towel over my face, waiting for the inspiration to strike. It didn't, but I was willing to wait.

"Thank you." I heard the melodic voice from under the towel shield. I peeled off one corner and saw the flight attendant guiding a young woman into the seat next to me. I couldn't help but stare at her through the gap in the partition between us. Tiny, exquisitely beautiful, and perfectly groomed, she looked like a princess, or maybe even Ariana Grande, in her tight black dress and shoes that could pass for art. Her platinum-blond hair was precision cut into a stylish bob, each hair perfectly smoothed into its place.

I peeled off the rest of the towel and attempted to smooth my own hair, but it was too late.

"Hello," the young woman said. "Are you all right?" She had just a touch of some accent, something that made her sound even more like royalty.

"Who?" I said. "Me? Yes. Why?"

Her lips curled into a hint of a smile. "I heard there was quite a commotion at the check-in."

"Oh," I said. "You heard about it?" A strange mix of anxiety and guilty pleasure washed over me.

"Are you by any chance Isabella Maxwell?"

"Yes," I said. For some reason it was easy to admit the truth to her. Maybe because it didn't seem likely that she would care to steal my backpack. "Right now, though, I wish I was someone else."

"Don't we all," she said with a laugh that sounded like tinkling fairy bells.

I looked her over again. Why she'd want to be anyone else was beyond me. I couldn't help staring at her perfectly smooth tan skin, which glowed next to the diamonds dripping from her neck, earlobes, and fingers. But even diamonds couldn't compare to her eyes, deep blue and bewitching, like those blue lagoons I'd seen only in movies.

Miss Perfect misinterpreted my staring. "Oh, where are my manners," she said and extended her hand. "I'm Vivien."

Her hand was slim with perfectly straight fingers, so unlike my own. I shook it, once. She had a good grip, not too firm, but not limp either. Dad would have approved.

Who am I kidding. Dad or any man with a pulse would've lost it already.

"Nice to meet you," I said. "It's my first time in first class."

Vivien chuckled appreciatively, and this hurt my feelings—I didn't mean it as a joke. "Actually, it's my first time flying. Not everyone can afford overseas vacations, you know. Some people have to spend the summer with Grandma."

She didn't flinch, which was impressive considering my sudden change of attitude.

"I hardly have time for vacations myself," she said in her angelic voice. "This is a business trip, and paid for by my employer."

Wow, what kind of a job comes with first-class tickets? Then I remembered I almost had one of those jobs once, and that I wouldn't want it back no matter what perks it offered.

A few moments of silence passed. "I really like your shoes," I said after I couldn't stand it anymore. "I've never seen anything that … blingy."

"Oh," she said, stretching one slim, well-toned leg in front of her, offering me another look at the shoe that belonged on a shelf in a museum or an art gallery. "These are my favorite Manolos."

So that's what they look like up close. "Are those … diamonds?" I pointed at the shimmering strip that hugged her petite toes.

She giggled. "Oh, no. If they were, I wouldn't wear them on a plane."

Right, I thought, glancing at her necklace and earrings. On second look, they appeared to be fake as well.

She misinterpreted my staring again. "These shoes are really comfortable," she said in a defensive tone.

"Are they?" The heels had to be at least four inches.

"And quite affordable. Comparatively, of course. You can't help it in my line of work. Sometimes you just have to spend money to make money, isn't that right?"

I had nothing, other than the same question about what it was she did for a living. I chose to nod thoughtfully instead.

"Certainly not like some of the shoes out there," she said. "You could literally spend millions on a pair if you wanted."

"No way," I said. "Millions?"

She smiled knowingly. "Oh, yes. Of course, you don't get to see them except at the Oscars, and the security there is just impossible. But you are in luck. India Couture Week starts tomorrow, and House of Borgezie will be showcasing their new platinum stilettos. You should see them—about a hundred thousand dollars, and every Cinderella's dream."

"House of … Bourgeoisie?"

She laughed, whole-heartedly this time. "It is, isn't it? Ah, you are so clever!"

I laughed along, trying to cover my embarrassment. *How could she be this beautiful, and nice, too? Some people just have it all.*

"I don't think I'll have time," I said. "I'm going to India to help the poor." It came out like the worst cliché possible.

Vivien raised an eyebrow. "Are you representing a charity?"

"No, I'm going by myself," I said, thinking that starting a charity wasn't such a bad idea. Perhaps it could be a joint venture between Prince Amar and me.

I was about to launch into the story about the prince and his scheming uncles, when one of the flight attendants started a one-woman show at the front, accompanied by a prerecorded safety message. I studied her every movement, more than a little worried that I wouldn't be able to find the life vest in case of emergency, however unlikely.

"By yourself?" Vivien said. She seemed utterly blasé about the correct brace position. "Will you have a bodyguard in Delhi?"

"No," I said, groping under my seat. Vivien must have read my mind; she pointed at a compartment in the armrest. I lifted the cover and saw a small package, still in plastic wrapping. I gave her a grateful smile, trying to suppress the urge to pull out the life vest and hug it like a security blanket.

"Sorry, what were you saying? A bodyguard? Do I need one?" My experience with bodyguards was limited to Kurt and Serge, and well, I wasn't going to hire *them*. Even if they were released on good behavior.

Besides, other than flying, nothing else scared me at that moment. The world was my tiramisu—I hate oysters.

"Judging by what just happened at the check-in, I would say yes," Vivien said. "And considering this is your first time visiting India, absolutely. You are in for quite a culture shock."

The plane jerked into motion, shocking me even more than Vivien's words. "We're moving!"

"Yes," Vivien said. "Just getting taxied to the runway."

She seemed so cool about it all, as if flying was on par with grocery shopping. Maybe it was. I took a deep breath. "Sorry, what were you saying about a bodyguard?"

"You will need one. A single blond girl like you in Delhi is sure to get into trouble."

I didn't expect a blonde joke from someone who was blond herself. *Maybe she didn't mean it.* Maybe I was just overreacting, which was understandable—it's not every day you get mobbed and then have to fly.

The plane's engines revved up. Suddenly, the whole idea of traveling to India seemed pretty stupid. I realized with painful clarity that, despite its fancy trimmings, the cabin itself was just a giant aluminum can. A can stuffed full of passengers and explosive fuel, about to hurl itself through the air at a speed of so many miles per hour, it boggled my mind.

"Excuse me!" I called out to the flight attendant.

She was at my side in an instant. "Can I help you?"

I didn't feel any guilt this time. "Yes, please. I'd like to get off the plane."

It took a moment for her to process my request. "I'm very sorry, ma'am," she finally managed. "I'm afraid it's not possible. We're about to take off."

"Oh," I said and groped the armrests in the same desperate way I do at the dentist's. "May I please have a drink then? Something strong? Make it two."

"I'm really, really sorry," she said. "I can't serve alcohol while we're still on the ground. The bar is locked. It's the license conditions. What about a glass of Perrier for now?"

"Does it have alcohol?"

The flight attendant chuckled, but I gasped for air with such angst, she almost choked on her laugh. "I will bring you a cocktail or anything you want as soon as we lift off. I promise."

"How long will that be?"

"Just a few more minutes," she said encouragingly. "Definitely less than five."

"Oh, God!" *I have just five minutes left to live.* On second thought, the cabin looked nothing like an office. More like a coffin, one of those expensive padded deals with satin pillows. *As if the dead really care about comfort.*

"What is wrong?" Vivien leaned over.

"I can't! Do this! Sober!" I managed between huge gulps of air. The good news was that all that hyperventilation was getting me lightheaded. At this rate, I was sure to pass out well before we became airborne.

"Just a few more minutes," the flight attendant pleaded.

"Just give her a drink, I will not tell," Vivien said.

The flight attendant looked back and forth between us. "I could lose my job."

Poor thing. The panic in her eyes brought back the not-so-distant memory of when I myself lost a job because of some irate customer who was unable to see the humor in my creative waitressing. "Oh. Sorry. That's okay, then," I said and burst into a flood of tears.

"I'll get you that water," the flight attendant said, and cleared out.

"Take this." Vivien pressed something into my palm.

My hand moved the small pill to my mouth on complete autopilot. "What is it?"

"Valium. It will help you relax."

The flight attendant returned with a glass of water and disappeared again before I could ask for an update on our preflight status. I took several quick gulps and turned to Vivien. "Was that really Valium? It's not working!"

"Give it a minute," she said. "Forget the bodyguard—you will need a lot more of these once you get to Delhi. Do you have any idea what's in store for you?"

I remembered Amar and why I was risking my life in the first place. "I'll be fine once we land. I'm meeting up with this prince."

Vivien raised an eyebrow. The engines revved up to the sound of a tornado whipping about a bunch of scared pigs.

"Yeah," I said a little too loud. "I'm gonna help him win back his inheritance, and then convince him to help the poor with all those billions of rupees. And of course I'll write another bestseller about it—"

The plane lurched forward. I scanned the cabin for any early signs of structural failure, desperate for a window so I could at least supervise the pilot's performance.

"A prince?" I heard Vivien say.

"That's right," I said, working my seat belt like a ratchet. The plane vibrated worse than my old washing machine on the spin cycle. Somebody touched my arm and I shrieked, jolting against the chokehold of the strap, which was threatening to cut off all circulation to my legs.

It was just the flight attendant, looking even more pained than I was. She held a tray with two shot glasses on it, full to the brim with a clear liquid. I threw back one, realized that vodka meant we were now airborne, and killed the other. The flight attendant darted back before I had a chance to thank her.

"So, the prince," Vivien said. "What is his name?"

"Who? Oh, yeah. Amar," I said, feeling the calming warmth of alcohol spreading through my chest. Or maybe that Valium was real, after all. It also helped that the plane leveled out a bit and the engine noise switched down from screaming to a dull grumble. I relaxed my grip on the armrest.

"Prince Amar?" Vivien looked surprised.

"Yes." I poked my head out into the aisle. I could see the flight attendant and one of her colleagues serving drinks to other passengers, none of whom seemed to be having panic attacks. In fact I could hear laughter, as if people were actually enjoying this experience.

"Are you certain?" Vivien said.

I looked at her, sitting there all relaxed and confident. I was still thankful for her help earlier, but something in her tone annoyed me. So what if I was wearing jeans and sneakers instead of a dress and stilettoes? I too had rubbed shoulders with billionaires. Not literally, of course, but I'd worked with them, and they'd paid me huge out-of-court settlements. Not only that, I myself was now a celebrity, earning seven figures in one year. Very low, beginner seven figures, a huge chunk of which had already been gobbled up by agent fees and taxes, but all billionaires had to start somewhere—and if the current trend continued, I was going to be one in about five years. Ten, at the most.

"Yes, I'm sure," I said, digging through my backpack for the phone. "I have his photo … here."

Vivien studied the phone screen in silence, stunned. I calmed down a bit. Maybe she was just genuinely surprised at the breadth of my social connections.

"I take it you've never met." Vivien handed my phone back, a curious look on her face.

"No," I said. "He doesn't even know I'm coming, it's a complete surprise."

"Then how do you know where to find him?"

Her questioning was getting on my nerves. "He signed off his email with an address…." I picked up my phone and swiped at the screen a couple of times before my groggy brain registered that it was in flight mode. I thought about it and turned it off; no need to tempt fate any further. "I'll have to look it up later. He did email me a couple of weeks ago, asking for help getting his inheritance back from his uncles."

"I see," Vivien said in the same irritating cool tone of voice.

"What is it?" I asked, thankful for the calming effect of the vodka-Valium cocktail. One of the unfortunate drawbacks of becoming a celebrity was that you could no longer afford to tell someone off.

Vivien seemed torn. "I don't know how to say this," she finally managed. "That man," she nodded in the direction of my phone, "is not a prince."

"Yes, he is," I said, surprisingly unruffled. "He might have lost his fortune, but his uncles can't take away his birthright title."

"That's not what I mean," Vivien said. "He is an actor."

"He has to support himself somehow," I said through the light fog setting about the edges of my consciousness. "Acting is a perfectly fine way to make a living. I considered it myself at one point. Actors aren't stupid. There was even a US president once who used to be an actor. And Schwarzenegger is also in politics. Of course, he wasn't smart when he cheated on his wife, but I think that's beside the point."

Vivien just kept looking at me, silent, and then it hit me. "Oh my God! Is he a porn star?"

She put her hands up, laughing. "Oh, no, no. He is a regular star, and a respected businessman. The picture you have is a still from one of his films, in which he does play a prince."

"Well, that makes sense," I said, defensive. "If writers are supposed to write what they know, I would imagine it's easier to get an acting gig as a prince if you already know how to be one."

Vivien looked at me a moment, as if waiting for a punchline. "That photograph," she finally said, "is from a classic film, I can't remember its name, but I do remember it is really old. This man must be at least sixty or seventy by now."

"What are you trying to say?" I prayed silently that she would say something like *No, wait, I was wrong. This really is a prince, lucky you.*

"Did he ask you for any money?" she answered with a question.

"No," I said, listening to that one syllable stretch for almost a full second. "Well, yes, but he said he was going to pay me back a thousandfold. That's a lot. And anyway, what does money have to do with anything? I don't get it...." And then I got it, all at once. "Oh my God!"

Vivien didn't say anything.

"How can I be so stupid?" I addressed the roof of the plane, wiping tears with both hands. "Only an idiot would believe in such a ridiculous story! Scheming uncles, my ass …"

"You are not an idiot," Vivien said.

"Yes, I am. Only an idiot would try to hand-deliver scam money."

She put a soothing hand on my forearm. "So you haven't given him any money yet?"

"No," I hiccupped. "I didn't."

"Great. Then what is the problem?"

I tried to think. It was ridiculously difficult, but I managed to form a picture of my bank account, still full to the brim. "I guess there isn't one. Except that I'm on this plane."

"In first class."

"Yeah, I guesth." My tongue wasn't fitting into my mouth the way it normally did. "I just have to watch ten movies and once we arrive, I'll get a return ticket and go thtraight back home. That'll be a lethhon I won't thoon forget."

"Don't be so harsh on yourself," Vivien said.

Her sympathy was so unexpected, I burst into another flood of self-pitying tears. The flight attendant swam into my field of vision. "Is something the matter?" she asked with a look of someone obliged to do so against their best judgment.

"I need to get off thith plane," I said, and saw she was dangerously close to calling in the air marshal. "Or, you know, maybe get another shot?"

"Make that two champagnes," Vivien said, and almost instantly, two bubbly glasses appeared, along with a promise of a never-ending supply of alcohol as long as I stayed put in my seat.

"I can't drink champagne," I said to Vivien. "It's for theb … lebarations. What are we theblebarating? The discovery of the world's most gubllible moron?"

"No. How about the fact that you were smart not to give this 'prince' any money? That you are going to have an adventure in India, regardless of the reason that brought you here?"

I looked at her with newfound hope. With Harden gone and Tara too preoccupied with sex to care, I'd missed friendship more than anything over the last few months. Finding a friend would make this overpriced plane ticket worth every penny.

"I know," she said as if she'd read my mind. "How about we celebrate the start of a new friendship?"

I felt my chin tremble, this time with soppy feelings. We clinked our glasses, and I sipped the divine potion, letting the bubbles fill my head with effervescent joy.

Then all the lights went out at once.

YOU SHOULD SEE ME AT THE DENTIST'S.

All alcohol ever gets is a bad rap for doing its job, just like the traffic cops. Of course, everyone hates liver cirrhosis and fines, but imagine the world without happy hour or road rules. What a nightmare that would be.

It's quite possible that my light dinner of Valium, vodka, and champagne prevented a nightmare in which I flipped out midflight, was arrested by an air marshal, forced an emergency landing, which could have easily turned into an international incident, causing airline shares to plummet, and perhaps even starting a mass exit of investors from stock markets. My panic attack could have been the beginning of the next global financial crisis—with the butterfly effect, you simply never know.

Instead, when I finally came to, there was little drama, other than the pilot bitching and moaning about the heat at our destination. My memory struggled to catch a lurid dream in which I might have been doing naked yoga on the banks of a sacred river and being chased by the enraged locals, I wasn't quite sure.

I unglued one eye, then another. I was lying down, my seat magically transformed into a bed. Some kind of fancy breakfast, complete with way too many utensils, a teapot, and tiny cakes, was on the serving tray over my legs. I popped open a bottle of water and chugged it, ignoring the glass. My head was pounding in a too-familiar way.

Vivien was already up, looking like she just came out of a beauty salon. She was reading a foreign-looking paper.

"Good morning," I croaked.

"Good morning," she sang back. "Did you sleep well?"

"I think so." The dream was still bugging me. *Can foreigners do yoga in public? Fully clothed, of course.* I looked over at Vivien's legs, elegantly crossed to one side. It wouldn't have surprised me if she herself was a yoga devotee. Or a dancer maybe. How else could a person obtain such a body? I tried to think of an icebreaker appropriate for a Q&A session on her diet and local customs.

"Do you speak ..." I nodded to the newspaper. I almost said "Indian," but remembered just in time how I was chewed out by one of my community college teachers for referring to the Chinese language.

"Hindi," Vivien said and nodded. "I was born in London, but grew up in Mumbai."

Half-British, half-Indian, one hundred percent perfect. God damn it.

"Wow, that's really interesting," I said, fighting hard against the undertow of the old friend envy and something new and weird that felt like yearning. "I grew up in LaGrange. Georgia. In the US. It's really nothing special. I'd love to live in Mumbai for a while."

Vivien laughed. "I'm not sure you would fit in. Have you heard of *One Night in Bangkok*?"

Holy crap, she's a porn star. That would explain her employer springing for first-class airfare.

"No." I shook my head. "Is it a recent ... film?"

"It is a song. You never heard of it? It makes a hard man humble?"

I shook my head again, hoping she'd used protection.

"Doesn't matter," she said, returning to her paper. "One night in Mumbai will make you wish for home, sweet home."

I nodded and reached for a cake, seriously doubting that one night in Mumbai could be worse than Christmas lunch with my family.

"This is so delicious," I said, inhaling the first little jewel, my hand already reaching for the second. "I can't believe I missed out on dinner."

Vivien didn't reply. I stole a sideways glance at her profile, her delicate brow furrowed in deep thought. She kept leafing through the paper, scanning its pages for some unknown bit of information. What was I thinking? This was no porn star or even a dancer—the woman was all business, despite her glamorous appearance. I must have been wasted last night to think that I was good enough to be her friend.

As if she read my mind, Vivien folded the paper and put it down. "Are you excited?" she said with another one of her luminous smiles that could probably heal a sick man.

"About what?"

She laughed. "Oh, you are just hilarious! Your comic timing is perfect! And that deadpan face … honestly, you should have your own show."

"Thank you," I said and took a sip of my lukewarm tea, embarrassed and hopeful all at once. *What if the language barrier, or the cultural differences, or whatever, mean that Indians will assume I'm clever when I'm simply too tired to think?* Maybe I could make a few new friends who were unaware of the stupid mistakes I'd made back home. The thought soothed at least some of the self-flagellation I'd done last night in the throes of regret over my decision to fly halfway around the world.

Shit, we're still flying. While I was wrapped in luxurious comfort at that moment, there was still one more obstacle between me and my new people—the landing.

"How long till we land?" I asked the male attendant who came around to clear the remnants of my breakfast.

"Less than half an hour," he said, startled. "Can I offer you a cocktail?" I could tell that he'd heard exaggerated stories about my little panic attack.

"No, thank you," I said with a royal indignation, which turned to regret as soon as he left with my tray. *What would be worse, going through customs drunk, or going down in a ball of flames sober?* I imagined my parents watching *Entertainment Tonight*'s feature story of Isa Maxwell boozing it up on an international flight, and stifled the impulse to press the service button.

"Is everything all right?" Vivien asked.

I wanted to joke about holding hands as we went down, like Thelma and Louise, but it sounded creepy and inappropriate in my head.

"Yeah, all good."

"You don't look it," she said. "Would you like another—"

"Yes."

She giggled while searching in her purse. "Are you always this funny?" she said, passing a bottle to me.

"Only when I'm stressed," I said, fighting the childproof cap. "You should see me at the dentist's."

Vivien threw her head back and laughed for a solid minute. *She doesn't get out much,* I thought, watching her wipe tears from her eyes.

The bottle capitulated at last. I fished out a pill and tried handing the bottle back to her. "Thank you."

"Take another one," she said, still laughing. "They are very low dosage."

"Are you sure?" I said while my hands produced the second pill and shoved it into my mouth, almost against my will. "Tell you what, I'm gonna stay in Delhi long enough to get a prescription for my flight back."

Vivien laughed as if that was the funniest thing she'd ever heard. A tingle of hope fluttered in my stomach. Maybe we were destined to be friends, after all.

"I wish I knew about these long ago," I said, handing her the bottle. "Would've made last Christmas a lot better."

And that's how we spent the last half hour before touchdown, Vivien laughing while I was hamming it up and wishing I'd come to know her a lot sooner, too.

WHERE IS YOUR LICKER?

Few things in life are sweeter than falling into a new friendship. *Maybe this isn't random*, I thought, walking beside Vivien through the carpeted tunnel, overwhelmed with the relief of surviving my first flight. Of course, it was silly to think she was sent to me by the Universe as a replacement for Harden and Tara, but how else could I explain feeling so content in her presence? We were like two peas in a pod, even if one pea was much larger than the other.

"You're almost as tall as me," I said, looking down at her heels. "I can't believe you can walk on those stilts."

She chuckled. "I can't believe you keep coming up with those one-liners. You should write a book or something. Oh, wait—you already did!"

We both laughed, and just then the tunnel birthed us into Indira Gandhi International Airport, as proclaimed by the Samsung-sponsored sign plastered high above.

I don't know what I was expecting, but there were no *Slumdog Millionaire* kids begging for coins, and no Bollywood dancers spontaneously busting moves, only businesslike people and families moving through the enormous hall of polished stone and metal. I didn't expect the airport to be so *modern*. There was nothing *Indian* about it, other than the huge collage of shiny copper plates and giant concrete hands in what looked like sign language poses.

"Wow," I said to Vivien, feeling deeply grateful she was by my side. Without her, I would have panicked hard at the mere sight of all the signs drawn in fanciful squiggles, even though they were all duplicated in English. They could have been in Braille for all that mattered.

"Not what you expected?" Vivien said.

"No," I said, once again impressed with her mind-reading skills. "I mean, I didn't have any expectations." That was a lie, of course. At the very least, I expected more women to be wearing saris.

We moved slowly through the waiting lines for customs and baggage claim together, chatting and laughing like sisters. I was already dreading having to leave India and my new friend behind. Surely she had to come back to the United States at some point. She seemed to be doing such good business there. I wanted to ask if she had any plans for traveling back to Los Angeles anytime soon, but held off. It's important in any new relationship not to appear too eager.

We were almost done with the whole process when a uniformed man came up to us and looked me up and down. "Random check."

"What? Why me?"

"Don't worry," Vivien whispered, ushering me toward him. "Just act confident, don't say too much, and be patient. I will wait for you over there." She motioned toward the exit doors.

"I don't feel confident," I said. In fact, I felt very close to peeing my pants. I should have gone to the first-class bathroom when I had the chance.

"Then fake it," Vivien said.

I turned back to the officer, who motioned for me to move to the cordoned-off area with chairs and tables. I followed him, trying my best to look self-assured, but all I could think of was Dad's stories of foreigners caught smuggling narcotics and left to rot in foreign jails. I didn't pack any drugs, I was pretty sure of that, but at that moment, I was also quite certain that the pandemonium in the economy check-in was created solely to sneak heroin into my backpack.

I heaved my suitcase onto one of the tables on a wordless command.

"How much money?" the officer said sternly.

"What? Oh, you mean declared … nothing." It was such a relief to be asked about something so benign and boring. I even took my wallet out from my backpack and showed him my new American Express. "Credit card, no cash."

He gave me a doubtful look, and then I remembered.

Oh, God. The stash of rupees in my bra. Mom gave it to me, along with her teary kisses goodbye. It wasn't much, an equivalent of a few hundred dollars, but I had a feeling it would be made into a huge deal if it was discovered in a strip search. I imagined being strip-searched by the stern officer and almost died.

Luckily, he just grumbled something and unzipped the suitcase to ruffle through my collection of brand-new sundresses and meds supplied by Doctor Mom. Normally I wouldn't take any medications on a trip, but Dad's lectures on the unsanitary horrors of overseas public toilets were still fresh in my mind. My supply could stop the diarrhea of a whole village.

"For sale?" the officer asked, holding up a box of pills.

"No," I said. "It's for me. In case I get sick."

He picked up two more identical boxes and looked at me quizzically.

"In case I get very, very sick," I said.

He sighed. "Where is your licker?"

"What? Oh, you mean liquor? I don't have any."

"What you buy in duty-free?"

"Nothing."

"Nothing?" He seemed unconvinced. "Why not? Much cheaper. Where your gifts?"

"I didn't bring any gifts," I said. I should have brought one for the prince, but at least that was no longer a problem.

The officer gave me a look of utter disdain for people who don't buy gifts, sighed, and moved on to my backpack.

"What this?" he asked, pulling out my brand-new tablet PC.

"It's my computer," I said.

"For gift?"

"No," I said. "It's for me. To write stories about my travels. I'm a writer."

He gave me another look, this one suggesting I was better suited to being a drug mule, but put the tablet back in.

It went on like this for a while, with him pulling out everyday items and me having to name them as if we were in an English-as-a-second-language class. He even took out a box of tampons, opened it, and checked inside, presumably for drugs or cash. Or maybe for undeclared gifts, I don't know.

"*Bevakoof,*" he said finally, and with a sigh, motioned for me to collect my stuff.

"Thank you." I was so relieved, I forgot to write down his name for a scathing complaint to the airport officials. Instead, I used all my weight to compress things back into their respective containers, zipped them up, and left. The sense of relief was so overwhelming, it wasn't until I was back, standing in the line, that it dawned on me that something was wrong.

Vivien wasn't there.

She wasn't waiting for me near the exit. She wasn't on the other side, either. I looked frantically for her in the faces of people passing through the cavernous hall, but it was no use.

My new friend was gone.

IT'S NOT LIKE I'M A TERRORIST WITH A HOMEMADE BOMB.

I told myself not to panic, over and over, until I was near hysterical. I realized I didn't even have Vivien's number, and kicked myself for all that needless self-restraint. *Fools rush in, my ass—the real fools are left behind.*

A woman's voice came on overhead with an announcement in Hindi, or Klingon, or whatever. I didn't understand any of it, of course. She then repeated the same in pretty good English, but in my panicked state, I once again failed to grasp its meaning.

Think, damn it. The adrenaline revved up my brain until it produced a somewhat coherent thought—obviously, Vivien was also singled out for a random drug/undeclared gift check. That was a pretty good guess, except there was no sign of her in the security area, where the tired officer had moved on to harassing another random unfortunate. The follow-up burst of logic was that she'd been taken away for an actual strip search. I almost yacked at that mental picture. *Poor thing will need me more than I need her,* I thought, settling down on top of my suitcase to wait.

The next thing I knew, I jerked awake from the back of my head smacking the wall behind me, making it painfully clear that my brain had decided to call it a day. It hurt, but at least the mental fog was gone, replaced by an alarms-blasting and heart-palpitating panic.

Did Vivien walk past me, unaware that the vagrant slouched on top of a suitcase is her new best friend? How long have I been asleep?

My brain screamed for me to get straight onto a plane back home, but I almost threw up from that thought. I had to get some sleep, fast. Somewhere in my emails was a confirmation of a prepaid hotel booking. If I got some rest and food, and managed to stop the constant vertigo attacks, I could probably think of a better plan. I could even find Vivien later, in the Yellow Pages, or whatever they had here.

I could see the exit from where I was sitting. The sunshine streamed through a glass wall, and there were moving cars, which promised a short trip to a shower and a bed. My legs were still catching up to that part of the plan where they had to haul me up and walk all the way across the hall with my luggage. I decided to warm up by telling the world, or at least the part of it that had Twitter accounts, that I'd arrived in an exotic faraway place.

I found the phone in my backpack and turned it on. *Switching off your phone during flight can save lives—at least the battery life.* I couldn't wait to tweet it.

Vivien would have lost her shit at that one.

The phone beeped, and I held it up, ready to snap a selfie with the spectacular feature wall in the background, when I noticed the "no service" message.

"What the hell?" I tried the settings, then restarting, then settings again, before I had to admit that my Horizon Wireless plan didn't extend to any destination more exotic than Hawaii. *That would have been useful information*, I thought, feeling angry with Dad and his stupid lectures, which never mentioned communication issues. Then again, it would have blown my mind if Dad knew anything about technology or overseas countries, let alone technology *in* overseas countries.

"Fine, this is fine. I can totally deal," I muttered to myself, looking around for help.

I didn't have to look far. Just a few yards away, a blue kiosk wallpapered with cell phone posters promised a ray of hope. I dragged my suitcase over and shed my backpack with a thump.

"I need a phone."

"Hello," said the turban-clad guy behind the counter. "How are you today?"

I stared at him in complete shock. I mean, he looked so *Indian*, but his voice didn't have the slightest touch of an accent. It was like watching a dubbed Bollywood movie.

"Wow," I said. "Your English is perfect!"

"Thank you very much," Bollywood said politely. "That's very kind of you to say."

"Oh my God, where are my manners?" I said, blushing hot red. "Hello, my name is Isabella. I would like some help with my phone service. Hope you're having a great day. Thank you. Very nice to meet you."

I would have preferred a quick death, but Bollywood just smiled, pulled out several brochures, and launched into a discussion of my options. He sounded like a college professor giving a well-rehearsed lecture, outlining all the pros and cons of each plan.

"Sorry," I said finally. "I'm so jetlagged I can't follow any of it."

Jetlagged and stoned. Shit, I shouldn't have taken both of those pills—

"Understandable," he said. "Perhaps we can start you on a simple prepaid plan? You can always upgrade later, if your needs change."

"That sounds good," I said, trying to appear as sober as possible by standing up straight and smiling wide. "I like simple."

He nodded. "Great choice. Now I just need a copy of your passport, your visa, two passport-sized photos, and your hotel booking confirmation."

"What? Why do you need all that?" I said, wary of his sleek-talking. After narrowly escaping one swindle, I wasn't about to fall for another one.

"That's just part of the government regulations." Bollywood shrugged. "I am afraid it would not be possible to issue a SIM card without it."

"A what? I don't want any games. I just need an Internet connection...."

"A Subscriber Identity Module card. Don't worry, I will configure it for you."

I dug in the backpack for my travel wallet, unsure of what to do. All that jargon talk was suspicious, but the thought of not having an Internet connection crippled my defenses. I had only one option.

"I have my passport and some spare photos," I said, "but no copies. Are you sure you need all this? I mean, it's prepaid, so what's the problem? It's not like I'm a terrorist with a homemade bomb." I looked around, worried that joking about terrorists and bombs in an airport might mean a quick end to my trip.

"That's no problem," he said. "I have a scanner right here. It will take just a minute."

"Okay," I said and handed him the little navy-blue booklet, which still had that new-ID smell.

Bollywood busied himself with the copier, and I tried to talk myself down from the ledge. *Who in their right mind would want to steal my identity?* I had to admit that at that point, it would have been a welcomed break from being me. Let someone else worry about being conned or mobbed on the street, not to mention the guilt trips.

I don't know if it was the new drugs or my old impatience, but everything seemed to be taking forever. I watched the guy slowly and carefully copy my name from the passport onto a paper form, surprised that he didn't lose his shit—though it was quite possible that news of my fake baby with a gay billionaire hadn't yet reached these shores. *Who knows, maybe Indians don't give a damn about Isa Maxwell.*

"Here you go," he said finally, handing back my passport. I carefully slipped it into my travel wallet, secretly relieved to have it back, as if it were a talisman or something.

I was zipping up the backpack when Bollywood spoke again. "Now I just need your credit card."

"What? Why?" *I knew there was a catch.*

"To pay for the plan," he said. "Or would you rather set up automatic payments from your bank account?"

"Oh, yes, of course— I mean, no. Not from the bank." I wasn't about to give him the keys to the vault. "Would you take cash?"

He agreed to let me pay with cash and politely averted his eyes as I dove into my bra bank, and even showed me how to insert the tiny SIM card into the back of my phone. I nodded appreciatively, certain that I couldn't repeat the magic trick of sliding off the back cover without tearing off every single one of my nails.

We had to wait a bit for my new number to be activated. A few minutes of silent smiling was all I could take.

"So ... where did you learn English? It's really good."

"In school."

"Wow," I said. "I had two years of Spanish in high school, and all I can say is '*Por que no los dos?*'"

He smiled. "I also spent a year in Florida as an exchange student."

"No way," I said. "That's next door to Georgia. I'm from Georgia." Who would've known I'd meet an ex-neighbor within an hour of landing in Delhi. *What a small world.*

"I was in Gainesville," he said. "University of Florida."

"You're kidding," I said. "That's a great college. Go Gators!" I would have killed to go to Florida, but that was always out of the question, what with their stupid tuition and even stupider SAT requirements. I mean, why would a writer need to know mathematics? I could always hire an accountant to manage my investment portfolio.

"We all we got!" he said.

"Huh?"

"That's the saying. I say 'we all we got' and you say 'we all we need' back."

"Oh, I get it," I said, embarrassed, although it was the Gators who should have been embarrassed for teaching international exchange students such poor grammar.

He smiled. I smiled back. He checked the phone, but there was no confirmation text yet.

"When were you there?" I asked. "I went to Orlando in the summer of 2012, I think. I'm pretty sure we stopped in Gainesville on the way."

"Oh, I was there much earlier," he said and checked the phone again.

"Ah, okay," I said. "Was that right after 9/11? That must've been hard for you."

"Why?" he looked up at me.

"Oh, you know," I stammered, unable to tear my eyes away from his turban. "Those were scary times. For everybody."

"I suppose," he said and busied himself with the phone again. I pretended to be extremely interested in one of the brochures.

A little old lady draped head to toe in green silk hobbled up to the counter and hunched over to look at the smartphones on offer. *Amazing,* I thought, *third-world country, my ass. Look at this grandma catching up to the twenty-first century.* I made a mental note to tell Dad about it. He still refused to get a cell phone of any kind, let alone a smart one.

Bollywood asked the lady something in Hindi, which shocked me again. *He really is Indian.* I tried to imagine how cool it would be to converse that freely in two languages, but it seemed as likely as running a four-minute mile or any mile at all. I also tried to remember how to say "My name is Isa" in Spanish, but it escaped me. Not that it would be useful now, anyway.

The lady did not share my awe for Bollywood's multilingual skills and just waved him off, instead rudely pushing me aside to have a look at more phones. I raised an eyebrow at him, but got no love back. I guessed he respected elders more than paying customers. Served him right, because she didn't buy anything and shuffled off.

I was trying to think of something else to say, something appropriate, when my phone dinged. "Confirmation text!" he said with visible relief. "You are all set now."

"Awesome," I said. "Leave it to Indians to figure out technology, am I right?"

Bollywood didn't get my joke, instead returning to his monitor. "*Bevakoof.*"

"No, thank *you,*" I said, trying to remember how to pronounce *bevakoof* for the next time. It seemed that most locals spoke English, but it would still be cool to learn at least a few Indian words. *I mean,* Hindi *words. Dammit.*

I shoved the phone into my bra, collected my belongings, and started the long trek across the shiny white floor, being careful not to slip. I'd once slipped on polished marble in a similar cavernous hall, on the other side of the world, in what seemed like another life. I landed in a whole heap of trouble then, but I was determined not to let it happen this time.

NO, AMERICAN GIRL. I DRIVE.

Not every significant moment in life is marked by celebrations. Some of them slip by without champagne and piñatas, and it could be years before you realize that walking through a particular door changed your life forever. It would take even longer to fully appreciate that you could never go back to the peaceful ignorance, much like you could never go back to the dark safety of your mother's womb.

These particular glass doors parted silently and unleashed a hot, humid wave of unfamiliar smells. I hesitated at the threshold for a moment, every cell of my body begging me to go home, back to the mundane and familiar, and then I stepped outside. *Into India.*

At first glance, India looked very much like the airport—disappointingly unexotic and surprisingly modern. I was still under cover, in the shade of a curved canopy soaring high above me on massive, tree-like columns, although it did little to combat the heat. And boy, was it hot. In less than a minute, my body went into shock, drenching my armpits and lower back in sweat, and frizzing up my hair into an eighties' homemade perm. The humidity was palpable, although there wasn't a drop of the rain I was so worried about; not even a single cloud marred the bright blue sky ahead. I dropped the backpack, then took off my rain jacket and stuffed it inside.

"Taxi?"

I looked up. A young man was fast approaching. He didn't look like a taxi driver—in fact, he looked more like a thug-in-training, with a thick gold chain glistening in the open neck of his shirt. One of Dad's warnings popped into my head, the one about the airport hustlers. I struggled to recall the rest of his advice, something about prepaid taxis.

"No, thank you," I said politely but authoritatively, hauled up the backpack, and turned to go back inside, almost knocking over a small older guy who materialized behind me. "Sorry!"

The man seemed not to notice my rudeness, instead latching onto the handle of my suitcase with a happy shout of "Taxi!"

"No." I tried to wriggle back my property. "I don't need a taxi."

The man pointed at my suitcase in confusion.

"Yeah, okay … I do need a taxi, but I'm going back to the airport to get one."

That made him smile again. "Taxi," he said, redoubling his efforts to wring the suitcase from my hand. The younger one grabbed the side handle, and we launched into a three-way tug of war to rhythmic chants of "Taxi!" and "No!"

Our game attracted the attention of a small group of other men nearby. They shouted something in Hindi at the two guys bothering me and started walking over to us. *Thank God.*

One of the newcomers, a bearded character in a red billowy silk shirt, pushed aside the small guy and grabbed the suitcase handle.

"Taxi," he said, and tugged, hard.

"No!" I yelled, pulling on the handle with one hand and trying to peel off his fingers with the other. "I said, I don't want a taxi. Leave me alone!"

I felt a tug on my backpack and spun around to see yet another dude trying to take it off my back.

"Please, y'all," I cried, trying to change my tactics. "Please, let me go back to the airport."

"Yes, yes." Silk Shirt nodded with his whole body and continued trying to tear the suitcase out of my hand.

It was hopeless. They were shouting and shoving each other, getting louder and more agitated. I had a moment of horrible flashback to the Los Angeles airport. It had been the same kind of free-for-all, except in this case they were more interested in my luggage than in my celebrity status.

My brand-new suitcase twisted, dangerously close to spilling various unmentionables onto the pavement. *Where's security when you need them?*

I was scanning the crowd for anything resembling a uniform when someone else caught my attention, an old man with a bushy white beard and fluffy white eyebrows. Something about his kind and wrinkly face and his hands folded on top of his jolly belly made him look like an ethnic Santa Claus. He seemed way too old to be capable of or interested in assaulting me, instead just standing there, on the edge of the mosh pit, watching the show as if it was *Survivor* on TV.

"You!" I pointed at him. "You! Taxi!"

It took a second, but then Santa snapped out of it and started making his way toward me through the ocean of waving hands and crushing bodies. Others tried to block him at first, but I kept pointing and shouting until they gave up and started to disperse, spitting what could only be insults at my savior, until it was just him and me, face-to-face.

"Hi," I said, trying to catch my breath.

Santa pointed at the suitcase, then pointed back behind him, at the parking lot.

"Yes," I said, relieved. At that point, I preferred sign language to any foreign one. "I need a taxi. Thank you."

He nodded again and shuffled off toward the parking lot, waving for me to come along. I followed him, dragging my suitcase behind me and trying to keep my hideously heavy backpack from slipping off my sweaty shoulder. We proceeded in silence for a few minutes.

"What a beautiful airport!" I said.

"Yeah, okay," he mumbled, half-nodding and half-shaking his head, kind of like one of those dashboard bobbleheads. He didn't look at me, instead closely examining the ground before his shuffling feet.

"It's so modern!" I gushed, trying to annunciate more carefully. "Very beautiful."

"Yeah." He bobbed his head in response. "Yeah, okay."

I didn't know what else to say, so I decided to give him some space and instead take in my new surroundings. There still wasn't anything particularly exotic about them, as we kept walking past familiar-make cars ranging from older Toyotas to shiny new Volvos. I was composing an introduction to my first article in my head, something about the Western influence on an ancient civilization, when my guide stopped.

"Taxi," he said, pointing at a rusty heap of an unidentifiable origin. It was kinda cute, with big round headlights that stared sadly over the mouth-like grill. It was small and curvy enough to remind me of my Beetle, and I felt an unexpected stab of pain at the memory. Beetle deserved a far better end than getting blown to pieces.

I pushed the memory away and tried to concentrate on the issue at hand. The car, if it could be called that, did not look land-worthy, or identifiable as a particular make. All of its paint was obliterated by corrosion, and more than one body part was secured to the frame with wire. I was seriously doubtful it would start, or that it would stay intact once it got going.

"I don't know," I started saying and turned to look back at the airport. In the blur of the heat waves emanating from the pavement, it looked like a mirage. There was no way I could make the trek back, not in my current state of exhaustion, dehydration, and drug-induced haze. Even if I did, I could fall prey again to the pack of taxi-driving wolves.

I looked back at my almost-driver, who regarded me without expression, his hands once again resting comfortably on top of his vast belly.

"Okay," I said finally. Surely, if the car survived the trip to the airport, it could get me to the hotel. I made a mental promise to plan better next time, helped Santa get my suitcase into the tiny trunk, and got into the passenger seat.

Which had a steering wheel.

What the hell? I thought, staring at the wheel as if it was a magical, talking white rabbit.

"American girl!"

I'd startled for a second, but thankfully it was just Santa at my door, shaking with laughter. It was so weird to see him so animated that it took me another whole second to understand that I was in the driver's seat. Which was on the right side of the car.

Santa was practically hysterical, so much so I was genuinely afraid he'd have a heart attack right here.

"No," he managed between choking coughs, "no, American girl. I drive."

That was the most he'd said since I'd met him. I climbed back out of the car and circled to the other side, trying to concentrate on the positives: my new driver spoke English, which meant we could communicate, and that meant I was more likely to end up at my desired destination.

The passenger seat looked exactly as I'd expected, except for the small issue of being on the wrong side of the car. I settled into the worn-out seat and searched the door for the window button, but there wasn't one. Instead, there was a funny little handle, kind of like the one my granny had in her Oldsmobile. I cranked the handle, and the glass moved down with a tired grunt.

All part of the experience. Is this exotic enough for you, Isa?

Santa squeezed in behind the wheel and took some time to get a key into the ignition. I should've noticed how hard it was for him to find the little key slot, but I was too distracted by trying to find the seat belt.

"Where's the seat belt?" I asked, digging in the crevice between my seat and the backrest.

"Yeah, okay," Santa said and turned on the ignition. "American girl." He bobbed his head in what had to be disbelief.

It took just a couple of sputters, but the car finally came to life and we moved, Santa leaning over the wheel, squinting through the windshield and his thick glasses.

"The seat belt?" I said again, making hand motions across my chest, when I noticed there wasn't one across his. I was about to remind him to put it on when we pulled out of the parking lot.

Into the wrong traffic lane.

ARE YOU SURE THIS IS THE RIGHT PLACE?

I t's fine to occasionally move out of your comfort zone, keeping in mind that it's not about how far you go, but about how fast. And trust me—you don't want to do it at fifty miles an hour.

"Jesus!" I shrieked and cowered down, bracing for impact. Time seemed to slow, and I managed a couple of stupid thoughts—*I hope there's an airbag*, and, *I need to make a living will*—before I took the risk of opening one eye.

I wasn't dead. We were still moving. Not only that, the cars around us were moving *in the same direction*. The upcoming traffic was on the right, safeguarded by a well-maintained planted median strip. I seemed to recall something about other countries driving on the wrong side of the road, but it had never occurred to me that I would one day see such an abomination for myself. It was worse than the metric system. Just looking out at the road was making me nauseated. It could have been the air, too, consisting mostly of fumes. If I had a handkerchief, I would have tied it over my nose and mouth, like most of the motorbike drivers that were passing by, farting exhaust in each other's faces.

"What, American girl?" Santa said, seemingly unperturbed by my outburst.

"Nothing," I lied. "It's so … beautiful." I waved my hand at the road ahead of us and felt a twinge of vertigo.

He bobbed his head in that half-agreement and half-disagreement thing. I willed my eyes to ignore the road and to study my driver instead. *I don't even know his name.*

You don't know where he's driving, either, Dad's voice said in my head. *He might be kidnapping you, for all you know.*

Well, you don't know anything, so shut up! Dad in my head sulked. It was better that way. Gave me some broadband to think.

"My name is Isabella," I said, thinking it wouldn't hurt to befriend Santa, just in case. "Maxwell. You can call me Isa for short."

"Good coffee," he said. "You rich, American girl?"

"What?" I said, terrified he'd recognized me. Then it clicked. "No, I'm not related to the Maxwell Coffee owners. My dad is a historian. And my mom is a nurse, but she was a housewife for most of her life."

A nice, decent family, utterly incapable of paying a ransom.

Santa didn't say anything, no doubt disappointed that I was so average.

I followed his gaze, which was a mistake; I almost threw up again. *Holy crap.* It seemed that neither Santa nor a single other driver on the road believed in the two-second rule. The pretty median strip was now gone, and the upcoming traffic was separated from us by nothing more than good will.

I turned to my side window, but it hardly helped—the madness was all around, with cars and mopeds way too close, swaying about without any regard to road rules, using only horns to warn each other of their next illegal move. The constant beeping of the horns seemed more like an appropriate overture to an accident, which was bound to happen any moment. *How ironic would it be,* I thought, *for the trip to end in a tragedy before it even starts.*

I was imagining the tributes by my devastated Twitter followers, and the outpouring of #IsaIsGone, when a strange green-and-yellow contraption passed us. It looked kind of like a three-wheeled scooter with a canvas canopy. The front was barely wide enough for the driver, and at the back, a couple huddled together on a bench seat. The woman held a baby, and the man balanced a sizeable suitcase on his lap. Neither was wearing a seat belt. Hell, the scooter thingy didn't even have doors.

"What is that thing? I mean, is that even legal?" I turned to Santa. He didn't answer, preoccupied with waving out the window for the other, moderately faster cars to pass us. He was using his other hand to periodically push his glasses back up his nose, so he was practically driving with his stomach. I turned away and tried to block that image too.

Another green-and-yellow buggy passed us, and then another, each with three passengers crowded in the back. *Holy crap*, I thought, *those are taxis.* It had to be the kind of "taxi" I would've been offered had I gone the official path. This really was a different world, so maybe different rules applied. I relaxed just a little, congratulating myself for following my gut to a more car-like transport, however ancient, slow-moving, and illegal.

We drove in silence for a few more minutes. I tried to figure out how long it had been since we'd left the airport.

You should've been there by now, Dad piped up again, and I pressed an imaginary red button in my head.

"Deluxe Castle New Delhi Hotel, D-166, Channa Market?" I'd read aloud the reservation on my phone, at a volume more appropriate for a busy nightclub.

Santa seemed to hear me this time. "Yeah, okay."

That settled my nerves a little more. I turned back to looking out the window. The highway had been replaced with a city street, and not a single thing—cars of foreign makes, enormous palm trees, and people dressed in every shade of the rainbow—appeared familiar. Everywhere I looked, there were dogs, and not one with a collar, much less a leash or an owner.

A gleaming, charcoal-gray monster of an automobile passed us, beeping its way through the thicket of moped drivers. Each one of its huge shiny rims had to cost more than my Beetle. I couldn't see the driver behind the pitch-black tinted windows, but the sight made me wonder if there were princes in India after all.

I'm in India! Just a few weeks back, I was a naïve and helpless girl, a pawn in the game of a powerful agent, unable to make a single decision for myself. Yet here I was, a grown woman, on the trip of a lifetime, perfectly capable of taking care of myself. I imagined staying for a while, really getting to know the locals, maybe learning to speak a bit of Hindi and making curries and that awesome flat bread. Eventually I'd figure out how to drive in this crazy traffic, maybe even buy a moped to get around and go shopping at the local markets….

I must've passed out, because I was in one of those markets, dressed in a sari, in the middle of an intense haggle over the price of flour and spices, when the merchant screamed in my face.

I jerked awake. The driver of the car next to us maneuvered close enough to spit curses at Santa and almost close enough to touch me. I reeled back. He was driving like an escaped mental patient, weaving closer and pulling away, only to veer toward us again. He was using his free hand to shake an angry fist and to occasionally address the heavens—I would imagine with prayers for a quick demise of my driver and me.

I rolled the window back up as fast as I could.

"What's his problem?" I cried to Santa, who was indifferently calm as usual.

"Ah, okay." Santa bobbed his head. "No problem. We drive slow."

With that, he turned the wheel and forced his way into another undefined lane to an accompaniment of beeping horns, angry shouts, and most definitely death threats.

I squeezed my eyes shut and recited the only prayer I knew, the one Grandma had taught me before I was cool enough to start questioning religion. I repeated the words over and over, like a spell that would make me invincible to unreliable foreign cars and their angry drivers. Images from Dad's presentation on the dangers of international travel kept floating up from my subconscious, and I did my best to stomp them out. *Those are things that happen to other people, nothing like that will ever happen to me.*

I continued this wishful thinking until a sudden stop almost launched me into the dashboard and my eyelids flew open.

"Deluxe Castle New Delhi Hotel," Santa announced.

I sighed with relief, stepped out of the car, and surveyed my accommodation. Its only feature reminiscent of a castle seemed to be its age. By the looks of the window air-conditioning units precariously sticking out into the void overhead, I would place the building sometime circa mid-twentieth century. There wasn't any signage anywhere to confirm Santa's statement.

"Are you sure this is the right place?" I asked, feeling a new wave of anxiety. "This can't be right."

"Yeah, okay," Santa said, heaving my suitcase out of the trunk.

It seemed I didn't have a choice. *Capable adult*, I repeated my mantra. I could always get another taxi, maybe even one with seat belts. I pulled the rubber-banded bankroll out of my bra and asked Santa how much he wanted.

"Three hundred rupee, yeah? Okay," he said, holding up three fingers. I looked at my stash. All I had was thousand-rupee bills. Three hundred rupees had to be something like a few bucks. Surely it wasn't right.

"Are you sure?" I asked him.

Santa bobbed his head, looked down, and finally said, "Two hundred rupee, yeah, okay."

I should have been happy for unexpectedly winning my first-ever bargaining argument with a local, but it made me sad instead. I looked down at his beat-up sandals and back at his beat-up car.

"No," I said firmly.

Santa was about to protest when I handed him one of the bills. He took it, head bobbing, then looked at me with the comical expression of a kid who'd just found a hidden Christmas present.

"No, no," he said, trying to give the money back to me. "Not so much, only two hundred. Two hundred rupee."

My heart almost burst with joy. Just one hour into my humanitarian trip, and I'd already made one poor man happy.

"Yes, yes," I said through a smile that was threatening to strain every muscle in my face. "For you. My friend."

Santa looked like he was about to have a heart attack again, or maybe burst into tears. I was so moved by my own generosity, I was about to burst into tears myself. It was best to leave on a high note.

"Thank you, my friend," I said, grabbed the suitcase handle, and dragged it toward the ancient front door.

DELUXE CASTLE NEW DELHI HOTEL.

Girls who babble on and on about how much they love surprises must be those who have sentimental childhood memories about princess-themed birthday parties, or those who get flowers without a "Sorry I called you a bitch" card. I, for one, am fine with knowing what's coming, whether good or bad.

I knew my digs were going to be substandard from the brief survey of the exterior, but the hotel continued to surprise me well past the entrance. The damn front door was so heavy, I had to lay into it with my shoulder, and finally with my whole backside. Nobody rushed to help me, even when I almost tumbled in butt-first. I managed to steady myself, got it together, and turned to take in my surroundings.

The lobby was dim and warm, despite the lazily moving ceiling fan and the noisy air conditioner firing on all cylinders. The walls were painted bubble-gum pink, which did little to hide the plaster cracks but provided a cheerful contrast to a huge black spider hanging from his ceiling web. A couple of backpackers were chatting in the corner, with a third lying, seemingly asleep, across a row of chairs. It would have been like walking into a frat house the morning after a breast cancer fundraiser if it wasn't for the wall display of keys above the front desk. Behind it, a hotel clerk surveyed my arrival with the indifference of an average voter during elections.

I dragged my suitcase toward him. "Hi, is this New Delhi Castle?"

I don't know what I was hoping for. Maybe that he would come to life and point to the correct hotel nearby, one where I wouldn't fear an appliance falling on my head. Instead, he looked at me with no perceptible change of expression. "Deluxe Castle New Delhi Hotel. Yes."

"Right," I said, kicking myself for not checking reviews on Trip Advisor or something. Or for allowing just twenty bucks per night for my accommodation budget. I did have excuses, plenty of them—like the stress of the last-minute booking and the price of the plane ticket. It was hard to spend so much money on the trip when I'd already earmarked it for the orphans and maybe a couple of saris.

I glanced back at the backpackers who'd stopped talking and watched me with a lot more interest than the staff member. A smart thing to do would have been to go out in search of another option, but I was simply too exhausted. "I have a reservation, Isa Maxwell."

The man's expression changed to slightly annoyed, as if I just woke him up from an afternoon nap. It took a few more minutes of repeating my name, spelling it, and finally writing it out on a pad, until he finally found my reservation.

"Yeah, okay," he said, even more irritated. "Isa-bela Max-vel. Passport and credit card."

What is it with all the passport requests? I thought, digging into my backpack in search of my wallet. I poked blindly at tissue packs, traveler's guides, random pens, and pillboxes until my hand dove into a large and empty pocket.

I looked down. My hand was sticking out of the backpack's side. I stared at it for a few seconds, unable to comprehend how it could be *outside* the backpack when my arm was still *inside* it. It took another few seconds to understand that it was sticking through a cut that wasn't there before. I pulled my arm out and held the backpack up to the dim light. The cut looked far too neat and large to be an accidental rip.

It took me close to an entire minute to get that I'd been robbed.

"Oh my God, oh my God, oh my God," I chanted, shaking everything out onto the floor and then searching through the wreckage for the familiar shape of my travel wallet, even though I already knew I wasn't going to find it.

"How you goin'?" asked one of the backpackers in a typical Hollywood-Australian accent. He was kinda cute, with beach-blond hair and long, lean body.

"Where? I just came here," I said, feeling close to tears. "Maybe it's in the taxi … oh my God, I've lost everything. My passport, and my traveler's checks, and all the credit cards!"

"Crikey! She'll be right, mate."

"What?" I had an easier time understanding Indians than I did this guy. I scrambled up to the front desk clerk. "I've been robbed!"

"Yeah, okay—no passport, no stay," he said, looking relieved not to be stuck with checking me in.

"What do you mean, 'no stay'? I can pay in cash…."

"No passport, no stay." The clerk bobbed his head like Santa. It didn't look cute on him.

"You can crash in our room," Australian piped up. His friend laughed. "We got bunks. You can get on top if you want."

"No, thank you," I said with exaggerated politeness. On the second look, Australian looked suspicious, especially with the tattoos covering up most of his left arm. Nobody would get that kind of artwork unless they'd been in a gang or worse yet, prison. I'd never met an Australian before, but I remembered something about them being convicts.

"No prostitute in rooms," the clerk said.

"Prostitute? Who are you calling a prostitute?" I said, trying to keep my right hand from flying up into his face. "For your information, I'm a bestselling author!"

The clerk studied my outfit and then cast his eyes around the lobby, returning to my face with a look that said that no bestselling author would ever consider lodging in New Delhi Castle Hotel, no matter how deluxe.

"Fair dinkum?" Australian said. "What'd you author?"

"An autobiography," I said, immediately realizing that it might not be wise to reveal my identity to a potential ex-convict.

"You go now," the clerk said.

"Where? Where am I supposed to go?"

"You should probably go to the police station," Australian said. I looked at him in shock. The last thing I expected was for him to suggest the authorities.

"That's actually a good idea. Thanks."

"No worries, mate." He winked at me in a way that made me wish I wasn't in such a mess. *Maybe he's misunderstood. Maybe he just craves the pain of a tattoo needle to replace the numb feeling of being alone in this world....*

I willed myself to return to reality, which was now dominated by the angry clerk, who wanted the undocumented prostitute out of his fine establishment, pronto. It took more negotiations and the waving of a thousand-rupee bill, but I finally got him to order me a taxi to the police station.

"Do you want me to come with you?" the Australian bad boy offered.

"No, thank you," I said. "I got this."

And I already got a bleeding heart, thank you very much. No need to discover that you're gay, or married, or just a kind soul without any interest in my ass.

No, thank you.

SO IT'S MY FAULT?

The taxi looked a bit more modern, and the driver was a lot younger, but I didn't give him a tip despite the debilitating guilt. It was no match to the fear of sleeping on the street, against which my only defense was the magic wand of cash in my bra. I kept nervously checking that it was still there until the driver became so distracted that we nearly ran into the back of the car in front of us. After that, I occupied my hands with hugging the backpack into my chest like a shield.

The police station looked more like an apartment block than an official government building, except for the red and blue sign and a large group of police officers hanging out at the front. They looked like military guerrillas in their khaki uniforms and berets, which made me more terrified than hopeful. It didn't help that they all stopped talking and openly stared at me as I dragged my suitcase up the stairs while pretending not to notice the attention.

This lobby, too, was warm, but it was brightly lit with overhead halogen lights, and the reception clerk was a lot more helpful. It was a uniformed officer, and a woman to boot, which instantly made me feel better about my situation and that of India's equal employment opportunities. She ushered me into a small room with a desk and two chairs and asked me to wait.

Minutes passed, and my earlier confidence in Delhi police forces began to wane as I took in my surroundings. The room was depressing, perhaps on purpose. It was painted the shade of mint green only Martha Stewart could love, and even that was already ruined by water-leak stains blooming in one corner. The barred window was open, but it was still smothering-hot in there. The only form of air conditioning was a desk fan, but for some reason it was mounted high on the wall, out of my reach. I tried my best to stay put behind the desk, which was covered in cryptic scratched-on messages, until I felt close to passing out on it.

"God helps those who help themselves," I mumbled, pulled the chair to the wall under the fan, and clicked the button on its now-vertical pedestal. Nothing. I clicked it again. The fan was dead.

"Isa-bela Max-vel?" said a man's voice behind me.

I almost fell off the chair. "What? I mean, yes."

Another officer in uniform appeared, only this one was distinguished by a pilot-looking hat. He looked like an exhausted field marshal, with a spectacular, meticulously groomed moustache and tired eyes set in deep, dark circles.

"Can I help?"

"Yes," I said, wishing I'd stayed in place and fainted behind the desk instead. "Sorry, I just wanted to turn on the fan. A bit hot in here."

I climbed down and carried my chair back to the desk. Moustache bent down, pressed a button next to the electrical outlet, and the fan whirred to life. I'd never before seen an outlet with a button on it—you'd think people who thought of putting it there would have thought of installing an air conditioner, too.

"Thank you," I said, relishing the breeze. I thought about asking for a glass of water, but Moustache motioned at the table so sternly I decided to choose my battles.

"Can I help?" he said again once we took our respective seats.

"Yes, please," I said, once again full of hope. "My wallet has been stolen, I don't know when, I only found that out, like, fifteen minutes ago. See, I was at this hotel, the Delhi Deluxe New Castle, and the clerk was very, very unhelpful, and then he wanted my passport, and then I was looking for it, and there's a hole in my backpack." I paused for a breath and to show the officer the cut. "So obviously somebody stole it, but I don't know who, or where, it certainly wasn't the taxi driver, he was very nice, although I suspect he isn't really an official taxi driver, but I know it wasn't him. I mean, I did fall asleep for maybe a minute in the seat next to him, but surely he couldn't have done it—he had a hard enough time just driving. And he was so sweet, there's just no way. I know I had the passport with me when I was buying the phone card, so it was probably one of the other taxi drivers who mobbed me afterwards, and let me tell you, I'm sure none of them were official, either. You should probably look into that."

The officer took a notepad from the desk drawer with the same tired look. "So your wallet is stolen?"

"Yes." I stopped my eyes from rolling just in time.

"Where it was stolen?"

"Like I said, I don't know," I said, trying my best to keep it together. I had a feeling that Moustache wasn't the kind of man touched or scared by a woman's tears. "I realized it in the hotel, but I'm pretty sure it was earlier."

"Was it taxi driver then?"

"No, like I said, I don't think so."

"So it was at airport?" Moustache said.

"Probably. Like I said, it had to be one of the other taxi drivers," I said, realizing I would never see my wallet or any of its contents ever again. "Please help me."

"Okay," Moustache said. "You need to report at airport police station. You need to make appointment...."

"Appointment?" I cried, no longer able to hold back the flood of hurt and disappointment. "Why at the airport? Aren't we in a police station right now?"

"This is rules." He shrugged. "You report where it is stolen."

"What about your duty to catch the perpetrators? Aren't we sworn to protect the public? I might be foreign, but I'm public!"

Moustache seemed unmoved by my outburst. "We probably not catch them," he said with a look of Buddhist-like acceptance of the fact. "Delhi has many of pick-pockets. You should be more careful."

"So it's my fault?" I sobbed, incredulous. "Vivien was right, it hasn't even been one night, and I already wanna go home…. Except I can't, because I don't have a passport and now it looks like I'll never get it back!"

"You can get new one." Moustache shrugged.

"I can?" My tears dried instantly.

"Yes," he said. "You need to file police report and pay fee. Then you get new passport."

New passport. Those words sounded like music. Sung by angels.

"You need proof of identity," Moustache said.

"What?" The angels choked.

"The proof that you are American."

"You've got to be kidding me!" I cried again. "The passport was my proof!"

"Do you have driver license?"

"No … I mean, yes, but it was stolen too. It was in the wallet."

"Yeah, okay," he said and fell silent for a moment. I wiped tears with my hands and studied his face for any sign of hope. There wasn't any—he looked close to falling asleep. Finally, he blinked a few times. "Birth certificate?"

"What? No. My parents have that. I mean, who brings their birth certificate to an overseas trip?"

"Okay," he said and returned to staring into space. "That is not good."

I had not one but two good comebacks for that—one about Captain Obvious, which was doubly funny because he was wearing that strange hat, and the other one I forgot, but I do remember it was awesome. Thankfully, and despite the heat, I had enough smarts to know that it wasn't in my best interest to insult an officer. I'd watched enough *Cops* to learn that lesson.

"There's got to be a way out of this," I said instead. *Surely I can't be the first idiot to lose their shit in India, both literally and figuratively.* That was pretty funny, despite the circumstances. I made a mental note to tweet it later when all this was just an amusing anecdote to tell at parties.

Moustache seemed to have done some more information processing. "Your parents fax copy of birth certificate?"

I didn't have a comeback to that because he finally made sense.

"Oh my God, of course!" I leapt across the desk on instinct to hug him but caught myself in time to change the hug into a painfully awkward handshake. "I can call them right now."

"*Bevakoof,*" Moustache said, wriggling his hand out of my grip.

"No, thank *you,*" I said, proud of having the foresight to shove my phone into my bra instead of the God-forsaken backpack. Not only that, I'd also installed Skype on my parents' desktop PC before leaving and promised to call them every day, although of course I had no intention of doing so. Funny how things work out sometimes.

"You go now," Moustache said, looking even more exhausted. "Go to airport to provide First Information Report. It is done at station close to where the crime happen. Then go to American embassy."

"But I don't know where it happened," I said. "Can't you pretty please do that report here? What if it did happen at the hotel? There's just no way to tell. I can't afford to waste more time going back to the airport. The embassy will close before I get it all figured out!"

Moustache stared at me, unblinking. "I can do, maybe, but what if I have trouble? There can be, what you call it, fee?"

"Is there a fee? I can pay a fee, that's no problem."

"No fee for you," he said, a touch irritated, "but great-great inconvenience and trouble for me."

"Oh," I said. "I thought you said there could be a fee. That's too bad. I'd rather pay a fee than go back to the airport."

He stared into space above my head for a moment, then tried again. "Maybe if I *compensation* for the trouble, I do the report. No problem."

A dim light flickered on and off in my head. *He wants a bribe.* The word sounded so dirty in my head, yet it fit the run-down room and my desperate situation. *Maybe it's not as immoral to give bribes under duress.* I fished in my bra for another bill. I didn't have to look at it to know that it sported a man in glasses and a number with three zeroes.

"Is that ... enough?" I asked, unsure if Moustache would ask for more, or arrest me on the spot for attempted corruption of a police officer.

The appearance of cash had a remarkable effect on Moustache's stamina—he leaned over the table and made the note disappear with a flourish of an expert card magician. It improved his mood, too. The next thing I knew he was off to prepare the damn report, leaving me alone with a task more difficult, more terrifying than climbing Mount Everest.

Calling my parents.

I BET IT'S NO POSTCARD.

It was about noon in Delhi, which meant there was still a chance that back home Dad was up, surfing the Net for proof of his latest conspiracy hunch. I clicked on the picture of my parents and listened to the dial tone. I was about to give up when it changed to the noise of a clicking mouse, shuffling chairs, and hushed voices.

"No, you're not doing it right!" I heard Dad say. "You have to click it."

"I clicked it already!" Mom said, irritated and excited at once.

The screen remained blank.

"Hi, guys," I said. "Your camera is off—"

"I told you!" Dad said, and I heard what seemed to be a struggle over the mouse control.

"Let me do it," I heard Mom say. "Stop touching it!"

"Dad." I tried to remain calm. "Let Mom figure it out."

There was a brief silence, permeated by heavy breathing and more mouse shuffling and clicking.

"Is it working yet?" Dad asked.

"Mom," I said. "Click on a camera button."

"I told her to click it," Dad said.

"Dad, just let her do it."

"Honey," Mom said. "There's no camera button."

"Yes, there is," I said as patiently as I could. "It's blue. With a white camera on it."

"They're all blue," Mom said.

"It's this one," Dad said. "This one. Click on it."

The line went dead. After a moment or so, I called them back. This time, the screen lit up with their faces, excited and way too close to the camera.

"Hey," I said. "I can see you guys!"

"How come we can't see you?" Dad asked. "I told you to click it."

Mom didn't answer him, but I could feel the tension across the thousands of miles. Funny how Dad was right next to her, and yet he couldn't tell she was about to lose it.

I looked at my screen. For some reason my camera was off. I was about to turn it on when I thought better of it. Maybe it was best that my parents didn't get to see exactly where I was.

"I'm not sure what's wrong with it," I said. "It doesn't matter. Let's just pretend we're talking on the phone."

"But we were looking forward to seeing you," Mom said.

"What does this India place really look like?" Dad asked. "I bet it's no postcard."

"It's better than a postcard!" I said. "It's exotic, and it's real, not like some Bollywood movie. And it's really hot."

"That sounds nice," Mom said. "It was quite chilly here this morning."

"It was thirty-nine degrees," Dad chimed in. "Did you know that this fall is already the coldest since 1987? Not in terms of severity, of course, the coldest day on record is still October 26, 1936. However, when we consider the *longevity* of the cold, as in the number of consecutive days below the average—"

"Dad!" I said. "What does the weather have to do with anything?"

"You said it was hot in India," Dad said, defensive.

"Yes, but I did not provide a breakdown of its climatic patterns!"

"I would be very interested in ..." Dad started, but Mom elbowed him. "What else, honey? How was your flight?"

"It was great," I said. "I got upgraded to first class. For free!"

Mom emoted extreme excitement, and Dad tried the same, although I could tell he thought he'd never fly, no matter what class.

"And you should see this airport. It's really modern. It's a modern country," I added, trying to push the images of green-and-yellow tricycle taxis out of my mind. "And the locals are very friendly," I added once those images were replaced by the mob of taxi drivers.

"That's so exciting, honey," Mom said. "Have you been on an elephant ride?"

"Mom! I just got here, like two hours ago."

Now it was Dad's turn to do the elbowing.

"Anyway," I said, remembering why I called them in the first place. "I've had a little problem, and I need your help."

"Are you okay?" Mom asked.

"What did you do?" Dad said. "Do not speak to anyone without a lawyer! Once they get a confession out of you, there's practically nothing—"

"I didn't do anything!" I yelled. "My wallet got stolen, and I just need you to scan my birth certificate and email it to me."

"Stolen!" Mom practically fainted, and Dad went on complaining that I never listen to him, especially when he talks about the prevalence of pickpockets in India. I asked him to explain how I was supposed to guard against my backpack getting cut open, and we went on screaming at each other for a few minutes until I threatened to hang up. I wasn't going to do it, of course; I needed the birth certificate. But my bluff worked perfectly: Dad backed off and just sat there, all puffed up and fuming, while I talked Mom through scanning and emailing the document. Good thing she was constantly copying recipes from borrowed books and updating Facebook with pictures of her baking achievements. I would've had an aneurysm if I had to explain how to attach a file to an email. They wanted to keep talking about India, but I made an excuse about having to go to the embassy, told them to say hi to Felicity, and hung up.

I AIN'T GOT A MADE IN THE USA STAMP ON MY ASS!

I t would be impossible for someone to have lived a full life without once bribing someone else. Mothers bribe their children with chocolate to get them into a car seat, then give teenagers new cars just to get them out of the house. No wonder those kids grow up bribing their dates with dinners to get them in bed, where those dates bribe them with epic blowjobs into committed relationships, thus completing the circles of life and corruption.

Still, never before have I bribed an official with cash, in part due to the fact that I never had any. *It's only a few bucks*, I kept thinking over and over, waiting for Moustache to come back with either my report or a set of handcuffs. To my overwhelming relief, he returned with the paperwork and a smile, and even ordered one of the younger officers to give me a lift to the embassy.

The trip over was short and cool as hell. We flew through the streets, sirens blazing, not that I wanted any more attention on my pale person. This time, nobody dared to bully us in traffic, instead getting out of the way as if we were starring in *Bruce Almighty*. Also, I had a seat belt, which hugged me with a promise that a bit more of familiar home, sweet home was just around the corner.

This time I knew we were in the right place as soon as I saw the golden eagle over the entry, its wings spread as if for a welcoming hug. I wasn't so sure about the rest of the building, which looked like an enormous trailer surrounded by a wrap-around porch, some scraggly bushes, and a reflecting pool with a few pissy fountain streams. I climbed the endless front stairs, dragging my suitcase up one step at a time, wondering why we couldn't afford a better building in a country where everything seemed to be so cheap.

Despite its humongous size, the interior overflowed with people of all colors, moving about, clutching their document folders, almost all smiling. I would've been smiling too if I had any documents to clutch. So far all I had was a copy of a police report and an email with an electronic copy of my birth certificate. *Hope this works,* I thought, getting in line for an airport-style security checkpoint. I was about to heave my suitcase up on the conveyor belt when a big Indian guy in official apparel stopped me.

"You can't bring it." He pointed at the suitcase.

"Why not?" I didn't care about the clothes anymore, although instinct told me to hold on to the medications and toilet paper, which made up half of the volume. Still, it was my property, and I felt entitled to drag it with me everywhere.

"Terrorism threats," the guard said.

"Look at me," I said, exhausted. "Do I look like a terrorist?"

He looked me up and down and shook his head. "Rules and regulations. You have to check it in. What's in the backpack?"

"My computer."

"You can't bring it."

"Why not?" I said, getting irritated. "They let me take it on the plane. Aren't you gonna scan it anyway? What kind of bomb can fit into a computer?"

The guy's quiet look suggested that his handgun trumped my logic. It was game over for me and my luggage.

"Fine," I said and dragged the suitcase and my feet over to the side counter, where I exchanged all my stuff for two slips of paper.

I returned to the checkpoint empty-handed but excited. The lobby was almost within reach, beckoning me with promises of help. The guard ignored my cocky smile and waved for me to walk through the metal detector.

It buzzed.

"What is it now?" I said, exasperated.

He swiped a magic wand up and down my body. It buzzed in front of my cleavage, and the guard's expression changed from bored to intrigued. "Do you have any body piercings?"

"No," I said, puzzled. "Oh! It's just my phone." I rummaged through my bra and produced the offending object.

"You can't bring it," the guard said. He was starting to sound like a windup doll.

"But I have to," I said. "It has my birth certificate copy on it. My parents emailed it to me 'cause I lost my passport."

The guard shook his head. "No."

"Are you kidding me? Why?"

"Terrorism threats." Maybe he wasn't a windup doll—he could have been one of those robocops retired from the field due to circuit board malfunctions.

I don't know if it was his brash arrogance, or the heat, or my general exhaustion, but just then my own circuit board malfunctioned.

"I'm not a terrorist!" I shouted, not caring that the random noise around me had hushed. "I'm an American citizen! I was robbed! I need a new passport so I can go home!"

I could feel everyone's eyes on me, but it didn't matter. *So what if someone recognizes me?* I was prepared to bribe or brag my way out of this.

"Do you know who I am? I'm *Isabella Maxwell*. But how am I gonna prove that, huh? I ain't got a *Made in the USA* stamp on my ass!" I smacked the area in question. "You have to help me!"

The guard leaned in, and for a moment I thought he was going to comfort me, but instead he snatched the phone from my hand.

"Give it back!" I yelled, rushing at him.

That's when the other guards rushed me.

I WAS JUST, YOU KNOW, MAKING SMALL TALK.

Despite its many shortcomings, being famous is great—seriously, a lot better than good. Celebrities might bitch about the invasion of privacy, but notice that they do it on Twitter, secretly hoping their moanings will get retweeted and score them a few more potential stalkers.

Personally, I was never again going to complain about fame, no matter how many mobs or *Star* reveals I had to endure. It was my bulletproof vest, heavy and cumbersome at times, but a welcome shield against life's random shootings.

"You're very lucky," the embassy representative said, offering me a tissue box. "Very lucky that your photos are all over the Internet. Otherwise, that little outburst coupled with the lack of identification would have meant a night in jail, pending further investigation."

I blew my nose and contemplated my answer. We were in a private office somewhere in the depths of the embassy building. This one was as small as the one at the police station, but it was modern, clean, and more importantly, air-conditioned. Even better—the rep, an American guy in his thirties, was nice enough to offer me a glass of water and let me use the staff bathroom, where I had a few quiet minutes to reflect on my predicament. Now, the quick trawl through the Internet reminded me that I, in fact, was a celebrity, and that it was about time I started acting like one. Humility and good intentions only get you so far in this world, whereas my connection to a powerful billionaire, real or otherwise implied, already got me out of the waiting line and possibly out of jail. The search also returned a few articles about my million-dollar advance, and if worse came to worst, I was prepared to pave a golden brick road out of this nightmare.

The rep must have misunderstood my silence as a veiled threat. "I'm very sorry, Ms. Maxwell," he said, shifting under my gaze. "We'll do our best to help you get your documents. In fact, we can issue you a temporary travel document right now."

I nodded, still unable to come up with anything half-intelligent to say. Maybe it was best I stayed quiet and just let him worry himself sick over a potential lawsuit.

"Is there anything else?" The rep hesitated. My silent treatment improved his disposition with every passing minute.

"Yes," I said. "Can you help find whomever did this to me? I spoke with the police, but they made it out to be my fault."

"Unfortunately, we don't get involved in the Indian legal system," the rep said apologetically. "American citizenship doesn't entitle you to any special privileges."

That irked me. "I'm not suggesting I need to be treated any differently from anyone else, but a crime has been committed against an American citizen and the local authorities seem to be uninterested in solving it. Somebody has to."

"We can certainly pass this information on to the FBI," he said politely while his eyes chastised me for attempting to take valuable time away from defending the homeland against terrorists.

"That won't be necessary," I said. God forbid the FBI discovered I'd smuggled undeclared cash into the country, or that I then used that cash to bribe a police officer.

He drummed his fingers on my police report in front of him. "I'd like to ask you a question if you don't mind, Ms. Maxwell."

Oh God. How could he possibly know I paid for that piece of paper? *He's just bluffing. Stay cool.*

"Sure. What is it?"

He kept drumming. "It's of a personal nature."

What does he know? "Personal?"

He blushed. "Have you and Mr. Hue, you know … before he got … there were these pictures, you know what I mean?"

"No, I don't know what you mean," I said, no longer scared and feeling a hot wave of anger, like a death ray, emanate from my forehead. "And frankly, I can't believe that an embassy representative like you would even suggest that—"

"I'm not," he said and put his hands up. "I was just, you know, making small talk."

"Small talk?" I said, aiming the death ray straight between his eyes. "I'd rather not. How about we return to the matter at hand?"

"Excellent idea," he said, needlessly folding and unfolding the report. "As I was saying, we'll provide you with the temporary travel documentation. We can even help you get access to your funds."

"Good," I said, feeling the heat beginning to dissipate from my temples. There was no point in getting worked up over some idiot's prying. At least it looked like I could stop worrying over my diminishing bra bank.

The rep picked up the phone and put it back in its cradle. "Um, Ms. Maxwell? Would you like me to call your bank for you?"

"That would be nice," I said with a queenly air of superiority. "It's Bank of United States."

The rep nodded and made himself busy with the phone. I was about to pull my own phone out, ready to update the world on the next act in this tragicomedy, when he turned to me with a look of shock and suspicion. "Ms. Maxwell?"

"Yeah?"

"They said you left the Bank of United States just twenty minutes ago."

"What?" I chuckled. "Obviously, that's a mistake."

The rep didn't laugh, instead studying me, like an FBI agent would, at least one of those I'd seen on TV.

"They said you closed your account."

THE SHOES! LOOK AT THOSE SHOES!

Some things in life are so traumatic that your brain does you a favor by wiping the memory clean. It's not exactly a perfect remedy, but it's certainly better than having an aneurysm.

I don't remember how I got to the bank. I think the rep gave me a lift, but at some point he disappeared, leaving me in yet another office room, alone, with only my suitcase, backpack, and a box of tissues for company. I blew my nose, which was unnecessary—I was so dehydrated there were no tears or snot left. I had to do something, anything. I blew my nose again.

The door opened, and an official-looking Indian man in a suit came in.

"Hello, Ms. Maxwell," he said and offered his hand.

"Hi," I put the tissues down for a moment and shook it. He took his hand back, looked at it, and discreetly wiped it on his pants.

"I'm Prateek, Bank of United States bank manager."

I looked at him, confused by his job title and his appearance. The staff at the embassy were all American, so it really wasn't all that racist of me to expect that the Bank of United States manager would be too.

"On behalf of Bank of United States, I apologize for your inconveniences, Ms. Maxwell."

"Thank you," I said, feeling grateful, hopeful, and scared all at once. "This is a mistake. It has to be some kind of mistake."

"As the Bank of United States bank manager, I assure you that we do not make mistakes here at Bank of United States."

"That's good, I guess," I said carefully. "Then can you please check my account balance?"

"Yes, of course," he said pleasantly. "May I please have your card?"

It took all the remaining energy I had to explain yet again that I was robbed and therefore did not have my card, but Prateek remained quietly wary. I finally had to google myself and show him the picture of me and Mr. Hue, attempting to compose the same exuberant facial expression I had back then, while he looked back and forth between me and my phone.

"This is most unsettling," he said and excused himself, leaving me alone again, with nothing to comfort me but a nearly empty tissue box and an endless supply of self-pity.

I was searching through the suitcase for any chewable meds when he finally returned.

"We have located a surveillance tape that may assist in your query," he said proudly, and popped a CD into his computer's drive. I zipped up the suitcase and wondered if he still Xeroxed things.

"Ms. Maxwell?"

I snapped to attention. "Yes?"

"Could you please have a look at this."

He turned the monitor toward me, and I watched a few seconds of grainy black-and-white action. Nothing interesting, just people moving soundlessly about the bank lobby, tellers counting out banknotes, and so forth. I was about to ask what I was supposed to see when I did finally have an aneurysm, because that could be the only explanation for what I was seeing.

I watched *myself* stride confidently into the bank, exchange a few words with the receptionist, and then take a seat in a chair opposite a small desk. I watched as an excited banker came over a few minutes later and shook my hand with both of his. I then walked off with him to the rear of the lobby, out of the camera view.

"What …" I managed. "What is this? I mean, *who* is this?"

Prateek bobbed his head apologetically. "That appears to be you, Ms. Maxwell. As I previously mentioned, it appears that you have already visited this branch earlier today. I didn't personally have the pleasure of meeting you, but as the staff assures me and as this tape shows, you were here. You also had your passport and your bank card with you."

"Passport?" I yelled. "And the bank card? That must've been the thief who stole my wallet!"

"I am very sorry for this inconvenience, Ms. Maxwell, but this person was most definitely you," he said and clicked a few keys. We skipped through more meaningless footage until I reappeared, carrying a large and seemingly heavy canvas bag. The doting banker was still shuffling alongside, while I—meaning the thief—seemed unimpressed, striding confidently in sky-high stilettos.

"Wait!" I shouted, and Prateek almost jumped out of his seat. "What was that?"

"Pardon?"

"Could you rewind it, please? Rewind it!"

For a second, I thought Prateek was going to call security, but instead, he clicked on the keys.

I watched myself glide across the floor again.

"There!" I shrieked. "Pause it!"

On the screen, I froze midstride.

"You see?" I pointed at the monitor, triumphant.

"What?" Now it was Prateek's turn to be confused.

"The shoes! Look at those shoes! They must be four-inch heels."

"Pardon?" He was hopeless. I bet he was the kind of husband who never noticed when his wife changed her hair.

"I don't wear heels," I said, sticking my sneaker-clad foot in the air. "I would've broken an ankle in those. Plus, I would have been over six feet tall in those shoes, and look at her!"

Prateek looked at me as if I was insane. Which, I was sure at that moment, I was not.

"Don't you get it?" I tried to slow down and point out the evidence for him. "Look—she's wearing stilts, and she still barely reaches that guy's shoulder. She's *tiny*."

Tiny.

The world slowed as I saw the truth unfold before my eyes, all at once. This was what Neo must have felt when he finally saw *The Matrix* for what it was.

"I know who it is!" I jumped up in a half-seizure, half-victory dance. "It's Vivien!"

That's when the security guards rushed me for the second time in as many hours.

AMERICAN WANT BHANG?

A lot has been said about rock bottom being a solid foundation for pushing off to go back up, but if you examine those quotes closely, all of them are by those people who'd managed to escape its gravitational pull. I bet if you asked someone who'd just landed in a deep, dark hole about his or her outlook on climbing back out, you'd get a different answer. I'm willing to bet you'd get a black eye.

"You've got to believe me!" I cried as the guards deposited me and my worldly possessions on the dirty sidewalk in front of Bank of United States, Delhi. "I'm the victim here!"

The guards moved back, and Prateek stepped to the front. "Ms. Maxwell. On behalf of Bank of United States, I would like to advise you to seek assistance elsewhere. I apologize for your inconveniences."

"My *inconveniences*? Are you freakin' kiddin' me? You handed all my money to a copycat, and all you have to say for that is *sorry*?"

"Bank of United States is committed to providing best possible service to our customers," Prateek said. "Safety and security are our priority. It simply is not possible that—"

"Shut up!" I said. "You and your bank can shove your *service* up your asses. As far as I'm concerned, you're an accessory to highway robbery."

He seemed wounded. "Ms. Maxwell, the facts are against you. I am providing you with a personal favor by not calling the police. Please be assured that customer service in local jails is not as excellent as in Bank of

United States."

"Can you just stop repeating the bank name, for God's sake? I know which bank it is—I'm a customer!"

"Yes, and I would like to thank you for using the services of Bank of—"

"Shut up!"

He pouted. My tough approach was not working in my favor here.

"I'm sorry," I said, trying to change tactics. "I didn't mean to yell at you. That's not how I usually act. I'm a good person, honest. I even recycle used batteries. Do you know how difficult it is to recycle them? You have to drive all the way to Home Depot, which doesn't even make sense 'cause you use gas, and that's not good for the environment, but that's the only option, and that's what I do. Most people just throw them in the garbage, but I don't. Because I want to help the environment. I want to help people, too—so can you please help me? Can you at least, I don't know, issue me a personal loan or a credit card for now? Some kind of emergency funding?"

"Yes, of course," he said. "We will need to see your passport, of course."

"A passport?" I laughed like a maniac. "You wanna see my passport? Did you not hear me when I told you that it was stolen, along with everything else?"

"I'm very sorry," he said again and disappeared behind the bank doors, leaving me on the sidewalk. The guards followed him, first giving me a look that clearly indicated that I was no longer welcome at Bank of United States.

I sat on my suitcase, hugged my wounded backpack, and bawled. Somehow new tears and snot appeared, even though I was more dehydrated than beef jerky. I finally had to admit that I was in deep-shit kind of trouble. I mean, a lot more than usual. Of course, I'd almost died before, and I'd lived in an abandoned shithole without a lockable front door, but that was nothing compared to where I was now, in a foreign country, without any documents to prove who I was. I missed my family and the little things in life, like food and shelter. With just a few bills left in my bra, I wouldn't be able to afford either for much longer. I needed a lawyer to get my money back, but first, I needed my money back to pay the lawyer who could get my money back so that I could pay him.

A Möbius strip of a clusterfuck.

I punched my overstuffed suitcase, but it only made my hand hurt. *Why didn't I pack at least a candy bar or something?* Sure, I had enough toilet paper to last me for weeks, but no food or water.

Water. Where was the monsoon when you needed it? I licked my dry, cracking lips and winced at the pain. I'd only had a glass of water and nothing to eat since I'd landed this morning. *The damn Bank Manager of My Bank didn't even bother to offer me refreshments.* The thought angered me, and I held onto the anger, the only force and only emotion left to carry me through. I wasn't going to be that tree in a forest with nobody to hear it fall.

Twitter.

How could I forget about thousands of my dedicated followers? *Thousands that will hear me roar all the way down to the ground.* I giggled hysterically as I typed "Lost in Delhi, documents stolen, please help!" into the text box, and waited.

Within seconds, notifications poured in. All around the world, strangers retweeted and hearted my plea, and my pulse throbbed, anticipating a miracle. I pulled down on the tab and scanned the replies.

"My prayers are with you!"

"Hubba-hubba."

"Increase your Twitter follower NOW!"

What the hell? I checked the stats. Within minutes, my cry for help was retweeted several hundred times, but not a single reply made any sense. I finally gave up when someone sent me a link, which I opened without thinking. I managed to close the window before I could figure out what they were doing, and hopefully before Big Brother got me on the radar. I hesitated for a second and turned off the phone. I was going to die from exposure long before Twitter managed to produce even one useful lead.

Doesn't matter. I'll come up with some kind of plan myself ... as soon as I find something to drink.

I shouldered the backpack, which now seemed to weigh a ton, grabbed the suitcase handle, and started off on my quest to find water. The quest encountered a major obstacle after just a couple of minutes, which was all it took to realize I had no idea what to look for. There were lots of businesses lining the street, but most of them had clothes and other dry merchandise laid out at the front. There were no 7-Elevens or anything similar offering drinkables or edibles.

"American! American!"

I stopped. An older man, his face decorated with colorful paint smudges, was waving me over. I came a few steps closer.

"American?"

"Yes," I said cautiously, trying to figure out if he had some bribe request in mind. There wasn't anything I wanted from him or his store, which seemed to sell mostly t-shirts.

The man clapped his hands in delight. "America! America good."

I nodded, thrilled that he spoke English. "Do you have water? Drink?" I mimed drinking from a bottle.

"American want *bhang*?" he said.

What the hell, is he propositioning me? Do I look that desperate already?

I was about to run away, if running away while dragging a huge suitcase was even possible, when the man called out something toward the dark cavity of his shop. An old lady appeared with a plastic glass of what looked like a milkshake.

"*Bhang!*" the man said happily and handed me the glass.

"Oh," I said, feeling like an idiot. "Milkshake? *Bhang* means milkshake?"

I held the glass, unsure of what to do. The old man made drinking gestures, still smiling ear to ear.

I tried a tiny sip of the drink. It was surprisingly good, like a mango slushie—cold, slightly sour, and incredibly refreshing. I took a bigger sip.

"Good?" the man clapped his hands and burst into giggles.

"Yes," I said. "Very good, thank you." I gulped the rest of the drink and handed the glass back to him.

"Two hundred rupee," the man said and held up two knotty fingers.

"Oh," I said, embarrassed. *How could you expect a poor man to just hand you free drinks?*

I fished in my bra for a note. There was that moment of panic when I couldn't find any, but then I pulled one out. My last treasure. I was about to ask the man if he had any change, but he looked at the note with such hunger, I couldn't bring myself to haggle. Plus, all that the first milkshake did was remind me just how thirsty and hungry I was.

"More *bhang*," I said, handing over the note. The man and the old lady looked at me in surprise, and my heart warmed at the thought that they now had enough money to eat for a week.

"More *bhang*?" he asked.

"Yes," I nodded enthusiastically. "More."

The woman went back under the awning and returned with a full jar. She filled my glass and then watched in awe as I drained four more glasses, one after another.

"*Bevakoof*," she said after I handed the glass back to her. Her husband just laughed, clearly ecstatic at making the sale.

"*Bevakoof*," I said, bowing to both of them, pleasantly aware of the milkshake filling my stomach with happiness.

It's amazing what a bit of water and nutrients can do, I thought, walking back outside and taking in all the beautiful, bright colors. The cruel sun had just disappeared beyond the horizon, or rather the jagged line of crumbling buildings, and it was already cooler by at least ten degrees. Somehow, everything felt lighter: my suitcase, my head, and my whole body. *I can do this*, I thought, watching the hustle and bustle around me, men, women, and children going about their lives.

I can figure this out.

Having taken care of basic sustenance, the next thing on my to-do list was to go back to the embassy before it closed for the day. This time around I wasn't going to take "Sorry, but we can't get involved" for an answer. I had rights, dammit, even if I didn't know exactly what they were. I checked Google Maps. The embassy was just a few blocks away. Good thing, since I had no money left for a taxi or even a bus.

The sidewalk was crowded with every imaginable activity. People walked between piles of goods for sale, makeshift outside kitchens, small tables, and plastic chairs. Everywhere people were hustling, be it selling, buying, cooking, delivering, haggling, or begging. A young girl with a baby on her hip approached me, motioning to her mouth with the free hand, then extending that hand to me.

"Sorry, honey, I'm broke," I said, feeling guilty as hell. The girl tried one more time, her eyes full of tired sadness, then moved on. Another child, still technically a toddler, followed her, carrying a plastic basket full of tissue packets and other small goods.

This is bullshit. Those kids should be in school, not begging on the streets. A new wave of anger, mixed with guilt, propelled me forward. My situation, however frustrating, was temporary, and nothing compared to the future they faced if I didn't get my shit together and help them. *How hard can it be?* I imagined myself picking up my travel documents from the embassy, then guilt-tripping my sister into sending me some emergency cash. I saw myself filing another report at the police station and getting a copy of the surveillance tape from the bank. Next, I was back in the flying aluminum can, except this time happy to be on my way back home. After that, it would be a simple matter of suing Bank of United States for misconduct something-or-other, winning back my money, and returning to India, only much better prepared.

I took a deep, relieved breath of air. It was a piquant bouquet of spices and exotic flowers, with just a touch of rotten fruit. Certainly unique, it seemed to fit the vibrant colors of the street life.

A car horn snapped me back to the reality, and I jumped back, narrowly avoiding being smashed into bits by a beat-up truck. A bearded man stuck his head out the window and took time to scream obscenities at me.

I clasped my hand over my heart, trying to keep it from jumping out. *Idiot—look right, then left. Or is it left, then right? Jesus, just look both ways before crossing a street.* I took a few more deep breaths, but couldn't get the heartbeat under control. It raced on, drumming its erratic beat against my rib cage.

I also couldn't recognize where I was, not that I would've expected to. I tried to think how long I must have walked on autopilot, but my mind refused to concentrate on anything for more than a split second. I got my phone out to try to figure out how much farther I had to go.

Nobody expects to be washed out to sea by the current, and that's how it felt when all of a sudden a wave of mopeds engulfed me. My scream drowned in the roar of a hundred engines while the drivers passed me on both sides, without as much as a look. I froze in the cloud of exhaust fumes, too afraid to breathe or move, crippled by the awareness that pain, or even death, was mere inches away.

What's wrong with me? First, I can't cross a street, now I can't even tell when I'm in the middle of it?

By some sheer miracle, the wave of mopeds continued to part before me as if I was a reluctant Moses. In a minute, they were all gone, and I was left alone on the *sidewalk.*

"What the hell?" I cried, shaking my impotent fist at the disappearing tailpipes. "Stay on the street, you bastards!"

I spun around to see if anyone else was hurt or witnessed this atrocity, but nobody seemed to share my concern for pedestrian safety. The street was practically deserted—I must've walked away from the busy commerce area.

"This is shit!" I said and moved as close as possible to the building line, away from drivers that ignored not only road rules but also the fundamental reasons behind the advent of curbs and sidewalks. Unfortunately, the move meant a whole new set of dangers, since these particular curbs and sidewalks were in dire need of maintenance, and the adjacent buildings were in need of bulldozing. I couldn't decide if I should be looking down, for cracks and trip hazards, or up, for falling bricks. A smart thing to do might have been to go back, but the embassy on the map beckoned me like a mirage.

After a hundred yards of slow advance, I was presented with a new obstacle course. A brick wall must have crumbled, and the rubble, entangled with remnants of orange safety fencing, took up most of the sidewalk. By the looks of it, the collapse took place a while back. Bags of trash had been deposited amongst the ruins, and a small cloud of flies hung in the air above them. A well-nourished cat was digging through one of the bags, looking pretty healthy except for the sickly, bald tail.

Must be ringworm. That's not too bad for a street cat.

Except it wasn't a cat at all.

The rat, as if sensing my thoughts, stopped digging and rose up on its hind legs, sniffing and searching the evening air for clues. I'd never seen one this big, not even in my craziest dreams. Our eyes locked. I saw no fear in them, only curiosity.

"Oh, God," I said, not sure what to do. It'd been a while since I'd last seen one in real life, but I was pretty sure that normal rats did not walk the streets in daylight, and especially with that kind of attitude.

There was a moment of paralyzed helpnesness, when I was caught between the fight and flight, but then the rat slowly lowered and skulked away, seemingly annoyed at having his dinner interrupted.

No way was I going to attempt climbing over the rubble after that, not even if it was for *Fear Factor*. I crossed the road, less scared of the mopeds than I was of mutant ninja vermin.

Breathe. That didn't work. I hyperventilated until I was lightheaded, but the shadowy feeling of danger didn't leave. Even the colors around me had changed, from bright and happy yellows and oranges, to cool twilight blues. The dark storefront openings now looked ominous, as if they too carried a threat.

You imagine things.

As if on command, one of the shadows pulsated and separated itself from the doorway, stalking its way closer to me. At first glance, my hysterical brain assumed it was another giant rat, but the shadow morphed into a dog-shaped monster. By that time I was used to seeing stray dogs everywhere, but they were mostly happy, tawny mutts with big floppy ears and friendly grins. This one was a mix between a German shepherd and a hellhound—black, emaciated, and missing one eye.

"Nice doggy," I wheezed and froze, hoping it would move on with its business.

The dog returned my neurotic greeting with a low growl and a spectacular display of bizarrely healthy white teeth. None seemed to be missing.

Run!

My mind was screaming, but my legs turned to mush, ready to play dead.

The suitcase.

I pulled on the handle, ready to use it as a shield. My hand felt numb and far, far away from my body, as if in a different zip code altogether.

Wha?

I looked back in horror, half-expecting to see my hand missing, or a stretched-out tentacle in place of my arm. The good news was that all the parts were still there—my arm looked roughly the same length, and the fingers were holding the suitcase handle like they were supposed to.

The bad news was that everything looked mottled, as if painted by Monet. I let go of the handle and brought the hand in for a closer inspection. It came unwillingly, and I could tell that something wasn't right, even though I couldn't focus my eyes enough to see what it was.

I'm sick!

The five glasses of milkshake leapt up in my stomach, dangerously close to coming back up.

Why did I have to tempt fate with thinking that I can get it together? I can't get anything together. I can't even get around in this country ... Dad was right ... it's malaria ... except I haven't seen a single mosquito yet—

Then I saw it. Where the emaciated black dog was just a moment ago, a monstrous thing appeared, like one of those creatures you only get to see in second-rate horror films. I swiped at it and watched my hand leave a flesh-colored rainbow in the air, as if it had been smudged on an invisible window glass.

If I was close to losing my mind before, I totally lost it then.

I screamed. At least I think I did. I took off running down the street, except it felt like swimming through thick molasses. Either my legs didn't appreciate the urgency of the situation or the malaria was rapidly taking control of my body. It was my worst nightmare ever, only about a million times more horrible.

I dared a glance back. The snarling creature was gaining on me, its shape now resembling a pulsating, possessed lava lamp. It howled, the sound bouncing inside my skull.

Not happening. This is not happening.

I redoubled my efforts of trying to punch through the thick air. Someone was on the sidewalk in front of me. I tried reaching out to him or her, but the person growled back, just as villainous and amorphous as the evil thing in hot pursuit.

Gun. Wish I had a gun. Wish I had anything.

I'd already lost the suitcase somewhere along the way, but I could feel the weight of the backpack slamming into my back with every step. I twisted one arm out of the strap, spinning around in hopes of knocking the evil thing out of the ballpark with the makeshift bat. I almost succeeded. Almost.

The next thing I knew, the dirty pavement was rising in front of me, kind of like in that movie with Leonardo. You know, the one that's so hard to understand, with all the multi-layered dreams and nightmares.

I'm gonna die in my dream.

Then the pavement punched me right in the face.

WHEN DID YOU GROW A MOUSTACHE?

I walked through the long and narrow corridor, running my fingers along one ancient stone wall. The light falling through the small windows on the other side painted a pattern of light and dark gray stripes across the floor. My mind wavered as I crossed each bright beam, coming closer and closer to the ornately carved wooden door at the end. *What's behind it?* I reached out for the heavy brass ring of a handle, and the door moved silently, with surprising ease.

The room was murky, but I could make out a human figure crouching in the center. I moved closer, trying not to make a sound, afraid that even my breathing was too loud in the cavern-like stillness.

Prince Amar.

So, Vivien lied to me on more than one occasion, because there he was, just as young and handsome as I remembered him. He was sitting on a large, embroidered floor pillow, smoking a pipe that was attached to a big bronze jar by a long tube.

I came another step closer. "Hi, I'm Isa Maxwell. You sent me an email...."

The prince nodded and moved to put down the pipe.

"What up, Izz?"

It was Harden, dressed in a colorful Indian costume, looking almost as handsome as the prince and nowhere near as gay.

"Harden!" I threw my hands around his neck. "I didn't even know you were here. I thought you were in Japan or something?"

"I'll always be here for you," Harden said. "I will never leave again, I promise."

I pressed my face into his neck. "Never again, you hear? Never again…"

He took my face into his hands and looked into my eyes, his thumb lightly stroking my cheek. The warmth of his hands and the heat in his eyes made my heart jump in its cage.

"I love you, Isa," he said finally and kissed me. It was so unexpected, yet so right, that I kissed him back, losing myself in his soft lips, eyes closed and head spinning. I pressed my whole body into his, big and hard as a rock. His mustache tickled my nose.

"When did you grow a moustache?"

I opened my eyes.

I was alone, lying on a narrow, stiff bed in a small, empty room barely lit by the morning sun through a tiny window. Harden disappeared, and it was something else tickling my nose. I brushed it away.

A giant cockroach fell onto the pillow next to me, right in front of my eyes. It landed on its back, and I watched as it struggled to turn over, the myriad of legs and various other projections kicking up. It succeeded and flopped over, antennae still moving as it considered its next move.

In an instant, I became airborne, my own legs springing from under me with the power of a hundred spooked horses. My scream, like a deafening airstrike siren, reverberated through the tiny room. I heard people's voices outside, shouting something I couldn't understand, but nobody came to my aid. I jerked the handle of the door with its funny window covered in vertical bars. It was locked. I pressed my face to the bars, and that's when it finally dawned on me.

I'm in jail.

IN ADDITION, YOU TAKE PURSE, ALSO.

A nother thing everybody assumes about rock bottoms is that they are flat, when in fact, they could be a slippery slope into an abyss from which even Captain Nemo couldn't return.

"Where is money, Miz Max-vel?"

I groaned, staring at the same pilot hat I saw just yesterday.

Deja-woe me.

"We've been through this," I said, smiling at Moustache in hopes that the language barrier masked the sarcasm in my voice, which, despite my best intentions, came through like the mildew on the walls around us. "Vivien took it all. Could you just please make one phone call to Manchester Airlines and find out the last name of the passenger in seat 3B? You already know her first name."

"Yes, yes, you already say this," Moustache said calmly. "And I explain to you that there is no evidence against anyone else in this crime."

"The shoes," I moaned. "What about the shoes?"

"But!" Moustache raised a finger to punctuate the dramatic pause. "There is good evidence that you did drugs, Miz Max-vel. Let's review."

"Let's not," I said, but he played the video anyway. It showed me running down the street, toward the asshole who chose to film me with his phone instead of helping the poor confused tourist. I could hear him laughing at the end when I finally face-planted.

"Okay, so maybe I was on drugs, but I didn't steal the money." My head hurt, and I just couldn't go through another spin of this nightmare-go-round. "It was *my* money—how could I steal from myself? And if I stole it—from myself—then where have I hidden it? I would like to know that myself!"

Moustache observed me with the cool attitude of the man who has the upper hand.

"I don't know," he said. "But I know you are on news, running on street with too much *bhang*. Where do you buy *bhang*? And why do you drink so much of it?"

"I've told you, like a zillion times, I can't remember." Maybe not exactly a zillion, but I did say it at least a hundred times already. "And I didn't know there were drugs in it." At least that was true.

"Maybe you didn't," Moustache said philosophically. "Or maybe you did?"

I pressed the heels of my hands into my temples in an attempt to squeeze out the reality.

I'm going insane.

The thought was strangely comforting—a plea of temporary insanity could get you out of anything these days. Wouldn't it be convenient and fun to slip into a world where I was a superhero and could fly away at any moment? Or at least burn Moustache with my laser eyes.

"In addition, you take purse, also," Moustache said, completely unaware of my murderous intentions.

What? I tore myself away from trying to choose the color for my superhero costume. Who was I kidding, it was going to be black.

"What purse? Somebody stole my *wallet*," I said. "Wait, are you saying I took somebody's purse?"

"Yes. Purse had money." He consulted his notebook. "Almost twenty thousand rupee. Also, somebody rob house last night."

"What house? What the hell are you talking about?"

"Nice house. Steal many furnitures, very expensive."

"What the hell? I didn't take a purse or any money, and I most certainly did not steal anybody's furniture! If I did, then where is it?"

"Is what I want to know," Moustache said.

"Listen," I said slowly. "I want a lawyer. I'm not going to say another word until I've had a chance to consult with someone who understands simple logic and basic human rights."

"You don't need lawyer."

"Oh yes, I do. I was robbed. Twice. You're supposed to help me. Instead, you're trying to implicate me in all of your random unsolved crimes. It won't work. Either I get a lawyer, now, or this is gonna be one of those international incidents with politicians and TV coverage."

"You already on TV," Moustache pointed out.

I groaned and facepalmed, which did nothing, other than remind me that I had one hell of a painful bump on my forehead. I patted it gingerly with my fingertips. It seemed to have deflated a bit, but I didn't need a mirror to know it was going to turn all the colors of the rainbow. I would imagine it contrasted nicely with the rest of my skin, which was sunburned to a glowing ruby-red.

"Forget the lawyer. I need a doctor for my concussion. My brain feels like it's hemorrhaging."

"Hemorrhoid?"

"Hemorrhaging! It means bleeding, in the brain. I might be dying."

"No, no," Moustache said, laughing. "No dying. You don't need doctor."

A slow, anguished moan escaped my chest, along with the last of my will to live. I was done. The scratches on the desk mocked me with their hidden meaning. I was more lost than ever, in a country where I understood nothing, not the language, or customs, or people, or why I should have to go to jail when I was clearly a victim.

Moustache took this as a sign that I was close to confessing. "Where is money, Miz Max-vel?"

I shook my head and pressed my fingertips into my eyes. "I didn't steal anything."

"You say you don't remember anything. How do you know you don't take it?"

"That's not what I said. I can't remember where I bought *bhang* ... but I do remember not stealing." It was shady logic, but it was true, and the truth had to count for something.

"*Bhang* is strong marihuana drink," Moustache said. "Five *bhang* is five times strong. Maybe you drink five *bhang* and don't remember you steal purse?"

"No." I moaned into my hands and pushed thumbs into my ears. It was nice and dark in there, and a soothing ocean-like sound replaced Moustache's annoying voice. *I could just stay like this.*

"Miz Max-vel!" Moustache rudely pulled one of my hands down. "I say you cooperate with investigation."

"I *am* cooperating," I said, trying my best not to scream in frustration.

He took a long pause. "This investigation not working."

"No," I agreed.

"I need to do search."

"That's great!" Finally, the first decent idea of the day. "Like I was saying, if you can find this Vivien—"

"I search you," he said categorically. "For drugs and money on your person."

"What do you mean?" Cold sweat rolled down my back. "Like, a strip search?"

"Yes. Strip."

"What do you mean, like right now? That's not right! Seriously, where's my lawyer? Where's my one phone call?"

"No lawyer," Moustache said. "You call embassy later, if you cooperate. If not cooperate, you go back to jail."

It really was shaping up to be an international scandal in the making. "Wait till *Star* hears about this!"

"I could charge you with many, many offenses," Moustache continued, unperturbed. "But I want to help you, Miz Max-vel. You are good person. If you help me, I help you, even if there is fine."

He raised both eyebrows, and I finally understood his smoke signals. *Of course. He wants another bribe.*

I was kicking myself for forgetting how this legal system worked when another policeman burst into the room and rattled something off. Whatever it was, it made Moustache jump off his seat and leave me alone trying to figure out how much public intoxication would cost.

Start with twenty thousand rupees and work it up from there. I didn't have any idea how high I was willing to go except that I'd pay anything not to go back to my cockroach cellmate.

I was composing a script for a phone call to Felicity, with the aim of extorting enough cash to get me out of jail and out of the country, when Moustache returned with a white guy in a black suit. I couldn't take my eyes off the newcomer—he seemed so confident, so clearly in his element. He was saying something in Hindi to Moustache, who looked almost sheepish, constantly trying to interject and bobbing his head like mad. Even his whiskers seemed to wither down.

"Good morning, Ms. Maxwell," the white man said in perfect American English.

I could swear there was a halo over his head. "Oh my God!" I cried. "Are you my lawyer? You have no idea how glad I am to see you."

"No, I'm not a lawyer," the man said. "I'm Consul General Grant Lawrence."

HOW IS WOMAN NOT WANT CHILDREN?

Everyone always assumes that doctors and lawyers are the most influential people and make the best possible husbands, but that's before they ever meet a politician. It's like they have a gravitational pull.

The man extended his hand. "Don't worry, Ms. Maxwell—you will not need a lawyer." He gave Moustache a piercing look. "This has been a misunderstanding. You are free to go, and I will personally do my best to make sure you are able to contact your family and have access to emergency funds. As a matter of fact, I already have your temporary travel documents." He handed me an envelope.

I pressed the envelope to my heart and shook his hand for a few moments too long, worried that if I let go, he might disappear. "I was robbed," I said finally, staring at him with a teenage-girl longing. "Can you help me with that, too?"

"I know," he said. "It's a major news story at the moment. I'm very sorry, Ms. Maxwell, but the embassy can't get involved in these types of legal matters. I think it would be best for you to return home and to seek an investigation with your bank. I'm sure the FBI would be able to help."

I nodded, once again disappointed by the official policy on matters pertaining to careless citizens. Yes, of course, the FBI seemed to magically appear at every TV crime scene, but where were they now? I mean, it was obvious that a highly organized international crime syndicate had targeted me and cleaned out a major bank, yet Interpol didn't seem to give a damn. Still, I was excited about going home—it was a much better option than going to jail.

"I can't thank you enough," I said to the Consul as we were walking out into reception. "I can't believe you found me. Thank you so much."

"Well," he said and for a moment, he seemed oddly awkward. "You should thank your friend. If it wasn't for him, I—I mean, we wouldn't have known you'd been arrested. The news story failed to shed any light on your name or whereabouts."

"Friend?" I scanned the lobby for Harden's massive frame. It should've been easy to pick him out in the crowd, but I couldn't see him anywhere. Instead, I saw Santa, making his way toward us.

I looked back at Consul in disbelief.

"Mr. Bhatnagar came to the embassy and made such a fuss that I had no choice but to see him personally," he said. "And of course, once I'd put two and two together, I had no choice but to resolve this mess myself."

"Mr. Bhat ... who?"

"Kabir Bhatnagar. Isn't he your family's friend?" He pointed at Santa, who was now in front of us, unflappable as ever.

Kabir. I finally knew my guardian angel's name, and I was overwhelmed by a hot mess of feelings, from gratitude for his help to the shame of referring to him as Santa.

"Thank you, Kabir!" I said, unsure if I should hug him. "Thank you so much, I can't believe you found me!"

"Yeah," he said without moving. "Okay, American girl."

"Isa," I said patiently. "American girl" was no better than "Santa," but the man had the excuse of advanced age, plus so many brownie points, I'd never be able to repay him. Quite literally, since I had no money whatsoever.

It took less than ten minutes for Moustache to arrange some paperwork and return my backpack. I still had my phone safe between my boobs, which was a relief—I would have died to know that someone searched me while I was out cold. After an awkward goodbye and more vague promises of ambiguous help, Consul left. I hugged the envelope with my pass to freedom and watched him disappear into the blinding sunlight.

"We go now?" Kabir asked after a minute.

"Oh," I said, snapping back to attention. "Yes. Where?"

"We go to my house."

A real local house of a real local.

"That would be so great, thank you!" Now that I had no money, I no longer had any reason to stay in Delhi, but I couldn't decline an offer to see how the real Indians lived. "I will pay you, later, when I get money from my sister, I promise."

"No money," Kabir said and bobbed his head on the way to the parking lot, looking offended. "You give too much money already, American girl."

"Isa," I said patiently. "And that wasn't too much. I have lots more. I mean, I'll make a lot more, once I publish my second book."

"No, guest don't pay for anything, and you are guest."

"Thank you," I said, touched.

"You are like my daughter," he added.

"Your daughter?" It was so unexpectedly sweet, I almost hugged him right there.

"Same *saal* ... same year old."

"Oh, I see," I said, noting the new word. "Will I meet her?"

"No." He bobbed his head. "She is like you—very much trouble. She move to live with her sister. Say she don't want to live with us."

"That's okay, isn't it?" I got into the car.

"No, no. Not okay. She not married. But she not listen. Very much trouble, that one." He squeezed behind the wheel.

"Is her sister married? I mean, your other daughter?"

"Yes. Four other daughters—all married. But not this one. We want to arrange her a very good husband, rich and very handsome man, but she not like him. We want grandchildren, but she say she not want children.

How is woman not want children?"

"I don't know," I said, thinking of Felicity and her twin terrors, and whether I myself would ever be ready to experiment with Maxwell family genetics.

He bobbed his head in quiet despair and started defibrillating the car's engine. It looked hopeless for a second, but then it coughed, and we rolled out of the parking lot. *Amazing how quickly you can get used to things*, I thought, surveying Delhi traffic with the cool indifference of an umpire. Perspective is a funny thing, even when you don't feel like laughing.

The traffic was just as bad as yesterday, so I had plenty of time for errands. I dialed my sister's number. *Pick up, Felicity! Pick up!* I squeezed my eyes shut, trying to direct all of my mental energy around the globe. We weren't twins, but surely she had to have a premonition about the hell I was in. Some kind of a gut feeling, other than the usual horniness.

"Hello?" I finally heard her voice and jumped in my seat.

"Felicity! Oh my God, I'm so glad I caught you. Is it late there?"

"Past midnight, but I can't sleep. How are you doing, kiddo?"

"I'm good," I said, trying to think of a clever way of coercing a few thousand out of her. Felicity was loaded, but not only because she made a lot of money. She also had a hard time letting go of it.

"I'm not," she said gloomily. "I think I'm pregnant."

I giggled, but she didn't join me. "Wait. You're kiddin', right?"

"I wish I were." She groaned. "But nope. I just did three tests, and I got a total of six lines."

"What?"

"I'm gonna have another baby!" she said and bawled.

Her pain kicked me in the stomach, right across the ocean and mountains between us. I didn't know what to say—she was nowhere near that upset when she got knocked up the first time around. "Congratulations" was definitely out of the question.

"I'm just hoping it's not true," she said once she got herself under control.

"But you said there were six—"

"I know, but maybe it's ectopic. Or it could be cancer."

"Don't say that!" I had a brief and terrifying daymare of a funeral, followed by a reading of the will awarding me custody of the twins.

"I'd take cancer over two years of night feedings. It's about time I got rid of the surplus internal plumbing."

"Jesus! Seriously, Felicity, stop talking like that."

"I can't," she wailed again. "How am I gonna handle three of them? I only have two hands."

"I'm sure it'll be fine," I said, slightly overacting my enthusiasm. "I'll help, and Mom will too. Have you told the parental unit?"

"That's what I'm afraid of most. Mom will probably want to move in. And no, I haven't told them, and you better not say a word either." Her voice changed channel into the usual business-like programming. "I'm still not sure if I'll keep it."

"You have to! I mean, it's your choice, of course, but … what does David think about it?"

"What does it have to do with David?"

"I don't know," I said, wondering what she'd been up to in the last month or two. "Isn't he the father?"

"Yes, of course," she said, indignant. "But it's none of his business. To tell you the truth, I don't even know if we'll stay together."

"Oh."

"Yeah, he's been distant lately, and he disappears for hours on end. And we've hardly had sex, certainly not like that first month. I don't even know how this happened. Maybe I'm just full of Holy Spirit." She snorted on the other end of the line. I couldn't tell if it was a laugh or a muffled cry.

"It'll work out," I said. "I don't know how, but it will."

Felicity went on bitching about David, and the pathetic excuse for legislated maternity leave, and how she was going to get fired regardless of her rights, while I tried to think of what to do next. I could no longer bring myself to ask her for money, now that she was on the verge of a mental breakdown and about to be swallowed by an avalanche of bills. There was only one other option, even though I knew I'd regret it for years to come. Just thinking about it made my skin crawl.

"I'm sorry, Felicity, I have to go," I said finally. "I'll call you as soon as I can, and I'll be back home soon."

"It's okay," she said in a tired voice. "At least now I feel sleepy. Thanks, kiddo."

I hung up, took several deep breaths, and dialed my parents on Skype. A wave of panic flooded my brain, begging me to push the red button, but I fought it off by digging my nails deep into my palm. It had to be done. Perhaps it was for the best, the kind of lesson I would never, ever forget.

The phone screen went black for a moment, and I heard Mom's voice. "Isa! Darlin'!"

"Hi, Mom," I said and then I saw them—pale and panicked, too close to the camera, pushing each other out of the way.

"Are you okay, honey?" Mom said. "We saw your tweet. I tried to call the police, but they said that their jurisdiction—"

"What? Since when are you on Twitter? Are you following me?"

"Yes, of course," Mom said. "You hardly call, how else would I know what's happening with my baby?"

I felt the pangs of overwhelming guilt at updating my followers more often than I had my parents.

"What's going on?" Dad demanded. "What have you done?"

It took a split second, if not less, for the guilt to be replaced by a flash of defensive anger.

"Nothing!" I said. "I was robbed, then robbed again, and then arrested. I almost died!"

The next wave was of intense regret as Mom sobbed uncontrollably into her hands.

"Mom, it's okay," I cooed. "It's all resolved now, honestly. I have—"

"Look what you've done to your poor mother," Dad said. "You've shortened her life by a good five years!"

95

"I've done nothing, not to her, or to anybody! Somebody has done a terrible thing *to me!*"

"I told you not to go!" Dad barked. "If you just stayed home, nothing like this would've ever happened. I predicted this, but as usual, you wouldn't listen—"

"You didn't predict anything!" I yelled, glancing at Kabir. He didn't seem to mind. Come to think of it, the conversation had to be similar to one he would have had with his own daughter. "I'm not gonna take travel advice from someone who never traveled."

"I went to Hawaii," Dad said defensively. "I had to *fly* to Hawaii. Let me tell you, if not for your beautiful mother, I'd never even consider getting into one of those deathtraps."

"You know what," I said, "you're the reason I have a fear of flying. Thanks very much, I know now whom to blame for this mess. If I weren't in such a panic, I would have never taken Valium from a stranger—"

"Are you on drugs?" he shouted so loud, I would have heard him across the world without Skype.

I was about to hang up and opt for begging on the street when Mom intervened. She didn't yell or elbow him, instead saying "Darlin'!" with such force, it stopped Dad's advance like a stone wall. The distribution of power had clearly shifted in the Maxwell household since the almost-divorce. It was a welcome change, but a little scary, too. I was used to having Dad as an adversary, but I had no idea what to expect from this new Supermom.

Dad and I waited in silence while Mom blew her nose and straightened her hair.

"So you're okay now?" she sighed after a minute.

"Yeah, all good," I said. "Some major official from the American embassy, Consul something-or-other himself, came to get me out of jail and to give me travel documents."

"Jail?" Mom looked close to losing it again.

"Not jail, police station. Sorry, my mistake." I silently cursed my loose tongue. "I was just there, you know, filling out paperwork. All I need now is some money for my flight back." The words came out with surprising ease—the warm-up screaming round did wonders for my assertiveness.

There was another near-disaster when Dad learned the price of the ticket and almost had a coronary, but Mom stopped all that drama with a simple hand on his shoulder. I felt a strong urge to take notes for future-husband management, if I was ever so lucky as to get one, of course.

It took forever to explain how to wire the cash to me, and another forever to say goodbye. It was as if they were afraid they'd hang up and never see me again. Frankly, I had the same feeling.

"This is almost behind me," I said to Kabir, and then a wave of unexpected sadness washed over me. Nothing about this trip worked out the way I'd hoped, and now I was going to head home, defeated. Worst of all, I couldn't even bring myself to post a blog or a tweet, even though I knew my Klout score was falling with every minute that passed without an update on my totally awesome adventure. That last panicked tweet alone had to have cost me half of my followers.

Kabir bobbed his head in agreement.

I sighed. "Just angers me that Vivien, the woman who robbed me, might get away with it. Not even might, she will—the local police are so incompetent, they'll never find her. Not just incompetent, they're corrupt! Between you and me, that officer was practically forcing me to pay bribes." I decided to omit the part in which he succeeded in doing so.

"Bribe is big problem," Kabir agreed. "Everyone make bribe business. Police is good business, and mafia is very good business, also. Bad people pay police good money."

"They do, don't they," I said, glad to finally have a conversation with someone who was on the same page. "And this Vivien, she was bad, bad people."

Kabir bobbed again.

"So even if she gets caught, she'll use my cash to pay her way out. How ironic."

Kabir puffed to indicate his displeasure with this predicament. I felt closer to him by the minute.

"If she has any left, of course. Now I understand how she could afford to fly first class. It's easy to spend money when you didn't work for it. I mean, who wears *Manolos* to the airport?"

Kabir was saying something, but my mind didn't register a word, overwhelmed with the memory of Vivien and her goddamned precious shoes. And it wasn't just the anger, either. There was something in it, a clue perhaps. My heart was beating fast while I tried to put bits of our mid-flight conversation together.

Just as I was about to remember something, something really important, Kabir slammed the brakes, and I almost head-butted the dash. Apparently, we'd arrived at his house. His parking skills were no better than mine.

His house was no better than mine, either.

WAIT, DID YOU SAY YOU HAVE A TV?

Everything is relative, and everyone is familiar with that concept. It's the one that causes your ass to appear either huge or toned, depending on whether you're in a yoga class or Burger King waiting line. The theory of relativity, I think it's called. It ruled my life, first driving me to make a million and then to give it all away, but I didn't expect it to punch me in the gut the way it did in front of Kabir's house.

It would have been a stretch to call it a house, really—it was more of a shack or a lean-to. It was shabby in the exact verbatim interpretation of the word, with literally no space left for chic. My old place was a palace compared to this eclectic collection of recycled materials, haphazardly squeezed between two similar structures. Looking at it, I realized I might have been wrong about Kabir's daughter. Perhaps it wasn't the family conflict that drove her away after all.

It hadn't rained since I'd arrived in Delhi, but half of the dirt road in front of the shack was still flooded. I climbed out of the passenger seat, being careful not to drown, and took in my surroundings. They stunk, both literally and figuratively. A skinny white cow was lying in the shade on the opposite side of the street, but I couldn't blame her entirely for the smell. There were piles of garbage everywhere, covered in hordes of flies.

There were hordes of children too, of different ages. Some of them were old enough to be in school in the middle of the day.

Maybe it's a public holiday. I tried to remember what day of the week it was, but gut feeling told me this was no Sunday picnic.

The kids stopped whatever it was they were doing in the puddle and watched us, quiet and serious. There was none of the boisterous screaming I was so used to hearing at playgrounds back home.

I took out my phone—this had to be documented, whether for Twitter or myself, in case I later thought I dreamt it. I snapped a photo of the cow, then the street, and posed for a selfie with the bright-blue sky and the kids in the background.

One of them, a boy on the verge of teenhood, said something.

"Hi!" I waved at him and smiled. He laughed, shouted something else, and then in an instant, they were flying down the street like a flock of spooked birds.

I turned to Kabir, who'd made it across the puddle and was now standing in front of his shack, waiting for me to finish getting acquainted with the locals. Custom dictated that "What a lovely home!" was in order, but I couldn't bring myself to say it.

The lovely home was rusty-brown, just like Kabir's car, partly due to the siding made of reclaimed metal roofing, and partly due to dust layers that settled in its many grooves. Kabir pushed aside the sheets that were hanging on the line in front of the house and waved for me to come in. I hesitated for just one moment, some primitive part of my brain screaming at me to run, but I shut it up, stooped down, and followed him through the small doorway.

It was hot and dark. Not like the police station, which now seemed luxurious in comparison, but more like the inside of an oven, subdivided into several smaller ovens hidden behind curtain doors. The ceiling was so low, I had to hunker down to avoid bumping my head into the beams. Thankfully, we walked straight through, into a small courtyard surrounded by brick-and-concrete walls on all sides. In the middle of it was a fire pit topped with a big metal pot and a wisp of smoke rising into the already hot air. An old woman in a sari squatted next to the fire, her head covered in a pretty red veil and her wrists decorated with dozens of bracelets that tinkled with her every move. She seemed at odds with the place, an exotic bird that flew into the slum by mistake.

Kabir said something and the woman jerked her head up to look at me. There was a moment of confusion, followed by recognition, then shock, and finally terror. She said something back, bobbing her head and smiling, but looking into her eyes, I didn't need to understand Hindi to get that she was less than thrilled to have me over.

"Is everything okay?" I asked Kabir after the woman disappeared into the house.

"Yeah, okay," he said. "My wife, she watch too much TV. She think you rob us." He chuckled and shook his head.

I looked back at the shack. "Rob you?" It seemed absurd to think there was anything worth taking inside. "Wait, did you say you have a TV?" The structure didn't look like it had plumbing or electricity, let alone cable.

"Yeah, TV," he said proudly, pointing behind me. I turned and saw the small box propped up in the open window. Something resembling a Bollywood film or maybe a soap opera was on. I didn't register it before, because the scripted argument was echoed by the neighbors' voices, rising over the courtyard's wall. Life in the slums seemed to be full of drama.

No wonder she's not happy, I thought, watching the wife return with two small plastic chairs. I moved to help her but she recoiled, almost losing her balance. After I saw that video of me, the one in which I ran through the street like a possessed banshee, I could understand why anyone would be reluctant to have a suspected thief and drug addict stay at their house. I touched the bump on my forehead and winced.

Kabir's wife deserved some credit for her courage. After practically forcing me to sit on a chair in the corner of the courtyard designated as the dining room, she even served me breakfast, some kind of awesome savory pancakes. I tried to refuse the food, but my stomach teamed up with my hosts and I caved in, feeling guilty for taking food from people who had so little themselves.

After I'd convinced Kabir that I simply couldn't eat another bite, we moved our chairs into the living room—the corner of the courtyard in front of the TV. The soap opera was still on, or maybe it was a new one, it was hard to tell. The scene pictured a young woman coyly pushing away a singing man. Both were wearing an inordinate amount of bright-yellow gold jewelry, blissfully unaware it was going out of fashion somewhere in the southeastern US.

"No good, this. We watch good show." Kabir shuffled over to the TV. After a rapid montage of random scenes and a heated argument with the lady of the house, he finally succeeded in changing the channel to the news.

Great, I thought, *this really* is *like hanging out with my dad*. I tried to get comfortable in my chair, which was impossible. At least it helped me fight the after-meal sleepiness. There was no way I could nod off with the hard plastic edges cutting off circulation to my legs.

Kabir's wife brought over a plate with little leaf-wrapped parcels and offered it to me in an outstretched hand, from at least two steps away.

"Thank you so much," I said, shaking my head. "I'm too full."

"*Paan*," Kabir said, took one of the parcels, and put it in his mouth. His wife did the same.

"Thank you, but I can't *paan* anymore, honest." I rubbed my stomach to show how close I was to bursting at the seams.

Kabir bobbed his head and went on watching TV and chewing his dessert. I drifted off a little, thinking how grateful I was to him for bailing me out and for the food. To think how badly I misjudged both him and Vivien, who turned out to be just as fake as her jewelry, and her—

Kabir spat blood onto the ground, right in front of our feet.

"Oh my God!" I jumped up from my chair. "Are you okay?"

He startled a little. "Yeah, okay."

His mouth was *full of blood*.

The first thing you have to do in that kind of situation is try to stay calm—that's what the operators always said on *Panic 911*. I took my phone out with trembling hands and turned to his wife. "He'll be okay—I'll call an ambulance. What is the ambulance number?"

"*Kya*?" A trickle of blood dropped from the corner of her mouth.

"Jesus!" I looked back and forth between them. The pancakes we ate were spicy, but not spicy enough to cause internal bleeding.

"That's okay, I'll Google the ambulance number."

I tried to type, but it was hard to do with shaky fingers and blurry vision. Google informed me that my gibberish didn't match any documents.

"Fuck!"

"You okay, American girl?" Kabir asked and spat blood again.

He seemed remarkably calm for someone experiencing the sudden onset of a deadly disease.

"I'm okay, but you're bleeding." I motioned to my mouth. "Mouth. Blood."

Kabir wiped his fingers over his mouth and looked at them. I expected him to scream, but instead he burst into giggles, chattering something to his wife. She, too, started laughing, both of them looking like happy zombies with their mouths full of flesh.

"No, American girl," he said finally, wiping his eyes. "Not blood. *Paan.*"

His wife picked one of the leaf-wrapped parcels, pretended to eat it, and then spat another bloody gob onto the ground. On second thought, it looked a little on the magenta side, not that I'd ever seen anyone spattering blood before.

"Oh," I said, sitting back down. "It's the food. I get it."

I forced a smile and they smiled back with their terrifying mouths, then settled back into watching TV, chewing and spitting.

I tried watching TV, but my heart kept racing. My mind was racing too, although now that the crisis passed us by, it went back to running circles around Vivien.

How could I think we were going to be friends? I should've known she was just using me. Who else could be that nice to strangers? Except Kabir, of course. She faked her interest in me just like she faked those eyelashes and those ...

I sat up a little straighter in my chair.

Holy crap. Those amazing blue eyes of hers. They had to be contacts.

Funny how your brain starts working properly as soon as you feed it with calories and adrenaline.

I bet her perfect hair was fake, too. Son of a bitch, I bet her name isn't even Vivien.

That was a terrible thought—if my hunch was right, and Vivien was indeed a talented kleptomaniac mimic, then there was no hope of ever finding her. The FBI would check a few leads and then lose interest. I mean, who would care about poor Isa and her philanthropy fund when there were drug cartels to take down and terrorists to catch?

The news turned to a spotlight on some fashion show. Gorgeous girls in long, flowy gowns paraded up and down the catwalk. The reporter was saying something, I assumed gushing over the outfits no mere mortal could afford.

Vivien could. For all I knew, Vivien was in some couture shop at that exact moment, trying on a dress that could feed a family for a year.

The reporter held the microphone up to one of the girls, who was also gushing, probably about how comfortable and affordable her sparkly stilettos were. The camera zoomed in closer on one of her feet, clad in what looked like a huge engagement ring.

The reporter kept on talking, but of course I didn't understand any of it. Maybe that's why when three English words popped into the long stream of her chatter, they hit me harder than lightning.

House of Borgezie.

VERY BEST JOKE.

I didn't scream.

Okay, so maybe that doesn't seem like a big deal to you, but the thing is, I *always* scream. I scream when somebody comes up from behind me and says my name, even if I'd been waiting for them. I scream when the lid on the pickle jar pops open, even if I'd spent ten minutes sweating over it. I scream at popping champagne bottles. I practically lose it every time I watch *Jaws*, even though I know exactly what's coming.

This time I froze, unable to breathe, all circuits madly trying to process what I just saw and comprehend what it meant. And I was sure it meant something. I didn't know what it was yet, but I knew what I had to do.

"Wow," I said in a too-high voice. "Those dresses look amazing. It would be so much fun to go to that show."

Kabir mumbled something indecisive.

"Look at all the pretty girls," I said, but he didn't react, content in his chair, full of pancakes and inner peace. I had to act fast before he nodded off.

I sneaked a peek at my phone. It took less than a minute to find out that India Couture Week was being held in Taj Palace Hotel, and another minute to find the Western Union about ten minutes away. Not as close as I'd hoped, but it was something.

"Kabir," I said sweetly. "Sorry to interrupt, but can we please go to the

Western Union? My parents have sent me some money." That part was true. I just wasn't going to tell him what I was planning to do after.

He seemed disappointed not to finish his after-meal ritual, but after a few more minutes and a few relieved glances from his wife, we were on our way. This time, I made sure to pay attention to what was just outside my window—and it was as close to hell on earth as I was capable of imagining. Occasionally, we passed a newish building, some even three stories high, but the majority of other homes were the same as Kabir's and worse, if that was even possible. Street dogs and children were everywhere, and at one point I even saw two pigs ruffling through the garbage. The smell and the flies seemed to follow us long after we left the squalor behind. I looked back, promising to myself I would return with something more than good intentions.

I glanced over at Kabir, and my heart ached in protest. *That's the only way,* I told it. I took a couple of breaths, getting ready to jump into the cold pool of lies.

"Um, so, do you like being a taxi driver?"

"Is okay," he said, and we drove on in silence while I struggled to resolve whether lying to one person was worth potentially helping many. *What he doesn't know won't hurt him*, I lied to myself.

"So, what do you like besides driving?" I tried again.

"I like TV," he said. "I like news."

It was hopeless. "Do you do anything else for fun?"

"I like potato chips," he said.

That wasn't what I'd expected, but it was a start. "Potato chips? What kind?"

"Vinegar and salt," he said. "And barbecue. And sour cream and onion. And cheddar. Very good."

"Great," I said. "Once I get my money transfer, I was hoping to take you and your wife out for dinner, to thank you for your kindness. But for now, how about I get you some chips, too?"

"Yeah, okay," he said, and I almost squealed with joy.

"I like chips very much," he said dreamily. "But my wife don't. She say too much money. She say she cook better too."

I nodded, wondering if a bag of chips could also be the last straw for his cardiovascular system. "Great," I said, feeling like shit. "I know just the place."

Half an hour later, we left the Western Union, my already sizeable bustier padded with close to two hundred thousand rupees. *It might take all of it to get back half a million dollars.*

"Let's go to Taj Palace Hotel," I said casually. "It's not far, and they have the best salt and vinegar potato chips."

"Why Taj Palace?" Kabir seemed uncomfortable with my choice of venue. "Twenty-Four-Seven have salt and vinegar chips...."

"No!" I said. "I mean, we could, but these chips are special. Just wait, they're worth it."

Kabir bobbed his head but continued driving, the promise of potato chips overcoming whatever internal conflict he had. It could hardly be called driving, though—we were practically inching our way through the traffic. It would have been faster to walk, but for once I was happy with the delay. I needed time to come up with a plan.

After ten minutes of really hard thinking, I had to admit that even ten hours wouldn't have been enough to figure out what I was going to do when we got to Taj Palace Hotel. I didn't even know what I was expecting to find. I mean, if Vivien could change appearances so dramatically, how would I even recognize her?

"We should go to another place," Kabir said and pointed at the dead traffic in front of us.

"No, no," I said. "We're almost there."

He shook his head.

"Tell me a story," I said anxiously. "Something about India. And if the traffic doesn't start moving in five minutes, I promise we'll go to Twenty-Four-Seven."

Kabir seemed pleased with this arrangement. "I tell joke," he announced. "Very funny!"

"Okay," I said, finding it hard not to smile. "Let's hear it."

"This is good joke," he said and chuckled. "Is like this: man come to doctor office, with his wife. Good doctor, he work on tooth."

"A dentist?"

"Yeah. Dentist. Very best doctor, very expensive."

"Okay."

"Yeah. The man ask how much to fix tooth. The doctor say price, but the man don't like, very expensive."

I nodded.

"The man ask how much to pull tooth," Kabir continued, emphasizing the plot twist by making hand gestures of ripping out the insides of his mouth.

"Aha."

"The doctor say price, but the man say no, too much!" Kabir acted out every emotion with the enthusiasm of Bollywood stars. "Very expensive! The man say, how much to pull tooth, but no drugs."

"No novocaine?"

"Yeah. No nothing. Pull tooth, but no drugs! Doctor say price, much less. Man say okay, and ask his wife, which tooth?" Kabir barely managed to squeeze out the last few words before he burst into such hearty laughter I couldn't help but join him.

"He don't want to pay for wife tooth drugs." Kabir wiped away tears. "Very bad husband."

"Ah, okay," I said, smiling. "That's funny."

"So, so funny," Kabir said. "Very best joke."

I nodded, and we sat in silence.

"We go to Twenty-Four-Seven now?" Kabir asked.

"No! I mean, wait, now I have to tell you a joke. Then we go."

It could have been the anticipation of a forbidden salty fruit, but his eyes sparkled.

"A man went to see a psychologist," I started.

"What is 'psychologist'?"

"A doctor," I said.

"You tell same joke?" Kabir asked, slightly wounded.

"No, it's different," I promised. "A psychologist is a doctor who works with the brain." I tapped my head. "So, the man said to the doctor: 'Doctor, my life is terrible. I live in a small apartment, by myself, I don't even have a girlfriend, and my job sucks. I'm lonely and depressed.'"

"Man not married?" Kabir asked.

"No. That's why he's—"

"How old this man?"

"I don't know. Why does it matter?"

"Why he not ask his mother to find him good wife?" Kabir said, genuinely surprised. "He not need head doctor, he need *shaadi tay karvanevaala*!"

"A what?"

"Matchmaker. Matchmaker find him good wife and make him happy." Kabir shrugged with a "case closed" expression.

"No. I mean, maybe, but that's not the joke. Just listen, okay?"

"Yeah, okay," Kabir bobbed his head, but I could see that his heart was no longer in the story.

"Anyway, where was I? Oh, yes, so the man is *depressed*," I said, trying to convey the gravity of the situation. "So the doctor says to him, 'Okay, what you should do is buy a goat, and let it live in your apartment.'" I tried to match Kabir's performance with my acting.

"Goat!" Kabir burst into laughter. "It is funny joke! This doctor is very bad doctor, very, very bad."

"Wait," I said. "I'm not finished."

"No?"

"No. The man bought a goat and came back a week later. 'Doctor,' he said. 'I'm even more depressed. The goat is constantly bleating, and there's shit everywhere.'"

"Of course goat does such things! Goat is not good to live in apartment. This man so stupid."

"He isn't. The doctor told him to buy a goat, so he did it. The doctor was very famous, a good doctor. Just wait, okay?"

"Okay," Kabir said, still bobbing his head, but now in an agitated manner.

"So the man said to the doctor that the goat didn't make him happy. 'Okay,' the doctor said. 'Now you must buy a pig.'"

"Pig? What doctor is this? He is not smart or good at all. At all! Did the man pay him?"

"I don't know," I said. "I guess so. That's not the point, just let me finish!"

"He should not pay," Kabir mumbled, pouting.

"Okay," I said and took a deep breath. "Long story short, the man was still not happy, so the doctor told him to buy a cow," I put my hand up to silence Kabir's protest. "So finally, the man came back and said: 'Doctor, the animals don't let me sleep, there's shit everywhere, and I'm very unhappy.'"

Kabir grasped his head with his hands and rocked back and forth in obvious distress.

"So the doctor then told him to sell all the animals and the man sold them," I said, ignoring Kabir's dramatics and speaking as fast as I could. "He came back a week later and said: 'Doctor, I'm so happy. Nobody is bothering me, I can sleep all I want, and my apartment is clean!'" I took a deep breath, like a diver finally coming up to the surface.

"Did he marry?" Kabir asked, dropping his hands down.

"What? No! That's not the point."

Kabir looked at me sadly for a moment. "You are nice, Isa but this not good joke, not nice. I tell you another good joke, very much better."

"You're right. It's not a very good joke."

Vivien would've loved it. I turned to look out of my window, just in time to see something my brain couldn't quite comprehend.

An apparition.

YOUR NAME NOT ON LIST.

I t wasn't a ghost, of course, and in fact, Vivien's skin looked several shades darker than I remembered. Her blond bob had turned into a shiny black updo, but there was no mistaking that profile, the clear, slightly rounded forehead, flawlessly arched eyebrow, exquisite nose, and that perfect pout. I stared as she inched alongside us in her Mercedes. I should have at least slid down in my seat, but luckily she paid no attention to the junker next to her or the two vagrants inside it.

I kept staring at the Mercedes as it pulled a bit farther along, far enough for me to see its trunk. I got my phone out and snapped a photo of the license plate and the back of Vivien's head.

Kabir broke into another fit of giggles, trying to deliver the punchline of his latest joke—it seemed we finally found something else he liked, besides the news and potato chips.

"That's funny," I said on autopilot. "Can you follow that black car, please?"

He studied the Mercedes with a wary eye. "Why?"

"Oh, I just saw that a movie actress is driving it. Actor, I should say. A starlet, really—you wouldn't recognize her. I saw her in this independent film, but I forgot its name. She was really good. I want to ask for her autograph." I did my best to avoid eye contact with Kabir.

At least the part about the actress is true. Best acting I've ever seen.

My acting wasn't too bad either—Kabir didn't question my motives, and we followed Vivien. Practically rode her tail would be a more accurate description, but Kabir was new at reconnaissance, so I let it go and tried my best to hide behind the dashboard.

Thankfully, it wasn't long before she turned into the driveway of Taj Palace Hotel.

"Oh, look." I feigned surprise. "She's going to the same place we are."

The festivities were in full swing. Guests in eveningwear and more sensibly dressed staff spilled out of the portico entrance. One of the staff jumped into the path of Kabir's car and forced us to back out of the driveway, away from the delicate eyes of the hotel's fine guests.

We observed from the curb as Vivien parked right in front of the entrance, handed her keys to a valet, and floated away in another pair of sky-high heels.

I watched her with barely concealed jealousy. She was a star even in this crowd of tall, skinny models and oversized businessmen, with a few aging first wives thrown into the mix. Her long white dress was deceptively simple, but an overlay of effervescent tulle, heavily embroidered in silver, gave her an almost regal appearance. One edge of the tulle fell from her shoulder, trailing behind her like a bride's veil. It draped over her large evening bag, which was the only accessory out of place.

The delicate veil billowed in the breeze, and then she was gone. A hostile voice inside my head urged me to follow.

"Kabir," I said and turned to him, feeling like proper scum. "It looks like there's some kind of an event here. Maybe you're right, and we should go to that other store instead."

"Yeah, okay." Kabir reached for the ignition.

"I'm just so disappointed I didn't get to ask that actress for an autograph. She's my favorite."

Kabir shrugged and tried to turn on the engine.

"Wait!" I pleaded over the screeching noises. "Could you please wait here while I run over there and ask for her autograph? It'll take me at most just ten minutes."

Kabir looked at me, confused, but I could see my general reputation as a crazy American girl working in my favor. "Yeah, okay."

"Thank you so much," I gushed, climbing out of my seat. "Just ten minutes, I promise. Fifteen at most. Then we celebrate."

Liar, liar. My head felt like it was on fire. *What the hell am I doing?*

I walked up the front steps, pulling my bangs down in a feeble attempt to hide the bruise on my forehead, and trying to resist the urge to check an armpit for its BO state. I was mere feet away from the entrance when a grumpy-looking man blocked me with his whole body and barked something in my face.

"Sorry, I can't understand," I said, trying to squeeze past him.

"I help you?" Grumpy said in a tone that wasn't helpful at all, and put his arm out to cut off my maneuver.

"Yes," I said, even though all I wanted to do was to turn and bolt. "I'm here for the House of Borgezie."

He scrutinized my dirty outfit with an expression suggesting that I belonged in the madhouse. "You on guest list?"

"What? I mean, yes. I'm Isabella Maxwell."

Grumpy made a quick job of scanning a printed page on his clipboard. "Your name not on list."

"It was a last-minute booking. Can you look again, please"—I tried to imitate the way Moustache had said my name—"It's Isa-*bela*. Max-*vel*."

I almost added, "Do you know who I am?" but remembered we were no longer in Kansas, or Texas, or anywhere even remotely close to home. I longed to be "that girl" again, but nobody seemed to recognize me on this side of the world.

Grumpy grabbed my upper arm in a viselike grip. It was painfully clear he didn't recognize me either.

"Ouch! Do you know who I am?" Pathetic, but it was worth a try.

"Yes," he said. "You are beggar."

"I'm not a beggar! Please, just wait," I begged as he dragged me away. "I'm sure we can find a mutually ... acceptable ... solution."

Grumpy ignored my pleas and proceeded to all but carry me out, his fingers digging into my flesh. People around us parted, leaving wide space for the guard and his catch, obviously relieved to be rid of the penniless bum.

Wait a second.

I remembered, a little late again, that I was no longer penniless, that I now had a golden ticket, or two hundred thousand golden tickets to be exact. I used my free hand to produce a note from my stash and wave it like a white flag.

"Ticket!" I cried. "I can pay for a ticket."

Grumpy stopped to examine the note but didn't let me go. "No tickets," he said, either not getting what I meant, or not willing to compromise his integrity.

"Um, I can maybe pay a fee then?" I said, pulling out a few more bills. "Late notice or something? Special access for members of, um, fashion fan clubs?"

It took a bit more negotiation, but twenty thousand rupees eventually bought me not only a backstage pass, but a sari as well. Part of the deal was that I shed my current garb, and I agreed, thrilled to bits about the victory and my very first authentic sari. Grumpy seemed just as excited, and even solicited the help of one of the catering girls in fitting the new dress about my sloppy person.

I emerged from the bathroom like a butterfly from a grubby cocoon. One end of the sari covered not only the bruise on my forehead, but my hair as well, which was handy, since there wasn't another blonde in sight. It was almost impossible to walk with so many layers of fabric binding up my legs, but at least they concealed my dusty sneakers, which I had to keep. I shuffled along, afraid to step on the edge of the sari and cause a wardrobe malfunction. The last thing I needed was more attention.

Grumpy snuck me in through the kitchen, straight into a big hall full of beautiful people and their less attractive, but equally well-dressed companions. The noise was overwhelming, like a stadium getting wound up for the last play. I half-expected someone to start a wave, but they were all too posh and nowhere near drunk enough for that. I hobbled along, dumbstruck by the contrast with the parallel world I left not even an hour ago.

How can they be so happy and carefree when around the corner there's such poverty and hopelessness?

All around me bejeweled women, more sparkly than Christmas trees, chatted and sipped champagne. I realized after a moment that most of them had to be models showcasing designer dresses. The truly rich were a bit more understated, but you could spot them by the real diamonds and the lack of interest in others.

I moved about aimlessly, not sure of what I was looking for and wondering about the retail value of all the clothes and jewelry in just this one room. *More than enough to build a hospital.*

I remembered the shoes that were worth at least an elementary school, and scanned the floor, trying to see if any of the models wore those engagement-ring stilettoes, but all I could spot were just your average Manolo-type deals.

One of the catering staff came up to me with a tray full of champagne glasses, but I waved her off. Either my hand gesture wasn't aristocratic enough, or she spotted my bruise, but she kept looking back at me as she walked away. I pulled the edge of the sari lower over my forehead and watched her say something to a guy in a matching uniform.

Don't panic.

He turned and scanned the crowd.

Oh my God!

I hobbled along, trying to blend into the crowd and cursing the sari, which seemed determined to turn me in to the authorities. I kicked it, but it retaliated by further restraining my feet in its many layers.

Why is it so freaking heavy?

It was like trying to walk through a clingy curtain, each step threatening to rip down the cover and expose me for who I was—an imposter, a liar, a fraud on her way back to jail. I bunched up the pleats in both hands and lifted the front edge, hoping nobody would notice the Nikes under it. A graceful older woman, herself cocooned in a sparkly shroud, raised an eyebrow as she glided past me. It was time to abort the mission.

I hiked the sari up another inch and speed-walked out of the great hall, trying not to knock anyone over and hoping security was too preoccupied with the new arrivals to notice any suspects leaving the premises. I kept my head down to avoid eye contact with anyone and to monitor the rhythm of feet versus fabric shackles, but I could feel the bright aura of freedom just a few yards ahead.

That's when I heard fairy bells tinkling right beside me.

YOUR HONOR, SHE STARTED IT!

Be careful what you wish for. It might have teeth.

I froze in the limbo somewhere between fight and flight. There was no mistaking that sound, just as there were no ifs, ands or buts about my impotence to confront its source. What could I do in the middle of a crowded hotel without a weapon or a right to be there?

I moved aside and peeped around the edge of my headscarf. Vivien was coming out of an unassuming service door, chatting with another gorgeous Indian girl, a full head taller than her but just as skinny. They paused and did a few of those Hollywood air kisses, then the tall girl walked toward the main hall.

Vivien turned and made her way in the opposite direction.

She's leaving.

I didn't know how it was possible, but I panicked even more. She was right in front of me, but what could I do? Call the cops? What would I tell them? That I have a hunch?

Vivien paused just outside the entry doors to give the valet a paper ticket. The valet bowed and left.

I watched her from behind one of the doors. She was waiting with one hand on her hip, her evening bag slumping from the other, as if she was posing for the red carpet cameras. I thought about taking a photo, but there's nothing illegal about vanity, unfortunately.

I can follow her again. She was bound to do something incriminating sooner or later. I could snap a few photos for the police or the FBI.

The black Mercedes reappeared and Vivien got behind the wheel. I waited for her to pull out of the portico and rushed out, waving madly for Kabir to pick me up.

The rusty brown bug he called a taxi was nowhere to be seen.

This is not happening.

"Have you seen my car?" I cried in the face of a young Indian valet. "I mean, it's not mine, but I came in it, like half an hour ago. It was parked down there, next to that Volvo. It's reddish-brown and vintage. Sort of funny-looking."

It was preposterous to expect the poor kid to remember each car that stopped by, no matter how unusual, but I sure as hell didn't expect what he did next. Poor guy mumbled something that sounded like an apology and held up a ring with a car key and a shiny new car remote. Behind him was a matching shiny silver sedan with the driver's door open. Before I knew what I was doing, my hand reached out and took the key from him.

"Thank you!" I said over my shoulder, marching over to the sedan, propelled by an explosive mix of reckless abandon and giddy excitement.

Grand theft auto. Maybe it was for the best—more evidence of temporary insanity to help throw my case out of a court.

I tumbled in, sari still doing its best to thwart my efforts. I cursed, shut the door closed, and hiked my skirts up to the knees, searching for the right pedal with my foot. Valet was saying something to me through the window, but I just smiled, pushed the door lock, and shoved the key into the ignition.

The adrenaline rush was wild, nothing like I'd ever experienced before. *If this is what skydiving feels like, then maybe certain death isn't that scary after all.*

The engine purred, and I reached for the gear stick, only to bump my hand into the plush side of the door.

Damn it.

It didn't help that the guy kept knocking on my window. I waved him off and surveyed the equipment on hand. The gearbox looked pretty normal, except it was on the *left side*. Luckily the car was automatic, and the gears were labeled with the familiar letters and not any mysterious symbols. I switched into drive and pulled away from the portico in jerky leaps. Thank God, at least gas and brake pedals were where you'd expect them to be.

Vivien's black Mercedes was still waiting to exit the parking lot, just two cars ahead. Perfect. All I had to do was follow her. *If she turns, I turn. If she stops, I stop. If she—*

"*Faaark!*" I followed the cars in front of me into the beeping, smoking, wild chaos of a Delhi street. I would have crashed the car in mere minutes if the traffic wasn't once again at a near standstill. The drivers on both sides screamed curses at the drivers in front, but I cheered, glad to be alive.

I inched along, keeping a close eye on the black shape ahead of me and occasionally risking a glance back and up, to see if any cop cars or helicopters were in hot pursuit. It seemed that Delhi police were once again unable to catch a thief, which was now ironic and awesome in equal measure. Eventually, I calmed down enough to once again start dwelling on Vivien and her crimes against humanity.

Your Honor, she started it!

I still didn't have a plan for what I was going to do once I caught up with her. Law enforcement would need something better than impossible stilettoes and blue contact lenses to issue an arrest warrant. So far she hadn't done anything obviously illegal, other than, well, dramatically changing her appearance. If only I could prove she had a fake identity to go with that fake blond wig ...

The two-car buffer between us eventually disappeared, and I had no choice but to follow right behind Vivien, too scared to lose her at a red light. She didn't seem to notice me, ignoring her rearview mirror just like every other driver in Delhi.

After a while we exited the main road, and I made myself slow down and fall back, even though I had a small heart attack every time she turned into a side street. This neighborhood was nothing like the slums, with its wide lanes shaded by magnificent large trees, smooth sidewalks, and neatly trimmed grass nature strips. There were hardly any people using the sidewalks and shade, but there were plenty of smug mansions on both sides, bursting with pride and square footage.

Are we still in Delhi?

Finally the Mercedes stopped in front of a modern two-story and multi-color thing apparently designed by a toddler architect out of giant Lego pieces and packaging cardboard. I hit the brakes and pulled over to watch Vivien while she waited for the security gate to slide open. The house was guarded by a tall, solid wall, designed to keep out any potential thieves.

Takes one to know one, huh, Vivien?

I watched her pull into the driveway, waited a good ten minutes, then slowly drove past, taking as many photos as I could without crashing into a tree. The house looked like an impenetrable fortress with its smooth walls devoid of any lattice or downspouts, or anything else a novice ninja could use for climbing. I parked a hundred yards down the road, killed the engine, and turned in my seat to watch the gate.

Minutes ticked by, slow as molasses, but Vivien stayed put in her cubist castle. My stronghold was getting hotter by the minute without the air conditioner. Worst of all, it was *so boring*. No wonder the stakeouts are always replaced with a montage in the movies. It would have been bearable with some popcorn, but I had nothing to eat, drink, or do, other than stare at the damn gate.

After half an hour I decided to leave, before somebody reported a blond weirdo in a stolen car. The problem was, I didn't know where to go. Running to the police was out of the question, and so was confessing my recent stunt to the embassy. I hadn't run into the FBI yet, but they were in the category of authorities likely to require evidence and facts. There was the bank security tape, but legal action would be required to extract it from the bank manager. It looked hopeless.

"Stop it," I said out loud. "Think. Where can you go?"

I stared at the steering wheel and its shiny logo, but nothing came to mind. "Damn it!" I punched the wheel, and it retaliated with a short, angry beep.

Shit.

I looked out the back window. Nobody seemed to notice the horn in a city used to the constant honking, but it was time to get the hell out of there before I was apprehended for the accidental car theft.

Your Honor, I didn't mean to take the car. He gave me the keys.

Crime turned out to be surprisingly easy if you were bold enough to follow through and had just a little assistance from the locals, whether bought or unintentional.

The locals. *What happened to Kabir?*

Maybe he got tired of waiting and went home. I could look for him there, but I didn't have his address and couldn't remember his last name. Heck, I didn't even have a photo of him….

A photo.

I tapped the *Photos* app and chose *Moments* with a shaky finger. There they were—the skinny white cow and the selfie with slum kids in the background. I tapped the *Vivekananda Camp, India* heading and zoomed in.

Well, look who's a genius after all.

JUST A LITTLE STAKEOUT?

I drove slowly through the narrow, bumpy streets, following Siri's directions and occasionally stopping to check how much farther it was to Kabir's house. Either my shiny new car or my erratic driving attracted so much attention from the locals that soon a convoy of vehicles in varying states of disrepair formed behind me. I didn't notice it at first, but then kids of all ages joined the procession, running alongside and shouting, determined to find out where I was headed.

I stopped and checked the map—I was just a block away from Kabir's house, or rather, the spot where I took that selfie with another slew of local children. It was time to lose my tail, and maybe the evidence while I was at it.

I looked in the rearview mirror, trying to ignore my face and not think about the laser treatments I was going to need after just one day without sunblock. At the head of the convoy, a driver of one of those tricycle taxis waited patiently for me to get going. I killed the engine and climbed out.

"Hey!" I jiggled the car keys high up for him to see. "Can you drive?"

The driver looked at me silently from behind the wheel of his questionable apparatus. It seemed to have an engine, so surely it couldn't be that different to drive.

"Drive?" I said and made hand motions to imitate turning of a steering wheel. "Can you drive this car?"

He climbed out of his seat and approached cautiously.

"Here," I said, holding the keys out to him. "Take it."

He was still hesitant, until one of the kids tried to snatch the keys out of my hand. The driver sprang to action, grabbing them and chastising the youngster at the same time.

"Great," I said. "It's yours. Have fun!" I hiked up my skirts and took off running down the street.

Shit. Fingerprints.

I turned back, intending to wipe the door handles and the wheel with my sari, but the car and its new owner were surrounded by people, elbowing each other out of the way to get a better look. In a matter of minutes the fingerprints, if not the whole vehicle, were going to be obliterated. I had a brief sting of empathy with the car's real owner, followed by a Robin Hood-like elation at my role in the redistribution of wealth.

I'm sure it's insured. Victimless crime.

~

I didn't need to consult the map again—I could hear Kabir's wife even before I turned the corner, her voice rising and falling like waves of an angry ocean. I was just rethinking my plan, quietly glad that her screaming hadn't been weaponized by some terrorist organization, when I saw what had riled her up so much.

It was Harden, standing in the front yard, a huge backpack at his feet. His hair was longer than I remembered, and he was wearing a strange loose blue shirt, but there was no mistaking his bulk. The old woman was attacking him like a bird trying to chase a fox away from her nest, going at him with a flurry of waving hands, then retreating to her front door, only to regroup for another attack. Harden had his hands up to shield himself, but he wasn't moving, like a boulder set in place.

"Harden!" I sprinted toward him. The old woman saw me and recoiled back to her house, which offered a false sense of security: a big bad wolf could blow the whole thing down on the first try.

Harden turned to face me, and in the next moment, we collided in a crushing hug. I pulled on the folds of his tent-like shirt as if I could hide in there in hopes he could smuggle me home. For a moment, I felt safe, almost happy, and then I burst into tears.

"Are you okay?" I heard him say, but I refused to let go, burrowing my face even deeper into his armpit.

After a minute or two, Harden managed to unlock my fingers and move me to arm's length. I finally managed a good look at him. Even through the teary blur, I could tell he looked different, more grown-up somehow. He was still big, but some of that mass seemed to have moved up into his thick, wide shoulders and barrel-like chest. He was very tan, and his normally smooth-shaved face was covered in stubble.

"Jesus, Isa! What happened to your forehead?"

"What? Ah, that's nothing," I said, crying and laughing all at once. With Harden by my side, everything was going to be okay. "Oh my God, I can't believe you're here! How'd you find me?"

"Easy," he said. "You broadcast the news all over Twitter, so from there it was a matter of callin' the embassy, who put me onto the right police station, who gave me this address."

"You're here," I said again, patting his arms and chest, just to make sure he wasn't a hallucination. He was real and solid as a brick. *Police*, my brain registered. "Wait, the police have this address?"

"Yeah. You were released into the custody of ... I have it here...."

"Kabir." *Of course.*

"Yeah, I think that's the name. Who is that? How do you know him?"

"I'll tell you everything, just let me look at you for now," I said. "You really are here. Where were you?"

"In Cambodia. I hopped on the first plane out as soon as I saw you got robbed. It only took a few hours. I mean, it was two planes. And the bus to Phnom Penh. What's wrong?"

"Nothing." I kept patting his arm. "Everything's all right now. What did you say? Cambodia? Isn't that where they make all the cocaine?"

He laughed. "You're thinkin' of Colombia. That's in South America. Cambodia's in Asia, between Thailand and Vietnam."

I tried hard to remember where Thailand or Vietnam were, but all I could think about was an all-you-can-eat Chinese buffet. "That's cool."

There was movement inside the house. If Kabir had a phone in there, which would no longer surprise me, his wife would have already reported two crazy Americans to the police.

"I'll tell you everything, but you have to help me." I pulled him by the shirtsleeve down the street. It only took a minute for two tricycle taxis to appear—their drivers had to be stalking us. Now they were engaged in a heated battle over the rights to the fare.

I climbed into the closer one. "Get in!"

"Where are we goin'?" Harden said but got in with his backpack. That hardly left any space for me, but with his arm around my shoulders, I was no longer afraid of anything.

"I'll explain, I promise." I got out my phone. It only took a couple of minutes of arguing over the Google Maps snapshot for the driver and me to agree on a five-hundred-rupee charge. It helped that his competition was right next to us, loudly undercutting his bids.

"Where are we *goin'*?" Harden asked again, once we were off. I held on to him and gave the elevator-pitch version of what had happened over the last two days.

"It's a conspiracy! I even know who it is, or at least I'm pretty sure it's her, but I can't do anything about it. The local cops are corrupt, and I suppose the FBI too, and I don't actually have any evidence, other than the fact that this Vivien changes faces like a chameleon changes colors. Oh, and she wears these ridiculous stilettoes, and the woman in the security video was wearing them too."

"Stilettoes?" Harden said. "I mean, I believe you of course, but I'm not sure if anyone else would. It all sounds like a bad movie."

"Tell me about it," I said, spent. "It's pretty much *Mission Ridiculous*—people wearing disguises, stealing identities, and robbing banks. I mean, there has to be a whole band of them behind her. It can't just be freakin' *Vivien's One*."

"Look, I don't mean to sound like a parrot, but where are we goin'?" Harden said.

"Oh, sorry! To this place I saw Vivien last. I think it might be her house."

"Her house? Can I ask why?"

I thought about it. "I don't know. It might not even be hers. All I know is that she robbed me and got away with it, and that just burns me up. Could we please just hang around there a bit, take some photos, get some kind of a clue? For the FBI."

"You want to stake out someone's house?" Harden looked at me as if I was crazy. I'd never felt saner, but I sure looked the part, with my bruised face, odd clothes, and over-the-top fervor. I tried my best to calm down.

"Just a little stakeout?" I begged, patting his arm. "Maybe an hour or two? And if she doesn't show, I promise to get on the first plane out of here." It was almost not a lie.

"What if somebody calls the police?" he asked, annoyingly calm and rational.

"Big deal," I said. "I'll just pay them off. I got plenty of cash now."

"You gonna bribe the police?"

"I already did it once, and it was easy. Why are you looking at me like that? I bet the police in Colombia are corrupt too."

"Cambodia."

"Stop acting so superior," I said. "I'm trying to make the best of a bad situation, and you're not helping."

"I'm tryin' to help, but I think the best thing for us would be to get on a plane outta here."

"Fine, suit yourself," I said, pushed his arm away, and turned to the road. "I'll do it on my own."

He was quiet for a moment. "I hate when you get like that. This is so childish, Izz."

I stifled a smile.

WHAT WOULD ISA SAY?

When life gives you lemons, make lemonade. When it deals you one crappy card after another—bluff. The worse the hand, the better your poker face has to be.

I tried my best to look carefree while we unloaded just a few yards away from the gate that kept me from pulling out Vivien's hair. Harden, on the other hand, was an anxious mess.

"We are so gettin' in trouble for this," he said, his eyes darting around and looking suspicious as hell. "Even assuming you could pay off the cops, there's still no point to any of this if someone spots two white kids loiterin' on their street."

"You're right," I said. "Let me see your backpack."

It took some convincing, but he finally submitted to wearing a turban I fashioned from one of his t-shirts. I covered my head with the end of my sari, and laid out his other clothes on the nature strip as if they were for sale. We sat down on the grass to wait, although neither one of us knew what it was we were waiting for.

Harden's backpack stash included a bottle of water and a pack of crackers, which we passed back and forth between us. The sun was setting, and if not for the constant gate-watching and the worry over being arrested, this would have been quite a picnic.

"So what were you doing in Cambodia?" I asked when the food and water were gone. "Saving whales or something?"

He chuckled. "No, nothin' that exotic. Just helpin' a local village set up their network. Teachin' kids some basic computer skills. Helpin' my neighbor fix up his fence. That kind of thing."

"That's still cool. I wanted to help kids too and look how it turned out. Maybe you should've asked me to come with you."

"Maybe I should've," he said, pulling on the grass blades in front of his crossed feet. "You were just so busy, first with writin' your book and then with all the promotion. I didn't think you had any time for me, let alone anyone else."

"I would have made time," I said, trying to imagine how Sandra would have reacted to my announcement about joining the Peace Corps. Knowing her, it would have led to another news story and even more copies sold. I pushed away all thoughts about Sandra and her emails, still unopened in my inbox. At least I didn't have to worry about her suing me, now that I had no money.

Harden continued his lawn maintenance efforts. "I'm glad I got to see you before, Izz."

"Before what? You're not dying or anything?"

"Nah," he smiled at me. "I just have these morbid thoughts sometimes, when I'm happy."

"Morbid? What are you talking about?"

"I don't know how to explain it. Have you ever felt so happy you could die?"

"What? What the hell is wrong with you?"

He laughed and threw a handful of grass at me. "I'm kiddin', okay? Where's your sense of humor?"

"I still have it," I said, indignant. "Lots of it. I'm just, you know, dead-tired. Tired of feeling like an idiot all the time. I mean, this was supposed to have been the trip of my lifetime, and all I've seen so far is an embassy and a police station. I won't even get to visit the Taj Mahal."

He cleared his throat. "Um … the Taj Mahal's in Agra, Izz. We're in Delhi."

"I know that! Stop treating me like I'm an idiot."

"Sorry. I was just jokin' around. You know, like we used to. Always 'yo' and 'fo shizzle' and the like."

"True that. That's what I … missed. Homeboy."

"I missed you too, Izz," Harden said. "Cambodia's been fun, don't get me wrong, but it's been kinda lonely. Strange how you can feel so alone in a place where you're a star attraction."

"Are you? What, like Cambodia's newest celebrity DJ?"

"No," he said and laughed. "They're not into my music, unfortunately. I'm talkin' about walking on the street—I mean, I've always been big, but I'm practically a Godzilla there. An average girl doesn't even reach to my shoulder." He held his hand up to his chest, and I saw a ghost of a dark-haired female head nestled there.

"Are you … dating anyone?" I asked, looking for crumbs in the bottom of the empty cracker box.

"No. I don't think anybody finds Godzilla particularly sexy."

"Stop it, Harden," I said, feeling strangely relieved. "You're not still moaning about being fat, are you?"

"That was a great joke!" he said in mock rebuke. "Take a nap and then I'll try it again."

"I'd kill for a nap right now," I said, yawning. "I just have too much to do. You know, get my money back. Try again with the charity thing. Write another book."

"You're amazing, you know that?" he said, pulling on the grass again.

"Very funny, Harden. You're killing 'em tonight."

"No, I mean it," he said, unnecessarily straightening jeans and sneakers laid out between us. "You're an inspiration."

"Inspiration!" I snorted. "Seriously, Harden. You've lost your mind. Look at me. I try to do one simple thing, and it all turns into a mess. You're mending fences in Cambodia, and I'm here working on an international incident. One hell of a role model for young women everywhere."

"You're too hard on yourself."

"Not hard enough is more like it. Maybe I'm just not ready. It's like that whole thing with the oxygen masks on planes. You're supposed to put one on yourself first, before you try to help others. Otherwise, you pass out and who does it help? Nobody. That's me, basically. Out of oxygen and useless. All my money's gone, and I haven't helped a single soul."

"You're not useless, Izz. You helped me."

"What? I mean, how?"

"You've always cheered me on, even when everyone else was tellin' me to quit the DJ business. You were the only one who believed in me."

"Stop it," I said, and meant it for a change. One more nice word from him and I was going to lose it. Thankfully the dusk was beginning to creep in, and it hid my quivering chin.

"You know what I did when things got hard during those first few weeks in Cambodia?" Harden said, staring at my stomach. I shook my head.

"I'd ask 'What would Isa say?' and then I'd talk to myself like you were actually there. Crazy, huh?"

"Yeah," I managed. "Harden, you don't have to say anything."

"Yeah, I do. I want you to know how much you mean to me."

Light from a passing car lit his face for a moment. He was now looking straight at me. Maybe it was just the headlights reflecting in his eyes, but I thought I saw that Viking determination again.

"I want you to know ..."

Behind him, the car slowed down and stopped in front of the gate we'd been watching this whole time. The gate jerked awake and began slowly moving out of the way.

"Oh my God!" I scrambled up on all fours for a better look.

"Wait, let me finish—"

"No, it's her!"

"Who? What are you talkin' about?"

"It's Vivien," I said and crawled closer to him, watching the black Mercedes from the cover of his shoulder. "Pretend that nothing's happening," I hissed when he tried turning back to look.

"Nothing *is* happening," he said bitterly.

The gate retracted all the way and the Mercedes eased forward. I jumped up and skulked through the shadows toward it.

I heard muffled cries behind me, but didn't turn, instead quickening my steps. The floodlights came on, and I could see Vivien clearly behind the wheel. She was alone, and she looked tired. I had a moment of doubt, an almost physical pull of common sense.

What the hell are you doing?

Then the gate started moving again, and I went for it.

I DIDN'T EXPECT HER TO BE SO LIGHT.

W *hy pay for drugs when you can have adrenaline for free?*
I dodged the gate and squatted on the driveway behind the Mercedes, trying hard to keep my breathing under control. A moment later, a heavy paw landed on my shoulder, and I turned to see Harden's eyes, huge and terrified.

"What are you do—?" I planted a hand over his mouth to keep him quiet.

The thing was, I didn't know what I was doing. I knew that it, whatever it was, had to be technically illegal, and that I would eventually regret it, but I was driven by a force more powerful than common sense. It was strong, and it was primal, and it said "Go get 'em." Or maybe "Aw, hell no," or something similar. The force knew I'd been wronged, and it wasn't having it.

Harden couldn't feel the force, so he kept trying to say something through my fingers. Good thing he was still in shock. I'd managed to keep him quiet until we heard the sound of the opening car door. Then we both froze.

We are going to jail for this, Harden's bulging eyes said.

I did my best to communicate a message of "I know what I'm doing" with my whole face and a random assortment of hand movements, and he closed his eyes in quiet acceptance. It could have been barely contained anger, but it didn't matter as long as he stayed out of my way.

I peeked around the bumper to see Vivien step out in another pair of ridiculously high heels. Another sari, this one a delicately embroidered gold cascade, swayed with her every step. I couldn't help but envy the agility with which she floated to the front door, not once stumbling or hiking her skirts. She fumbled in her purse for a moment. There was a jingle of keys and finally, the click of the door lock.

I still blame adrenaline for what happened next. I pushed Harden away, jerked my skirts up well past my knees, and sprang forward, ignoring the roar of "Isa!" behind me. My eyes were on my prey, which turned to face me in surprise. Her delicate eyebrows flew up and her mouth formed a surprised pout, and then I tackled her like a star lineman.

We tumbled through the doorway and into the hall in a passionate lovers' embrace. I scrambled up, ready to fight, but Vivien just lay there, on the floor, like a broken china doll.

A moment later, Harden dropped to his knees next to her. "Jesus!"

"Is she? Is she … dead?" I was deepshitting myself—things were not going according to plan, which I didn't actually have.

It took Harden a few excruciatingly long moments to check Vivien's pulse and breathing. "No, but you knocked her out," he said finally. "She could have a broken neck for all we know. We have to call an ambulance."

"Oh my God," I said. "I'm going to jail now for sure."

"You should've thought about that before you attacked her like a rabid dog," Harden said, more preoccupied with the unconscious villain than he was with my pending fate.

"Rabid dog? Did you just call me a dog?" I had never in my life heard him call anyone a bad name. For a moment, I thought I misheard him.

Harden looked at me, more angry than apologetic. "What's gotten into you, Isa? It's like you're a different person!"

"What's gotten into me?" I said, mocking him. "*She* did. Well, technically, she got into my backpack, and then into my bank account!"

"So that's your excuse for tryin' to kill her?"

"I wasn't trying to kill her! I didn't expect her to be so *light*."

Harden returned to fussing over Vivien, taking off his makeshift turban to put it under her head. I watched him cradle her neck in his huge hand.

"I didn't mean for this to happen," I said.

He chuckled. "What did you think was gonna happen after you knocked her down? That she'd offer us coffee?"

"You're not funny, Harden. And you have no idea what I've been through over the last couple days. It's been hell! Do you think you'd be thinking rationally after waking up in jail and being interrogated by corrupt cops? Or being attacked by monsters?"

"Monsters? Jail? What the hell are you talkin' about?"

"Nothing," I said, remembering that I forgot to mention the *bhang* incident in my earlier debrief. Bringing up the hallucinations now certainly wasn't going to help me win my case. "I mean, metaphorically. I've had to deal with human monsters."

Harden paused his nursing for a moment and straightened up to look at me. Even on his knees, he was still as tall as me. "Okay, I'm sorry you had a rough couple days, but that's still not an excuse for violence. You almost killed her. I thought you wanted to help people."

"Good people, yes! Not the ones who help themselves, especially to others' property."

"Maybe you're havin' a post-traumatic stress episode or somethin'," Harden said, and sighed. And that's when Vivien moaned something.

"Oh, thank God she's okay," I said. "Help me sit her up."

"I still think we should call an ambulance," he said.

"Nonsense. Look at her. She's fine."

Vivien was not fine, but at least she wasn't dead. She moaned some more as we moved her up against a wall, and finally opened her eyes.

"Hi," Harden said. "Can you hear me?"

She looked back and forth between us, like a drunk. Then I saw a spark of recognition in her eyes. "American girl?"

Why does everybody call me that?

"Yep. I bet you never thought you'd see me again, huh?"

"I don't know what you mean," Vivien said, touching the back of her head and wincing. "I waited for you at the airport for an hour—"

"Liar!" I practically exploded with rage. "You're such a liar. And a thief! How are you enjoying my money, thief? Just wait till the FBI finds out about all this."

Harden put one arm between us. "That's enough, Isa."

"You should listen to your companion," Vivien probed her neck. "My lawyer will certainly hear about this."

"Oh, good, 'cause you're gonna need a lawyer where you're going," I said, slapping away Harden's attempts to control me. "Cause you're going to jail, that's why."

"I'm afraid it is you who will be going to jail," Vivien said coolly.

"Yeah?" I said, trying to shoo away visions of myself behind bars, feverish with malaria, surrounded by other destitute women fighting over gruel. "Well, you're the one who should be afraid. You have no idea what I have planned for you!"

"Let's all calm down," Harden said and extended a hand to Vivien. "Please, let me help you."

Vivien eyed him suspiciously. "And who are you?"

"I'm a bystander," he said. "I'd like to make this right."

He didn't even say he was my friend.

I watched while he helped her up and she leaned on him for support, all weak and feminine and disgusting.

"Thank you," she said, batting her eyelashes. "It is all such a shock, to come home at the end of the day, only to find a psycho stalker waiting in the bushes to ambush me."

"Whom are you calling a psycho, you ... you psycho?" I said. "I can't believe I ever thought we were going to be friends! All that laughing and sharing prescription drugs was just a ploy. You might be a good actress, but I'm not buying your act anymore, and a judge won't either!"

"Isa," Harden said and made a face. I made a face back, hoping it adequately explained just how pissed off at him I was.

Vivien squinted at me and for a moment I could almost feel her probing my mind, looking for a weak spot. "You poor, silly thing. Do you have any idea how they treat foreigners in Indian jails? Especially exotic creatures like you?"

I reeled from another flash of my possible future behind bars, although a part of my brain registered that nobody had ever called me an "exotic creature" before.

I still hate you.

"The consul general might have something to say about this," I said, trying hard to fake confidence, or if not, at least determination. "Maybe the FBI, too."

"I would like to lie down." Vivien motioned toward the back of the house and let her knees buckle. Harden lifted her up as if she was nothing more than a kitten, and carried her off.

"She's faking it," I said to his back. "This is all an act!"

"That's enough," Harden said without turning.

I followed them and watched as he gingerly laid her on the plush sofa in the living room. He never once looked back to see if I was still there, or if I cared that he was now literally and figuratively on my enemy's side.

My Viking deserted me yet again.

THAT'S WHAT WE WANT TO DO, TOO!

other Teresa was just fine without a boyfriend.

M   I steeped in resentment while Harden continued to fuss over Vivien, arranging and rearranging pillows, taking off her ludicrous shoes, and dashing to the kitchen for a glass of water.

"Thank you ever so much," Vivien purred, sipping delicately from the glass. "I feel quite a bit better now."

"Thank you ever so much," I mocked her and got a steely look from Harden. I mocked that, too.

"I still think we should call an ambulance," Harden said, kneeling next to the couch where she reclined like Cleopatra. "You could have a concussion."

"Oh, no, there is no need." Vivien laughed her tinkle-bell laugh. "You are such a darling."

They looked at each other, Vivien the Queen, and Harden the ever-obedient dog.

"She's playing you," I said. "Stop looking into her eyes like a love-sick puppy."

"All I'm trying to do is help, Isa," Harden said, tearing himself away from Vivien long enough to reprimand me with another hard look. "Could you, maybe, apologize?"

"I will not!"

"She's usually not like this at all," Harden turned back to Vivien. "It's the culture shock."

"It's so not the culture shock!" I said, exasperated. "It's a nightmare that won't end. Everyone is conspiring against me, and now it's *et tu* Harden?"

"I'm not against you," Harden said. "You imagine things."

"I think you might be right," Vivien said. Her eyes, which were plasticky-blue on the plane, were now dark and foreboding. "Now, Isa ... weren't you on the news yesterday? What was it? Something about you being on drugs, hallucinating, and then robbing a bank?"

"You, bitch," I said. "You know perfectly well that the bank heist was first."

"What's she talkin' about?" Harden asked. "Jesus, Isa, are you on drugs? Is this why you came to India?"

"No, I'm not on drugs. I mean, I had some *bhang*, but I didn't know it had dope in it. I was thirsty, and it's delicious. You would've drunk a bucket of it."

"Oh my God," Harden moaned. "I always thought Tara was a bad influence on you. Dope is a gateway drug, everybody knows that."

"Oh, please," I said. "Stop this 'I'm so perfect and saintly' show. You're the one who supplied us with alcohol. Isn't buying alcohol for minors illegal? Huh?"

Just when I had the upper hand, Vivien decided to intervene. "This is making my headache worse."

"I'm so sorry," Harden said. "Can I get you anything else? An ambulance?"

"Enough already," I started, but Vivien put up one hand. She used the other one to cover her eyes in the most melodramatic manner. Completely overacting, but Harden still bought it.

"Shut up, Isa," he said, and my heart skipped a beat, and not in a good way. I squeezed my mouth shut, not because he told me to, but because I once again felt like crying.

"I'm afraid I can't take this any longer," Vivien whispered with a pained look.

"I'm so, so sorry," Harden said.

"I have a big event tomorrow," Vivien said, lifting her hand just enough to glance at my reaction. "I can't afford to stay up all night dealing with the police and reporters."

"Thank you," Harden said. "Thank you so much."

I don't know what pissed me off more—his revolt against me, or his subservient attitude. "What are you thanking her for?"

"For not throwin' us in jail," he hissed.

I was about to spell out where and how I was going to throw him when Vivien interrupted us once again. "I would like for you to leave. Now."

Leave? Just like that?

Harden was saying something, I think promising her his firstborn, but I couldn't hear a word through the pounding of heartbeats in my ears.

"Not so fast!" I said.

Vivien stopped her drama for just a moment. A reflection of surprise passed across her face, which was to be expected, but there was something else, too.

"What are you doin'?" I heard Harden's pained whisper.

"Don't you see?" I said without taking my eyes off Vivien's. "That's what she wants us to do."

"That's what we want to do, too!" Harden said.

"Maybe you—but *I* don't," I said. "I've done nothing wrong, apart maybe from trespassing, and maybe breaking and entering. Okay, and the assault, but that's nothing compared to what she's done. She stole my identity and my money, but more importantly, I'm willing to bet that wasn't her first crime."

Vivien stayed silent, but her eyes bored into mine.

"Why did you go to that couture thing today, Vivien? You left before the show even started."

She said nothing but her chest heaved, and I knew I was close to the target.

"Let's go," Harden said.

I ignored him. "Yes, I was there. Are you surprised? What were you doing, casing the joint? Planning on stealing yourself a new pair of shoes by the House of Borgezie?" I made sure to pronounce the name correctly.

Vivien stopped breathing for just a second.

Right there. That's the bull's eye.

"Oh my God," I said, flashing back to the unnecessarily large purse she carried to the show. "Have you've done it already? Is it here somewhere? It's here, isn't it?"

"I don't know what you're talking about," Vivien said in an infuriatingly calm tone.

"Then call the cops," I said. "Better yet, let us do that for you." I fished out my phone. "What's the number for the police? On second thought, don't worry about it—I'll find it."

I was busy trying to type "Delhi police number" into the tiny search window, so I missed the moment when Vivien sprang from the couch like a spooked gazelle. By the time I looked up, she was halfway across the room.

"Isa, no!" I heard Harden yell as I took off after her. She turned the corner in a flurry of streaming fabric and pounding little feet, and I almost landed on my butt trying to do the same. When I regained my balance, she was just a glimpse of shimmering gold silk disappearing down a staircase.

Shit!

I caught up with her in the basement, where she fumbled to get another door open, a solid-looking one with metal edges. I grabbed her arms, thin and almost childlike but surprisingly strong.

It was like trying to wrestle an enraged cat. She spun and twisted in my arms, small fists flying everywhere. I managed to get hold of one of her wrists and was trying to tangle it up in the end of her sari when she nailed me in the solar plexus with her elbow.

"Bitch," I managed with what little air I had left in my lungs. My whole body seized up, and all I could do was hold on to her and wait for my diaphragm to cooperate again.

A moment later I felt Harden trying to pull us apart. "Let her go!"

"No," I croaked, kicking blindly, tangled in a mess of limbs, hair, and clothes.

"You will be sorry when …" Vivien huffed into my armpit, and then my foot finally connected with something. Harden hollered in pain and the three of us hit the door, stumbling into the room in one heap.

Motion-sensor lights came on, temporarily blotting everything in bright whitewash. I squeezed my eyes shut, trying my best to hold on … until I noticed there was no longer any struggle.

"Oh my God," I heard Harden say, and opened my eyes.

We were in the strangest room I'd ever seen, even stranger than my neighbor's exercise studio, although this one was flawlessly neat. It was almost entirely white, set up like a Hollywood makeup trailer, with a huge mirror surrounded by lights and a built-in counter lined with brushes in matching holders and shiny makeup cases. The mirror looked like one of those *CSI* investigation boards, plastered with photos of women, some torn from magazine pages, others printed in color and black-and-white. In one corner, a curio cabinet sported plastic mannequin heads with wigs in just about every color and style. In the other corner was an office desk topped with a computer monitor.

"This … this is it!" I scrambled to my feet. "Look, Harden, it's the proof. This is where she works on her makeup forgeries. I bet my photo's somewhere here too."

Harden said nothing.

"Are you okay? I'm sorry I kicked you, but I had no other choice, and look at this—turns out I'm right after all."

He just pointed at the other wall.

The one covered with human faces.

GO SCREW YOURSELF, HUGE TITS.

For one agonizing second, I thought I was in *Silence of the Lambs*, surrounded by at least two dozen trophies, carefully scalped from their previous owners. They all seemed to be screaming, their eyes and mouths dark, gaping hollows. I heard my own excruciatingly long scream reverberate from the walls like the sound of someone falling from a ridiculously tall building, say the Empire State one. It ended almost as abruptly when I saw Harden reach out and stick his finger through one eyehole.

"Don't touch it," I managed, even though it was obviously too late. "Gross. And also evidence."

It seemed that Harden was never going to listen to me again. He pulled the face off its plastic half-ball holder. "It's fake," he said, rubbing the skin between his fingers.

I came closer and dared to touch the thing. It wasn't slimy at all, and not scary either. It was the kind of a fake face Tom Cruise would peel off to reveal that it was game over for the bad guys. I turned to Vivien for an explanation, only to find it was game over for me.

I was staring down the barrel of an unfamiliar revolver. Strangely small, almost cute, but the bullets peeking from its fully loaded cylinder meant business.

"Hands up!" she said, trying to straighten her sari. I froze, letting just my eyes dart about the room to see if she had any more guns lying around.

"Don't even think about it," she said, slowly cocking the gun.

I shot my hands up, and so did Harden.

"Please," Harden said. His voice was deep and slow, as if he was trying to hypnotize Vivien. "Please, put the gun down."

"Shut up," she said.

"What are you gonna do?" I asked, watching the way she held the gun. Instead of bracing for a shot, she was now using her other hand to straighten her hair. She certainly didn't look like a woman who'd spent any time at the gun range.

"Please," Harden continued his hypnotic séance. "Please. We didn't mean for this to happen."

"I told you to shut up," Vivien said, and Harden finally did. "I have to think. What the hell am I going to do with you idiots?"

"Let us go?" I suggested. "I *will* leave this time, I promise." I meant it, too. Funny how your plans change once a gun is pointed at your head.

"Please," Harden said. "I promise, I'll carry her out of here—"

"Shut up!" Vivien screamed and fired a shot into the ceiling. The sound was deafening in the small space. Bits of plaster rained down and I screamed too, covering my head with my hands and waiting for the second shot. It didn't come. Instead, I heard a muffled thump and a pained cry.

I opened my eyes to see Harden clutching Vivien in a bear hug, the revolver on the floor at her feet. Her updo was a complete mess, and if she still looked anything like a doll, it was now a possessed one. She thrashed about, trying to wriggle out of his vise grip, and when that didn't work she started kicking and screaming.

"Jesus!" Harden bellowed. "Help me!"

"Stop it!" I screamed at the top of my lungs.

Surprisingly, it worked—Vivien stopped struggling for a moment and glared at me from behind a curtain of tangled-up black locks. Her nostrils were flaring.

"Okay," I said, putting my hands up. "Let's talk about this. I'm sure we can figure out a mutually acceptable solution. Give me back my money, and I promise not to call the cops."

Vivien considered my proposal for a moment. I thought it was a good one, but she turned it down by biting hard on Harden's arm.

I'd never heard Harden scream like that before. To his credit, he didn't let her go, instead spinning and hopping about the room as if the two of them were engaged in a weird contemporary dance. I tried to get in there, but I was poorly equipped for taming the wild beast. I had no choice.

The second shot brought down even more plaster. Harden and Vivien paused their routine, wheezing in unison.

"What are you doin'?" Harden said. Vivien shrank behind the same arm she was determined to devour just a moment ago.

"I'm helping you," I said, irritated. "Let's tie her up."

"How about you put the gun down?" Harden said, not moving.

"I will, but tie her up first."

Vivien stayed quiet while Harden bundled her into a chair with a strap from one of the makeup bags.

I surveyed his handiwork without lowering the gun. "That's not enough. She's a mini Houdini."

He rummaged through the countertop drawers for more restraints, finally settling on another strap and two scarves. With those safety measures in place, I finally dared to tuck the gun into the back of my sari.

"I think I'm havin' a heart attack," Harden said as he sank to the floor.

"No, you're not," I said. "Stop being such a drama queen."

He shook his head. "You're crazy."

"You're welcome," I said with seething sarcasm. "Remind me not to get involved next time you get attacked by a rabid dog."

"I thought she was gonna kill you," Harden said simply, but for some reason, the words stung.

"Thanks," I said. "I mean, for helping me. Did she hurt you?"

Harden held up his arm for me to see. There was some blood, but otherwise it seemed okay.

"She'll pay for that," I said.

Vivien swore in Hindi. I didn't need a translator to know it was ugly.

"Girl, please! Don't waste your breath. I don't know what you're saying, and frankly, I don't care."

"I will translate for you," she said. "Go screw yourself, Huge Tits."

"Oh, no!" I mocked her. "You hurt my feelings, Itty Bitty Titty Committee."

She said something else. "Do you know what that means, Loose Vagina?"

"Is that all you got?" I said. "Bitch, please. I can shoot better than you, and I sure as hell can swear better, too."

"Isa," Harden said. "What's the plan here?"

"Oh yeah, right," I said, giving Vivien one last nasty look. "Let's call the cops."

"And tell 'em what? That you've assaulted someone in their house, and now have 'em tied up at gunpoint?"

Right.

Vivien laughed. "You are a stupid girl."

"You are a stupid girl," I taunted her.

"How about we just go?" Harden said.

It made sense, of course. Everything he said so far made sense, but that didn't mean I had to like it, or follow it, at least not right away.

"Give me a minute." I took out my phone.

"Seriously? We're facing jail, and all you care about is Twitter?"

"Do you think that, maybe, you might be underestimating me?" I said, snapping photos of the room, making sure to document every wig, fake face, and magazine page plastered onto the mirror. "This is evidence."

Vivien observed my work with cold indifference. "Fascinating," she said finally. "What are the charges? Makeup addiction? Possession of illegal mascara with intent to supply?"

I stopped for a second. "Who are these women?" I asked, motioning to the mirror.

"Since when is it a crime to follow celebrities?" she sneered. "Will you be arresting the whole of Twitter, too?"

"Not unless they steal something, let's say, an identity. Are these celebrities perchance missing something valuable? Like jewelry? Or millions of dollars?"

"If this is your proof," Vivien said, "I am looking forward to watching my lawyer tear you a new one. You are not familiar with the local judicial system, are you? It is almost not fair."

"She has a point," Harden tried again.

I thought about it. "You're right, Vivien."

"Thank God," Harden moaned, getting up. "Can we please—"

"We need some better evidence," I said.

"Isa!" His face was bright red. Maybe he was having a heart attack after all.

Serves him right for helping she-devils.

"Stop yelling and help me search for it," I said, pulling out drawers and throwing their contents out onto the floor.

"I'm gonna leave without you," he said but didn't move.

"Suit yourself," I said, searching through the piles of makeup paraphernalia on the floor. It was no use. "It's probably somewhere in the rest of the house," I said, getting up. "In a hidden safe. That's where you'd keep cash, right?"

"So now you are going to rob me?" Vivien said.

"You robbed me first!"

"I did not."

"Yes, you did!"

"Isa," Harden said. "She's right. Even if you find cash, how will it be proof of anything, other than your breakin' and enterin' was premeditated?"

"Why are you always on her side? I'm not sure what we'd find. There could be stolen jewelry. That's proof, right?"

"I dunno, Izz." Harden slid back down onto the floor and buried his face in his hands. "I don't think gold can be traced."

I sat down, too. It *was* hopeless. Harden was right. Any police officer or judge would take just one look at poor, tiny Vivien, and, after hearing about her torment, would jail me for a million years. I looked at her. Somehow, even with the messed-up hair, she still looked gorgeous, her cheeks flushed with color and her eyelashes fluttering.

"What are you looking at, Vivien?" I asked, watching her face. Her eyes darted back at me.

"Isa! Please ..."

"I think I know where she keeps the evidence," I said, not taking my eyes off her.

Vivien's eyes flashed toward the monitor again.

Of course. How did I not think of that to start with?

I turned to Harden. "It's in that computer. Maybe something in the search history, or," I looked around the room, "judging from her obsessive-compulsive organizing, it's all in a spreadsheet somewhere."

"Bra-*vo*," Vivien said. "What are you going to do? Shake it until the spreadsheet falls out?"

"You underestimate me," I said. "I mean, you underestimate *him*. He's a hacker."

Vivien laughed, overly loud. It made me feel even better about my hunch.

"That's gonna be your last laugh, Vivien. For your information, Harden here," I thumbed in his direction, "makes a living out of hacking bank systems. Yeah, it's a job, did you know that?"

"Isa, I can't," Harden said.

"Yes, you can. I can hold a gun to your head if it helps."

"That's not funny."

"It could be, like that scene in *Swordfish*," I said, and then remembered that the scene also involved a blowjob. Harden must've remembered it, too, because his already-red face turned an even more intense shade.

"You won't find anything," Vivien said.

I ignored her. "Please, Harden, you came all this way to help me, don't bail on me now. Help me catch an international criminal and clear my name. Help me get the orphans' money back."

"Orphans," Vivien scoffed.

"Yes, orphans," I barked at her. "This money was on its way to the poor, and you knew it. There's no way I'm gonna let it buy you any more cars, or shoes, or makeup. Have you even seen how people live in the slums of this very town? Have you?"

Vivien rolled her eyes.

"Please, Harden," I said. "If not for me, please do it for the kids. You saw how Kabir lives. If we leave, Vivien wins. She knows my name. Without the evidence to defend us, we'll end up in jail anyway and the beggars will go on begging."

Harden was silent. I realized I'd been patting his shoulder the whole time, and took my hand away.

"You're crazy," he said finally. My heart sank.

"You are right about that," Vivien said.

"But you have a good heart," Harden continued. "That's what I've always … liked about you. You care about others."

I nodded and waited for him to say something so my heart could go on beating like normal.

"Okay," he said. "I'll do it."

Vivien went into a seizure-like attempt to wriggle free of the restraints, cursing in Hindi. I didn't bother to ask her what it meant.

"Thank you, Harden," I said, elated. My guardian angel was back at my side. "I promise, I will let it go. You don't even need to break into her bank or anything, just find some evidence that she stole from me, or from anybody."

I wanted to hug him, but he went straight to the desk and sat in the small office chair, which creaked in protest.

"Isa," he said after a moment. "I think we might have a problem."

"What?"

He pointed at the keyboard. It looked pretty average, black and plastic, until I noticed what he meant. The keyboard was covered in the same squiggles I'd remembered from the police interrogation office.

"That's okay." I pointed. "It has English letters, too." Under each of the squiggles were the familiar faces of our home alphabet.

"Yeah, but I bet the password and the commands are all in Hindi."

"Idiots." Behind us, Vivien laughed. "You know I can hear everything you say. It's quite silly for you to do this right in front of me."

"Don't even try," I said. "You're staying right here. I'm not taking my eyes off you again."

She didn't reply, instead redoubling her wiggling efforts. It was pointless—Harden did a good job with the restraints.

I put my hand on his shoulder. "Can you, I don't know, Google Translate it or something?"

"Sorry, Izz," Harden said, squeezing his temples. "I don't know where to start."

"It's okay," I said, although I didn't feel okay, not at all. "Can you maybe hot-wire it or something?"

"It's not a car," Harden said, and Vivien laughed again. That got to me.

"Fine," I said and marched over to her. "If we can't do it twenty-first-century style, let's go medieval on her ass." I pushed her chair closer to the desk.

"Calm down, Isa. What the hell are you talkin' about?"

"What I'm talking about," I said, looking for a suitable weapon in the mess on the floor, "is old-fashioned torture. The kind favored by the Spanish Inquisition."

"What?"

"You heard me. We're gonna torture her until she spits the password, and the bank account numbers, and then the passwords to those bank accounts." I found a curling iron and held it up for both of them to see.

"Don't be crazy, Isa," Harden said in a measured tone. "We're not gonna torture anyone."

"Maybe you won't, but I will. I'm crazy. You said so!" I stepped behind Vivien's back and tried to give Harden a reassuring wink, but it came out like a crazy tic. I tried to wink with the other eye, but that one was even worse.

"I won't let you," Harden said, looking scared. Who could blame him? In my delirious state, armed with the curling iron, I must've looked like Britney during the umbrella episode, or Lindsay during ... well, every day.

"You're bluffing," Vivien said almost calmly, twisting in her chair to look at me.

How does she know that? The woman was a mind reader.

"Oh, yeah?" I said, sticking the iron in her face. "Wait till I plug it in."

"You are all talk," she said. "But I will be sure to remember this for the court proceedings."

"Isa," Harden said, putting his huge arm between the iron and Vivien's thin shoulders. "Stop this nonsense this instant! You can't torture anyone. You're not capable of it."

"Stop it this instant," I mocked him. "Who are you, my mother? And you don't know what I'm capable of!"

I reached in past his arm, grabbed a handful of Vivien's silky hair, and jerked it hard to demonstrate my torturing capabilities. It had a little too much effect—Vivien squealed like a hurt puppy and burst into tears.

I was fine fighting with her as long as she was fighting back, but not when she cried like a little kid. "Sorry!" I cried and reached in to pat her head, only to be slapped away by Harden.

Vivien sobbed, flopping in her chair like a wounded bird in a hunter's trap. Harden pushed me away and bent down, trying to undo her restraints.

"I didn't mean to pull it that hard!" I said, and suddenly I saw myself for what I was—a maniac, a self-serving bastard, no better than this thief herself or a corrupt cop.

This is madness.

I could no longer blame adrenaline for what I'd done. Maybe Harden was right. I must've gone insane from the stress, or drugs, or perhaps even an early onset of malaria. There was no other way to explain it.

"I'm sorry," I cried. "You're right. I can't torture anyone…."

"Then perhaps I could help?" said a voice behind me.

JUST WAIT TILL 2REAL HEARS ABOUT YOU!

Once again, I didn't scream, which was a shame, since it would have at least temporarily incapacitated the intruder. Instead, I just gaped. Even my tear ducts went offline. Either the repeated shocks to the system fried my circuitry, or maybe it was because of the way he looked, so young and not even remotely scary. For a moment, I almost wanted to hear what he had to say—something I learned to regret soon enough.

"Who are you?" Harden said. Behind me, Vivien groaned.

"A colleague," the young man, barely out of his teens, said in an accent as smooth as his finely tailored black suit. He was equal parts androgynous and exotic, with his straight shoulder-length black hair and smooth brown skin. Even the way he arranged himself in the doorway was somehow artistic, as if he was posing for the Indian edition of *GQ*. He bent his long neck to make eye contact with Vivien, who seemed to shrink behind me. "Hello, Divya."

"Divya?" I said, turning to her. "So that's your real name?"

Vivien, or Divya, or whoever she was, just looked at the floor. For some reason, she seemed deflated by the appearance of this man-child.

"Do you two know each other?" I persisted.

"Yeah," Divya said. "You really are screwed now."

"Yes," GQ marveled, looking me up and down. "She is right, you know. You're screwed, baby."

"I ain't your baby, junior," I said, getting a bit of my confidence back. I had a gun in the back of my skirt and Harden by my side, and if need be, I felt pretty sure I could head-butt this scrawny insect straight into tomorrow. "Who the hell are you?"

"Too real," he said. Despite his youth and featherweight class, his voice and face carried a tangible threat. Not that it scared me. I knew kung fu. I mean, I'd never tried it, but I'd seen all the *Matrix* films. Even *Matrix Reloaded,* although that one might have been a spoof.

I looked him up and down. "Are you serious?"

He stepped closer, like super uncomfortably close, as if we were squaring off in a prison yard.

Fine. I pulled out Divya's miniature revolver. It got caught on the fabric, and it took a few seconds to get it out, which kind of ruined the effect. Still, it was a gun, and I pressed it straight into his chest. "How's this for real?"

"Jesus," Harden hissed but stayed put.

The newcomer looked down at my almost-weapon without a trace of fear, or respect. "It's 2ReeL—number two-capital R-double E-capital L."

"What?"

"It's my *brand,*" 2ReeL said with such contempt, I almost shot him right then and there. "Are you familiar with the concept of personal branding?"

Behind me, Divya groaned again.

"No," I said with a matching attitude, "but I'm familiar with the concept of intellectual rights infringement. 2Real is a rapper, and I'm pretty one-hundred-percent sure he's black." Actually, I wasn't—these days any white kid with an Apple could be a rapper. I was, however, pretty sure the kid in front of me couldn't drop a rhyme.

"It's spelled differently," 2ReeL said, defensive. "Like I said, it is number two-capital R—"

"That's great," Harden said. "Nice to meet you, 2ReeL. Now, Isa, how about you put the gun down?"

I was about to launch into an inspired monologue on how I was large and in charge, but then there were heavy footsteps, and two large men appeared in the doorway. They also had guns—massive, steroid-infused biceps, plus a couple of chunky pistols. In an instant, two muzzles stared me down, like two merciless black eyes.

"Yes, Isa," 2ReeL said. "Why don't you put your little toy down?"

I took a defiant second to stare down his pitbulls before throwing my revolver to the floor. One of the beefcakes was older and looked like he just got out of prison. He had a thick bushy beard and blue tattoos all over his arms and hands. Perched on top of a Harley, he'd be a perfect addition to the Hells Angels. The other guy wasn't much older than me, perhaps still only a Hells Apprentice and better suited to playing a heartthrob in some B-movie, but he too looked perfectly capable of pulling the trigger.

"Okay, let's talk," I said, putting my hands up.

Unfortunately, 2ReeL wasn't in the mood for talking, which became obvious when he ordered his buddies to tie my hands behind my back. They tried to do the same to Harden, but couldn't get his wrists close enough together, so they settled on tying his hands at the front. They liberated Divya from her chair, but then tied her hands too.

"What are you going to do with us?" I asked 2ReeL as the mean biker-dude pulled me up the stairs.

"You will soon find out." 2ReeL smiled in a way that made me sick to my stomach. "Anticipation is the best part."

I tried yelling and wriggling, but this only got me a massive slap on the back of the head. I didn't know it could hurt so much. Hard to believe boxers could take one of those straight on the chin and still keep going. I whimpered quietly, trying my best to move my feet along as the old biker dragged me out. In the driveway, behind the Mercedes, a black van was waiting for us. The apprentice thug put a bag over Harden's head and shoved him into the van. I heard him cry out in pain.

"Stop it." I turned to 2ReeL. "What do you want with us? I don't even know who you are!"

"I don't know who you are, either," 2ReeL said. "However, it does not matter. You're a witness—and you know what happens to witnesses."

My heart pounded. "Just wait till 2Real hears about you!" I yelled, struggling against my restraints. "You're so going to regret this!"

2ReeL just laughed in my face until some kind soul pulled a bag over my head.

WE'RE NOT GOING TO A PICNIC.

There's no need for expensive lab experiments to prove that time is relative. If you don't believe me, try waiting in the dark, tied up and blindfolded. Ten minutes will turn into an eternity.

After a while, I heard them load something heavy into the van, a big box or something, it was hard to tell.

"They're gonna need a bigger van," I mumbled and was instantly rewarded with an enthusiastic kick to the kidneys.

I kept quiet after that, not because I had nothing to say, but mostly out of fear that the next intervention would come in the form of a bullet. Both of my companions got the message a lot sooner; I couldn't even hear Harden or Divya breathing.

Somehow, I could tell they were still in there with me. After a while, the darkness of the bag quieted my mind and sharpened my other senses. I could hear our captors arguing about something outside, and I could smell something acrid, like a cleaning solution, or maybe a cheap aftershave.

This is how ninjas do it.

I no longer had a gun, but I still had some hope in this dark gloom, and it took the form of my phone, safe next to my pounding heart. Somebody should have been looking for me already. If not Kabir, then maybe the consul general. Maybe even Moustache, in search of the next bribe installment. I would take any of those options over whatever 2ReeL had in mind.

I willed my mind to concentrate, the way I practiced every time I was on a crowded bus, mentally urging other passengers to leave at the next stop. I envisaged a shadowy figure, a yet unknown hero coming to my rescue. Someone who'd been watching over me all this time and had picked this desperate moment to strike in my defense.

The van door banged closed with the force of an artillery recoil.

"Jesus!" I jumped with my whole body, smacking my already sore cranium into the metal wall behind me.

At least nobody bothered to slap me again. The van rolled backward, presumably out of the driveway, turned to the left, paused, and drove off. I concentrated my ninja powers on mapping out the route in my head, but it became impossible after the van made a few sharp turns. *This must be against some kind of law*, I thought, rolling back and forth on the floor, bumping painfully into the walls, and occasionally—and less painfully—into Harden. I could hear both him and Divya groan, but nobody said a thing. The darkness had an either a calming or stupefying effect on all of us, a bunch of parakeets quietly griping in a cage covered with a throw.

During one of those maneuvers, my head bag got caught on something, and I managed to wriggle out of it. I blinked a few times. My eyes, already used to the darkness, could make out the shapes of Harden and Divya on the floor next to me. The guards had to be in the front of the van.

"Harden," I whispered, scrambling up to my knees on the rocking floor. "Untie me."

"I can't," he whispered back hotly. "I'm tied up too."

"Just try, please. With your teeth, maybe?"

He sighed. "And then what? They have guns, Isa."

"I know," I said, refusing to accept that fact. "At least we'll have the element of surprise."

"Surprise!" he growled and waved his tied hands.

He was right, of course. In the game of rock-paper-gun-surprise, gun won over all the other options. Still, I couldn't just sit there.

"I'm sorry, Harden. I fucked up. I should've listened, I should've thought things through, but I didn't. And now it looks like we're gonna die. All I'm asking is that you help me try to fix this. I still have my phone, I just need to reach it. I'll call the cops and this could be over in minutes."

"I hate to say it, but she is right," Divya piped up from the dark. "We are not going to a picnic."

"Thank you for that, Divya, or Vivien, or whoever you are," I said. "So incredibly helpful of you to start cooperating when it looks like it no longer matters. Perhaps you could also enlighten me as to what warranted your friends to show up at your place with guns?"

Divya snorted in the dark. I ached to get my hands on her.

"Please, Harden?" I tried again.

He didn't say anything for what seemed an eternity, but then reached up with his bound hands and pulled the bag off his head. "Okay."

"Thank you," I said, and turned around to let him tug at the rope. "I'm so sorry, Harden. I'll listen to you from now on, I promise."

He snorted a rebuff but kept on pulling at the rope.

Oh God, please let me get out of this one, and I promise I'll go to church every Sunday and give ten percent to the parish....

I had a premonition, a warm knowing that everything would turn out okay, and then the van screeched to a full stop. I fell backward and would have broken my back or at least dislocated something, if Harden's body didn't break my fall.

"Jesus!" I cried. "Are y'all okay?"

"No," Harden said, and then the door opened and the Hells Angels fell upon me.

YOU THINK I LOOK LIKE BRADLEY COOPER?

Religion is a lot harder than what they lead you to believe in Sunday school. It's all fun in the beginning, with Christmases, and angels, and promises of heaven. But then you grow up and learn there's also hell, poverty, and war, plus George Bush.

I was so mad at God for standing me up, I hardly cared that the Hells Angels roughed me and Harden up for taking our bags off, whacked on new blindfolds, and dragged us out of the van. I didn't even try to threaten anyone with the consul general, mainly because it was unlikely these thugs understood English. They did, however, say enough to Vivian—I mean, Divya!—in Hindi, for her to scream something back. She had to be shit at cursing—whatever it was, it did nothing other than to entertain the bastards.

I didn't get to see where we were, but it smelled like my grandma's garden: Wet soil, manure, and roses. We walked across a crunchy gravel path and climbed several steps, and then, after a few more moments of getting prodded along, someone finally took off my blindfold.

We were in a kitchen, which was large, but so full of stuff, there was hardly any room left for our group. The stone walls were almost entirely covered in hanging pots and baskets, and the countertops were crowded with more bowls, containers, and jars of all sorts. Even more pots were simmering on the stove. It was dark, with the light from the small windows and stove reflecting in shiny copper, giving the room the ambiance of a Brothers Grimm storybook.

In the middle of this chaos, an old woman in a sari abandoned her dough and was wiping her hands with a towel. She looked so sweet and wrinkled, the sight made me long for my grandma. For a moment, I thought she was about to offer us cake.

2ReeL said something to the woman, who could have been his grandma, although it would be hard to believe such a sweet, cake-baking tree could bear an apple as rotten as him. Plus, Grandma seemed less than happy to see him—she put down the towel, aimed an accusing finger at 2ReeL, and launched into a long, angry rant. 2ReeL tried to say something, but even though I couldn't understand a word, I knew she wasn't having it. I gloated in silence while I watched her every word slap the brand straight out of him.

"What's she saying?" I asked Divya. I still hated her guts, but she was the only one around willing to translate Indian swear words.

"What do you think," she said. "The old hag is not happy he brought you here."

"Well, that makes two of us," I said. "So, are we free to go?"

Divya laughed, but there was no joy in it. "This is Naanaa-ji Aadarsha. Grandma Aadarsha. You have no idea who she is, do you?"

"You can't be serious," I said. "I've been in this country for, like, five minutes. Do you know *my* grandma? I mean, she's dead now, but did you know her?"

"Aadarsha is sort of a legend."

"Well, whoopity-doo. My grams was an eminent member of the LaGrange community."

Divya snickered. "What was she famous for? Jam?"

"She should've been," I said, trying to pull my slapping hand out of the rope handcuff. "You haven't tried it, so don't knock it."

"How sweet. Well, this one will make jam out of you."

That was it. I was about to head-butt her to the ground when Grandma Famous finally noticed our bickering. 2ReeL had a momentary reprieve when she moved the spotlight onto Divya, shuffling over and shoving that persistent finger into Divya's chest, prattling on with a look of disappointment normally reserved for family members.

"What's she saying now?" I asked, but Divya ignored me, instead cooing something in Hindi. It hardly made a dent in Grandma's tirade.

I was about to intervene by bringing attention to my still-tied hands and maybe requesting a glass of water when a side door opened, and a plump teenage boy came in cuddling a fluffy little kitten. He was wearing shorts and a tank top that did little to cover his belly or side boobs.

"Harshit!" Grandma scampered back to fuss over the boy, seemingly forgetting there were hostages in her kitchen. 2ReeL and Divya groaned in unison.

Harshit, if that indeed was his name, pushed the old woman away, shifted the kitten into one hand, and plunged the other one into a bowl of chips. Grandma clasped her hands in a universal gesture of maternal delight, went back to the table, and attacked the dough with a vigor of a much younger woman.

I was about to ask for that water and the untying, and maybe also for some chips, when, as an afterthought, Grandma paused her dough punching to say a few words to 2ReeL. The next thing I knew, we were being dragged away, down a hallway.

"Wait," I cried over my shoulder. "What just happened?"

Nobody answered me. The Hells Angels didn't speak English, and everyone else was either pissed off at me or hardly noticed my existence.

"This is bullshit! I'm a celebrity!"

Of course it was pathetic to resort to that, but how would you like to be tortured for someone's amusement and not even get a charity donation in return? My pleas had just as little effect as they do on prime-time TV, but at least there were no cameramen trying to frame my anguish.

"Celebrity," 2ReeL snorted, not even turning back to look at me. The farther we moved away from Grandma, the more his attitude came back.

"Yes, I am," I said, stumbling. This time Hells Apprentice was in charge of dragging me along, and he was taking the whole roughing-up-the-prisoners thing way too seriously. Even if he did make it to Hollywood, he'd blow his auditions by overacting.

"You're lying," 2ReeL said.

"I'm not lying, honest!" I said, trying hard not to roll my eyes at the irony of the situation. "I was in all the papers in the US. I was Mr. Hue's protege, and then everybody thought I was pregnant with his baby, and then I wrote a book about it. It was a bestseller, and I made a million dollars."

"Do you think I'm stupid?" 2ReeL stopped, and I almost head-butted his back. "Mr. Hue is gay. Everyone knows that. Do you expect me to believe you were romantically linked to a gay billionaire, or that a bestselling author, a millionaire no less, would dress like this?" He waved his arm over my disheveled person.

"I had to pay taxes," I started, but he moved on, and Hells Apprentice shoved me to follow.

Son of a bitch. I had to think of something else, and fast—we'd arrived at a heavy wooden door, and 2ReeL was looking for a key on a huge keychain.

"Wow," I said. "You know who you look like when you're mad like this?"

"Like a murderer?" Harden said behind me. It was good to hear him talk again, except of course he picked the worst moment to start.

"No," I said and shot a warning look back at him. "You kinda look like that actor, he was in that movie, what was it? God, he's so famous— what's his name?"

"I don't know, Isa," Harden said again, louder. "What does it matter if we get executed by a Bradley Cooper look-alike?"

2ReeL looked up from the keychain. "You think I look like Bradley Cooper?"

"No," Harden said. "I'm trying to think of a way out of this, preferably in one piece."

"Yes!" I exclaimed, trying to cover up Harden's last words. "You look just like him. The way your eyes sparkled just then. And the jaw—you totally have his jaw. And the jaw is, like, the sexiest thing on a man, if you ask me...."

"I've been told I look like a young Tom Cruise," 2ReeL said, smoothing his already sleek hair. "Bradley Cooper has blue eyes, doesn't he?"

"Yes," I said. "But the color doesn't matter, it's in the look, you know what I mean? It's the *brand*, and your brand is, like, so Bradley Cooper. And Tom Cruise, yes, I can see that too."

It could have totally worked if I had another five minutes, but 2ReeL returned to the keys, found one, and unlocked the door. A musty smell of rotten vegetables and earth hit me. One by one, we were shoved in through the narrow opening into what seemed to be a cellar of some sort.

"Don't try anything stupid," 2ReeL said.

"Me? Why do you assume it will be me?" I said, but he shut the door in my face. I could hear the key scraping in the lock.

"What a jerk." I turned around. I didn't exactly expect compassion, but I didn't expect to be pounced on, either. The dying light from the tiny window high above the floor was just enough to see the fury on my companions' faces.

"This is it," Harden said. "We're dead. We could'a been on a plane by now, but instead, we're gonna be murdered and most likely buried right here, in this cellar."

"You don't know that," I said, backing away into a shadow. "It's a root cellar, and that would be unhygienic. And anyway, you could die on a plane, too, you know. Have you taken crash statistics into account? Cause, really, if you're gonna compare the two options—"

"Just stop talking," Divya said. "The more you talk or do, the worse it gets."

That was rich, coming from her. "So what, now it's my fault Grandma Famous is mad at you? Or that 2ReeL showed up at your house with his armed buddies? What was he doing there? He has no idea who I am."

"You have no idea the mess you're in," Divya said.

"Oh yes, we do," Harden said.

"Speak for yourself. Why don't you enlighten me, Divya?" I said, struggling to free at least one hand. Maybe I was going down, but not before I slapped the hoity-toity out of her.

"That woman is the mother-queen of Delhi mafia," Divya said and sat down on the floor, disappearing into the shadows. "We are already dead."

Harden moaned in agreement and, unexpectedly, so did I. It wasn't just what she said. It was the way she said it, sincerely scared and hopeless. I let my knees buckle until my butt hit the floor. "But why? Why would she want to kill us? What have I done to her? I've never seen her before in my life."

"It's not personal. You're just in the wrong place at the wrong time. Your boyfriend is right—you should have gone home when you had the chance."

"He's not my *boyfriend*," I said. Harden stayed quiet in his corner, seemingly no longer interested in what I had to say. "Anyway, I would go home now. Can you tell her I'm sorry for whatever it is and we'll get on the first plane out of here?"

Divya laughed, but it sounded like she was close to tears. "It is too late. Aadarsha wants the big tuna—she doesn't care that some mackerel was caught in the net."

"Mackerel?"

"She doesn't know who you are, and she doesn't care. She wants the necklace back, and now she knows about the House of Borgezie stilettoes, too."

"What necklace? So, you admit you pinched the shoes?"

"Sure," Divya sighed. "It was all over the news, and apparently she knew it was me right away. I should've just stuck with the necklace and your cash, but I was just so worried I may not have enough to cover my tracks. Or perhaps I have a problem with shiny things."

"You have a problem, all right," I said. "Hope they have Kleptomaniacs Anonymous for assholes like you."

"Look, I know I did a wrong thing," she said earnestly. "Believe me, I had my reasons. And I would gladly give it all back for a chance to start a new life, one where I'm not afraid all the time and maybe even have a hope for the future. I would give it all to Aadarsha if she would only let me go, but she is taking my betrayal a little too personally."

"What did you do?"

"It's a long story," came another sigh from the dark.

DIAMONDS, OF COURSE.

The next time a curveball threatens to ruin your day, try imagining what it would be like to become an orphan at eleven. It helps put things in perspective. And if that's not enough to equate to whatever middle-class crisis you might be experiencing, imagine getting "adopted" by a criminal mastermind with special plans for your personal development.

"Did you have to, you know, do stuff?" I dared to ask.

"What?" Divya snapped. "Prostitute myself? No. Fortunately or unfortunately, I was a great deal more useful in other ways. You wouldn't believe how easy it was for a sweet young girl to pick up goods in exchange for a forged check. Especially for a girl who never looks the same twice."

"I don't get it."

"I stole things," Divya said. I could practically hear her roll her eyes in the dark. "I wore disguises, stole expensive things, and got away with it. First it was watches, then jewelry, then later artwork and even—"

"Bank accounts?"

"Sure," Divya said.

"So you admit that too?"

"Whatever. Neither one of us will live long enough to enjoy that cash."

"I wasn't planning on enjoying it," I said haughtily. "It was for others."

"Look, for whatever it's worth, I'm sorry. For some reason, I didn't want to believe you were a philanthropist. I mean, the way the media portrayed you, I thought you were more like one of those Real Housewives."

"The way the media portrayed you," I mocked her. I wasn't going to admit it, but she had a point about the *Real Housewives*. Who would care if one of them was robbed? They all needed to get a job as far as I was concerned. "I *am* a philanthropist. Who else flies all the way to India to help the orphans?"

"Who else?" She mocked me back. "How about every other celebrity in need of fresh PR or Instagram pulp? Or the sheltered middle-class overachievers in need of spiritual enlightenment? Cuddling babies for the camera does not make you a philanthropist, just like putting on a sari does not make you cultured."

"I wasn't going to cuddle babies!" I said. I mean, I did think of posting a picture or two of myself surrounded by the children whose lives I was planning to change, but how would *she* know that? "I came all the way here to give my money to those who need it."

"Well, I needed it, so consider this a job well done."

I laughed, but my heart ached. We could have become best friends under different circumstances, and if she wasn't such a cold-hearted bitch.

"Plus, someone was bound to rob you sooner or later," she continued. "You were a sitting duck, leaving your backpack on the floor like that, and in the airport no less."

I had a vivid flashback to the airport, to the last time I could remember dropping my wallet into my backpack. "So that old lady in a head scarf looking at the phones—that was you?"

"Yes. It wasn't planned, so I had to improvise."

"That was quite a performance."

"Thank you," she said. "When I was young, I had dreams of becoming a proper actor one day. I even fooled myself into thinking that putting on makeup and lying to people was helping to develop my acting skills. Of course, Aadarsha wouldn't hear of acting lessons. She'd already cast me as her lead villain for the rest of my life."

A weird wave of empathy washed over me. We both had others to blame for our career choices, although hers was more creative, come to think of it. My ideas for making a living never went further than going to an office and trying not to get fired for eight hours.

"So why is she mad at you?" I asked. "I mean, if you were such a star thief?"

"I was," Divya said with a note of pride in her voice. "The trouble is, I became so good I thought I could steal from *her*."

"You stole from the mafia queen?"

"I know," Divya groaned.

Another wave of empathy rolled in. It was comforting to know that even seemingly flawless humans sometimes made pretty stupid decisions.

"What did you steal?"

"A necklace. The one I was wearing on the plane."

"That piece of—" I almost said "crap," thinking back to the ridiculous costume jewelry. Surely it wasn't worth more than a few bucks.

"That exact one," she conceded. "Just over a hundred carats."

"Of what?" In my defense, that particular combination of words must've caused a small aneurysm somewhere deep in my brain.

"Diamonds, of course," Divya said as if diamonds were a common occurrence in her world. "Set in platinum. The center stone alone was almost five carats."

A one-carat solitaire had been my personal dream ever since I first found out about the whole jewelry-in-exchange-for-monogamy arrangement. I couldn't imagine a diamond five times that size, especially in the company of a hundred other precious stones.

"Funny," I said. "It didn't look like much. Of course, I've never seen a diamond necklace in my life, but I sort of expected it to sparkle more."

Divya chuckled. "That's because I painted it with pink and silver nail polish."

"Why would you do that?"

"Well, it was reported stolen by a certain Hollywood celebrity just hours earlier, and I didn't want to draw attention to the millions I had draped around my neck. I walked through security like it was nothing." There was that tone of pride again.

"Millions? With an 's' at the end?" My brain was definitely bleeding.

"Yes, but that is the retail price," she said defensively. "It is worth only a small fraction of that on the black market, and it is hard to find a buyer, anyway."

I thought about the mysterious black market and where you could find one. There had to be one in the pawnshop around the corner from where I used to live with Tara, although it sold mostly TV sets and car stereos.

"Wait, did you say you stole it from a celebrity? I thought you said it belonged to Grandma Aadarsha?"

She groaned. "It's another long story."

"I have some time to kill."

She didn't laugh. "I shouldn't be telling you this." There was more than pride in her voice now—she sounded like Mom bursting at the seams with new goss about Aunty Kelly's escapades.

"Why? Cause I might run straight to the authorities with this? We should all be so lucky."

Another sigh came from the dark. "It was my first overseas job. Aadarsha arranged for me to fly to LA under an assumed identity, where I managed to get invited to a pool party for a certain well-to-do producer and connoisseur of rare jewels and beautiful women. I was introduced to him as the exotic new bird, the up-and-coming Hollywood darling, not to mention fresh meat, so it wasn't difficult to get him panting after me like a fat old dog after a bone."

Eew. "Did you ... you know ..."

"No," she said. "That is not how to get what you want from a man.

You have to tease them, drive them wild, until they can't think clearly anymore."

Sandra would have agreed with her. *Does everyone know how to play this game except me?*

"At any rate, the more I resisted, the more he chased me, until a few days later I was invited back to his house for a romantic dinner. It was just the two of us, but he pulled out all the stops—sent a designer dress for me to wear and a limo to my hotel, had flower petals all over the driveway and more flowers inside, and even arranged for some famous chef to come in just for the occasion."

Nobody's ever done anything like that for me. "Did he propose?"

Divya laughed. "Propositioned is more like it. You crack me up."

I was actually serious about the proposal question, but another warm wave swept over me. I much preferred when people laughed with me, rather than at me, and were talking, rather than pouting in the corner, hell-bent on giving me the silent treatment for the rest of my life.

"*Eew,*" I said. "I mean, sorry. What did he do?"

"*Eew* is right," she said. "We had dinner, and he kept drinking while I kept flirting. He was so sure about closing the deal, he dismissed the chef and his staff, and I just pretended I didn't understand what was going on. It's easy to do with an accent."

"You don't really have one."

"Yes, I do. This is such beautiful dinner, and this is such beautiful wine, and this is such beautiful house," she said in a stereotypical Indian accent.

I snorted. "Sorry!"

"That's okay," she said, and I could hear a smile in her voice. "So we had more drinks, and then he asked if I wanted to see the rest of the house, and of course I said yes. So there we were, in his study, and he asked me to close my eyes."

"Oh my God," I said. "You didn't, did you? He didn't rape you, did he?"

"I wasn't anywhere near as drunk as he was, or as I was letting him believe," Divya said. "Of course I pretended not to look while he wobbled off and fumbled with a safe door. Then he came back with a box and told me to open my eyes, and there it was, on black velvet, the most unbelievable string of diamonds I'd ever seen in my life."

"That sounds like the *Pretty Woman* plot."

"It does, now that you mention it. I guess he wanted to impress me, and what can I tell you … I was impressed. It was like being hypnotized. All I could hear was 'take me' and of course, I reached out to touch it."

She paused.

"And?" I said, there with her, myself reaching out for brilliant sparkles.

"The drunken idiot slammed the box on my hand."

I snapped out of my vision. "You're kidding."

"I wish," she said. "It wasn't funny when I thought he broke my fingers."

I cringed, but couldn't stop myself from giggling. "Sorry. I just thought you were lucky to escape a *Pretty Woman* bath scene he probably had planned for later."

Divya giggled too. "Let's not go there. So I'm crying, and he's panicking and running around trying to find a Band-Aid, but of course he has no idea where anything is without his housekeeper. And that was when I slipped a little something in his drink."

"What?"

"Rohypnol. Undetectable in cognac."

"You gave him a roofie? It's a date-rape drug, isn't it?"

"Yeah, but I was not planning on raping him," she said, once again reading my mind. "He was so relieved that I didn't leave right after that disaster, he put the necklace around my neck, and kept on gushing how I was more beautiful and special than the diamonds. It was kind of sad. We went to his bedroom, and then five minutes later he was asleep like a huge, bloated baby. I slipped outside, caught a taxi, and that was it."

"That's unbelievable," I said. "No wonder you managed to swindle Bank of United States. Practice makes perfect."

"Yeah, but it didn't make me happy," she said, and sighed. I couldn't see her, but it was easy to picture her face, those doe-like eyes welling with tears. "I mean, there's excitement in it, and for a moment you feel like a champion, even though your chosen sport is highly illegal. But then reality sets in, and in that reality, you are nothing but a pawn in the hands of a mean old witch."

"I know exactly what you mean," I said.

How can we have so much in common? I had to remind myself this woman was a cunning criminal, partly responsible for my current predicament. Still, under different circumstances …

"So there I was that night, in a crappy motel, waiting for my flight out. I can just see it now—I am lying on the bed, looking at the diamonds sparkling on the pillow next to me, and it hits me."

I was hardly surprised the necklace had magical powers as well.

"It was my ticket to freedom. Just like that, it all seemed possible. Aadarsha was not expecting me back for at least a week, which gave me enough time to find a buyer, get enough cash to leave town, and start somewhere fresh, with a new name. Maybe even a new nose. It was a sign. Something like when I met you and your easy money."

"Thanks for that," I said. "Couldn't you just, I don't know, sell your house? And that car?"

"I wish," she sighed. "I don't own any of that. Aadarsha lets me have a certain lifestyle, but no independent means. On her books, I am actually in debt to her, basically her slave."

I thought back to my days of being a slave to Visa and one payment away from repossession. "I know. Once you get in debt, it's impossible to get out, unless you do something drastic about the situation."

"Maybe," Harden piped up from the darkness, "you two could stop bondin' and start thinkin' what to do about this here situation."

So the silent treatment lasted at most ten minutes. "Why?" I said, not bothering to hide the poison in my voice. "Aren't you on top of this? I mean, you always have the answers to everything, right?"

"I never said that. Look, Isa, I'm sorry I yelled at you, but there was no other way to get through. You were off your rocker—"

"Off my rocker?" I said, incredulous. "So now you're calling me crazy?"

"I didn't say that!" Harden exploded. "This is how we always talked before, and all of a sudden it's offending you? We're in deep shit here. Could you maybe stop arguing with me for one minute and help me get this rope off?"

"I'm not arguing with you," I said. "And I'm not gonna help you ever again. You'll probably figure out later how I didn't do it right and screwed up everything."

Harden moaned.

"I will do it," Divya said. I heard her shuffle over to the side, toward him.

"Fine," I said. "Live dangerously, why don't you."

Neither one answered. I heard more shuffling, followed by whispers and puffing that could have been taken off a porno soundtrack.

"What the hell are you doing?" I said.

There was still no answer, and I considered going over there myself when the lights flickered on.

"What the hell are you doing?" 2ReeL echoed from behind me.

Divya rolled away from Harden, both of them blinking stupidly in the fluorescent light. For once, I didn't protest when Harden got kicked.

THE MORE ACCURATE WORD FOR THAT IS 'ASSHOLE.'

I t's funny how you don't appreciate law and order while it's constantly in your way but fall in love with it as soon as it's gone.

I was trying to remember which convention established fair prisoner treatment rules while being pushed and shoved down the narrow hallway. It was on the tip of my tongue, but as usual, the stress short-circuited my brain into worrying about something else. That was why I never bothered applying for *Who Wants to be a Millionaire?* Given my track record, I'd most likely forget my own name, instead preoccupied with how my butt looks on TV.

This time I was preoccupied with what was going on between Harden and Divya. *Nothing is going on,* I tried to tell myself. *She was just trying to untie his hands with her teeth.* I tried hard to block the image of her head in Harden's lap. It was like trying not to think of a white elephant.

I expected to be paraded in front of Grandma Aadarsha again, but instead of the kitchen, we were taken to a living room. I think it was meant to be lavishly decorated, although I couldn't appreciate it, my eye focus being thrown by so many patterns on the curtains, rugs, furniture, and other random ornamentation.

2ReeL took a seat on the couch, camouflaged by a dozen embroidered pillows and throws, and motioned for Harden, Divya, and me to be seated on the other couch, across from him. Harden sat down next to me,

174

but I just stared straight ahead, pretending not to see him.

"I have some bad news," 2ReeL said after a pause so pregnant, it was overdue for a caesarian.

I tried to imagine what could be worse than kidnapping at gunpoint. Death came to mind, but surely that wasn't it.

"Does anyone want to know what it is?" 2ReeL continued, slightly irritated.

"Is there good news, too?" I asked automatically, and cringed for a blow, but none came.

"Sort of," 2ReeL said. "The good news is we've found your hidden safe, Divya."

He looked at her for a reaction, but she just stared moodily at the rug, probably just as annoyed by all the visual mishmash around us.

"Aadarsha is not happy about the damage to the walls," 2ReeL continued, "or the fact that you'd installed one without consulting her."

Divya didn't even move an eyebrow. If the four of us were playing poker, I would have been out after the first hand.

"We managed to open it," 2ReeL continued, "but it was empty. Where is the necklace, Divya? And where are the fancy shoes? Aadarsha would like all of it back."

"The shoes were never part of the deal," Divya said.

"They are now. Grandma is an old woman. She was truly saddened by your betrayal."

"She didn't look sad to me," I said.

"She deserves a fair payment for the pain and suffering you have caused her."

"Pain and suffering?" I said. "That's rich. How about the pain and suffering you've caused us?"

2ReeL's sigh was overly dramatic, I thought, as he said, "I almost forgot about you, Isabella."

He remembered my name. For some reason, the thought scared me.

2ReeL seemed pleased by my shocked reaction. "Yes, I have looked you up. It appears you are indeed Isabella Maxwell and that at least part of your story is correct."

"Which one?" I said, trying to shrink into a valley between two throw pillows.

"The one about a million dollars."

Shit.

"Imagine my delight," 2ReeL said, "when I'd discovered that the annoying backpacker who needlessly complicated the whole operation turned out to be a bonus."

"You're the one who's annoying," I mumbled.

2ReeL ignored my jab. "I'm prepared to let you go in exchange for a sum of one million dollars."

"A million!" I puffed from my pillow fort. "More like half a million. I had to pay taxes and the agent's fee. And the expenses, too. I didn't know you have to pay for the book tour yourself, but it turns out that the publishing business—"

"Fine!" 2ReeL said. "Half a million. Wired to an account in the Virgin Islands. Then you're free to go."

Free. If I had to choose the best word in the English language, *free* would have to be it, even ahead of *love*.

"I don't have it," I mumbled, hating Divya's guts. In this game of each woman for herself, she had all the good cards.

"Pardon?" 2ReeL said.

"I don't have any money left," I said, louder. "Divya took it all."

Divya groaned.

"Is that true?" 2ReeL asked her, perplexed. "When did that happen?"

"Yesterday," I said. "We were on the plane together, and she gave me Valium—"

"Shut up," Divya snapped. I was hoping Harden would say something, even if it was more anti-drug nagging, but he didn't even look at me.

"On the contrary, please continue," 2ReeL said.

I did. I mean, how could it make the already bad matter worse? I told him most of the story, starting with our plane conversation and finishing with the fouled-up breaking and entering. "We were going to try and hack into her computer, and then you came in. You remember the rest."

"Yes, I do," 2ReeL said. "So I guess you're useless to me now."

I didn't like the tone of his voice. "I wouldn't say useless. It's such an ugly word. But you don't need me, that's true. And you don't need Harden, either." I darted my eyes over to see Harden's reaction, but there was none.

"Pity," 2ReeL said, redirecting his gaze to Divya. "So it looks like all the eggs are in this basket-case."

They stared at each other for a full minute, long enough to win a contest of some sort.

"You owe me half a million dollars, a diamond necklace, and a pair of bejeweled shoes," 2ReeL said eventually, "and that is final."

"Actually, she owes *me* a half-million," I said.

"Fine," Divya shot back. "I will give Aadarsha everything, but on one condition. I want out."

"That would not be a problem. Consider yourself *terminated*." 2ReeL laughed when he said it, but my skin crawled.

If that at all bothered Divya, she once again didn't show it. "Everything is in a safe-deposit box in Delhi National Bank."

"A bank?" 2ReeL rolled his eyes. "Honestly, Divya, why do you make things so much harder for yourself?"

Divya said something I didn't quite register, distracted as I was by a loud slurping noise behind me. I twisted around to see Grandma's favorite boy waddling in from the hallway. He wore the same shorts and tank top, but instead of a kitten he was cuddling a huge plastic drink cup.

2ReeL said something to him, but Harshit, or whatever his name was, walked over to me with the confidence of someone who owned the place. I pulled back but he just leaned in closer, sucking on the straw with a Dyson-like force. I got a whiff of a vanilla milkshake and a kick from my furious stomach.

"What do you want," I said, sick and tired of getting bullied by privileged minors. *This is how the working life must be for seniors, bossed around by adolescent supervisors.* Maybe Dad was right, and his last principal really was a wet-behind-the-ears, useless prick.

This current prick said nothing, just reached out with a free hand and patted my hair, the way one would pet a kitten. There was no menace in the gesture, but I almost threw up.

"Looks like Harshit has a new favorite," 2ReeL said.

"Can you tell him to leave me alone?" I tried dodging the patting hand, but it was hard to do, wedged into the corner of the couch.

"He is harmless," Divya said. "He just likes pretty girls. And he is an idiot. Aren't you, Harshit?"

Harshit just sucked on the straw, looking me up and down.

"That's harsh," I said. "I mean, he's annoying, but I don't call people idiots. Even when they steal my money or kidnap me. The more accurate word for that is 'asshole.'"

2ReeL stood up and put his arm around the boy's shoulders. "Your new love thinks you're an asshole, Harshit."

I squinted at him. "I meant you and Divya. Y'all are lying, conniving, kidnapping, criminal assholes, and now you pick on the kid who's nice to me."

"Don't worry," Divya said. "He doesn't understand a lick of English."

"Not of English, or business, or accounting for that matter," 2ReeL said and hugged the boy closer. "And yet Aadarsha intends to put him in charge of her empire. Why, that would make both of you idiots, wouldn't it, Harshit?"

You didn't have to know English to feel the poison in his voice. Harshit woke up a little, shrugged off 2ReeL's arm, and walked away, giving him an evil look over his shoulder.

Maybe you underestimate him. Maybe you underestimate a few people.

Harshit left, but a twinge of new hope remained. I thought back to Mr. Hue. My previous experience with self-assured pricks showed that the degree of self-assuredness directly correlated to the ease with which one could manipulate them. Or was it counter-correlated? Definitions aside, I had a feeling 2ReeL and his brand were no match for my double-talk.

"Did you say Grandma, I mean Aadarsha, is going to put him in charge?" I said innocently. "I thought you were the boss around here."

You could almost hear the words hit the sore spot. 2ReeL chuckled bitterly. "Why? Because I am trying to move this shambles of an organization into the twenty-first century? Because I look like a businessman? Because I have developed a *brand*?"

"Yes, all those. It would be a pity for your brand to fade away."

That produced a small meltdown—2ReeL spat accusations at Aadarsha, Harshit, and the incompetent workforce while the incompetent workforce didn't seem to get any of that, continuing to stand guard behind us.

"I had no idea it was that bad," I said. Unfortunately I had no other ideas either, except for a suggestion that he needed therapy. Obviously 2ReeL detested his current position, but how to take advantage of that was clear as mud to me.

"So now I have to look forward to that retard being my boss," 2ReeL said bitterly. "This is the thanks I get for working my butt off."

"Working your butt off?" Divya snarled. "I have been the workhorse all along, and what thanks do I get? Executed for seeking alternative employment?"

"No," 2ReeL said. "Executed for stealing from your employer."

"Jesus!" I yelled, startling both of them. Of all the English words, *executed* had to be the worst. "Why are you guys fighting? Y'all should be working together against this old hag and her pet. Join forces, mutiny, start your own company. Something, anything, but not this."

They stared at each other. "I'd give everything to whomever lets me go," Divya said slowly. "At this point, I don't care if it's you or Aadarsha, as long as I get to leave."

"As long as all of us get to leave," I corrected her. "Me and Harden, too."

"Sure." She didn't take her eyes off 2ReeL.

"Aadarsha doesn't even know about the half-million," I said. "You can definitely pocket that, I don't mind."

2ReeL stared reflectively at the ceiling. "That sounds good in theory, but how do I know you will deliver and not just skip town, disguised as Aadarsha herself?"

She would, too. I tried to remember the old woman leaning on me back at the mobile-phone kiosk. That was some impressive improv.

"You can send someone to the bank with me," Divya said, nodding to the band of ex-convicts behind us.

"I could do that," 2ReeL said dreamily. "But what if you pull some kind of a stunt, like that time you'd triggered a fire alarm in the National Museum? You just walked out with everyone else and a … what was it?"

"A gold-and-diamond buckle," Divya said quietly.

"That's right," 2ReeL said. "Now I remember. Rather poorly cut diamonds, weren't they? Good thing there were so many of them."

That hardly surprised me. *She's too far gone even for Kleptomaniacs Anonymous.*

"Then what about the time you got caught red-handed by the shop owner, and you made a scene as if he was trying to molest you? Who knows what happened to the good Samaritans who came to your aid."

Divya said nothing.

"See what I mean?" 2ReeL said. "How can I trust that you won't just disappear once you're out in the public?"

"What other option do you have?" Divya said. "I can't wire the safe-deposit box to you, now can I?"

"You're the one without options," 2ReeL snapped.

"Time out!" I said. I would have done the t-sign, but my hands were tied. An almost suicidal arrogance emanated from my empty stomach—when my blood sugar drops, I can eat or kill anything. "You want the money, but you won't let her get it. You can't have the cake and keep Divya in the basement, too."

"Interesting metaphor," Divya said. "Weird, but correct."

2ReeL squeezed his head with two fists. "Dear gods, why is this so hard? Why didn't you just bury it somewhere in the backyard?"

"Can you imagine me digging in the dirt?" Divya said. "With what? My silver cake knife?"

2ReeL punched a pillow again and again. His tantrum was more befitting a diva than a gangster, but I wasn't going to tell him that.

"I need some kind of collateral, Divya," he said once the pillow was sufficiently fluffed up. "Damn it, I would hold these two hostage, but something tells me you wouldn't mind seeing them dead. Why don't you love something I could maim and torture? Like a boyfriend or a puppy?"

"Because I am not stupid," Divya said. "Maybe because I always knew this day would come, and you would finally blow your top for no reason."

"I do have a reason," 2ReeL said, looking dangerously close to blowing up. "Five-hundred-thousand and one-hundred-carat reasons. The same reasons Aadarsha will use to put her precious Harshit in charge. This disaster may cost me my life's work."

"Your life's work?" I said, mocking his tone. "You must be eighteen, at most."

2ReeL glared at me. "Perhaps you are right, and I don't know what I'm doing. Perhaps I should start cutting off your fingers until *you* come up with a better idea."

I gasped. Sure, 2ReeL was a first-class weirdo, but not the finger-cutting kind.

"I have a better idea," Divya said. "Why don't you send her?" She nodded at me.

What the hell? I couldn't keep up with the punches. "*Why don't you send her?*" I mocked Divya's posh accent. "This is your problem, Divya—why don't you try harder to solve it?"

"You see what I mean?" Divya said, not looking at me.

"*You see what I mean?*" I mocked her again. "I see exactly what you mean. Once again, you want somebody else to do the hard work for you. Mark my words, this attitude will catch up with you sooner or later."

She didn't say anything, just gave 2ReeL a knowing smile. He looked back and forth between us, then paused to stare me down. "Do that again."

"Do what?"

He pointed a finger at Divya. "Her voice. Say something again, and pretend to be her."

What a sicko. "Why?"

"Do it or I will kill you!" His shout made all of us jump.

If stage fright is a way to get a truthful performance, I had all the motivation I needed. Either that or maybe I was born to be an actor after all. I stuck out my chin, pursed my lips in that annoying coy way, and said, "Please, like I am going to believe that!" in Divya's voice.

"That's impressive," 2ReeL said, deep in thought. Even the Hells Angels watched in awe while I fluttered my eyelashes, crossed my legs, and prattled on in Divya's drawn-out accent.

"A bit overplayed if you ask me," Divya said. "But imagine the same in full makeup and a black wig. She won't need to say much of anything if you go with her."

"Go where?" I asked, barely able to breathe. I wasn't exactly excited about going somewhere with 2ReeL, but I wasn't keen on sticking around, either.

"You have her collateral right here." Divya nodded at Harden. "That's her boyfriend."

"What the hell are you …" I started saying, but 2ReeL shut me up with just one finger in the air. He looked back and forth from me to Harden.

"I presume we could get the makeup from your house, Divya? I will need you to write a list."

"A list?" she snapped. "As if one of your dogs can tell a difference between a bronzer and a blush?"

2ReeL smirked. "Make it a good one."

I had just about enough of their cryptic exchange. "Do you mind explaining to me what's going on?"

"Certainly," 2ReeL said. "You can rest for now, but tomorrow morning we will go to the bank. Divya is going to do her magic with your face until you look enough like her to pass the security check. Then you will collect the goods she had stashed away in the safe-deposit box."

"Why would I do that?" I said.

"Because if you don't, I will cut off more than your boyfriend's fingers."

"Please," I said. "Like I'm gonna believe you would ruin Aadarsha's furniture with blood? The most you're capable of is waterboarding, or playing Enya on repeat."

2ReeL didn't answer, instead giving an almost imperceptible nod to the Hells Angels. Before I knew what was happening Harden was on the floor, being kicked with such force that it dawned on me—the psycho wasn't bluffing after all.

"No!" I screamed, no longer caring what would happen to my fingers. "Wait! Please!"

One of the convicts stopped long enough to pull out his gun and press the barrel into Harden's cheek. It was more than I could bear.

"I'll do it!"

NO PEENY IN KAKA!

I don't know in which culture "having a rest" equates to being handcuffed to a bed, but apparently this was what 2ReeL had in mind. Despite my protests, I was taken away to one of the guest bedrooms before I got to see whether Harden was okay.

He's okay, it was just a few punches, I lied to myself. *I got kicked in the kidneys, and I'm fine. Dandy, in fact. I just need some sleep.*

Those were lies, of course. I wasn't dandy, and I couldn't sleep. It didn't help that I could hear men outside my door, first talking, then snoring, but not once leaving the post. I had visions of Hells Apprentice coming in and taking me by force. Terrible, appalling, yet strangely arousing visions, vivid enough to make me consider chewing off my own thumb. He didn't come in, so I just languished there, tense like a guitar string.

Even worse, my brain returned to that whole not being able to think under pressure state. I should've spent the free time practicing Divya's accent, or trying to come up with what I might say at the bank, but all I could do was regret things. I had a whole list of them, starting with opening that damn email. Asking for the upgrade to first class. Taking drugs from a stranger. Not keeping an eye on my valuables. Not calling the bank the moment I realized my wallet was gone. Trying to stalk Divya like a Nancy Drew-wannabe. Each one just a small wrong step, yet together they brought me to this hotbed of evil.

And oh my God, was it hot. If there was air conditioning, nobody bothered to turn it on. Nobody bothered to give me any food or water, either. I tried to find solace in the fact that I wouldn't pee my bed in this dehydrated state, since I wasn't about to ask my guards to take me to the toilet.

I stared into the darkness, barely able to make out different shapes in the moonlight coming through the window. I was sober, but the longer I stared, the more menacing the shapes became, threatening to come at me the moment I closed my eyes. There was no other choice but to hold vigil until morning.

You know how sometimes you're sure you didn't sleep all night, except later you remember weird dreams, and then you can't tell if it really happened or not? I didn't have any dreams that night, but I must've fallen asleep for just a moment, because the next thing I knew there was somebody sitting next to me on the bed.

My first thought was that it was Hells Apprentice, and my whole body tensed up in anticipation. I blinked a few times, and Hells Apprentice's muscular shape morphed into a young boy.

"Harshit?" I asked, disbelieving.

"*Haan*," he said back.

Hon? Holy crap, they were not kidding—he is into me. The vision of being taken against my will suddenly got fifty shades more disturbing. *This can't be. He's just a kid.*

No, he's a weird and horny teenager, said the devil on my shoulder.

"What are you doing, Harshit?" I said, trying to pull away as far as my bindings allowed. I could tell he was still dressed, in something dark. *Thank God.*

Harshit reached out and stroked my arm. "*Peene ka.*"

His touch was electrifying, in the sense that it set off every panic alarm in my entire body. If I wasn't tied down, I would've bolted faster than Bolt himself. *What did he say? Pee? Penis? Kaka?*

"No, please, no," I begged, wriggling in what probably looked like an epileptic fit. "No peeny in kaka!"

185

Harshit leaned toward me, and I was about to scream when he shoved something in my face. To my surprise, it wasn't a ball gag, but another huge plastic cup. The familiar smell wafted into my nostrils.

Bhang.

"No," I shook my head. "No *bhang*." At least for now, my legs were still free and able to kick if necessary. If I got stoned in addition to being tied up, I was guaranteed to wake up with a sore kaka.

"No *bhang*." Harshit laughed. It was a surprisingly genuine sound. "*Lassi*."

A dog, too? I squeezed my lips shut against the stubbornly probing straw, moaning in protest.

"*Lassi*," Harshit insisted. "*Peene ka*."

I should've held my breath for longer, but after just a few seconds, my mouth betrayed me, gasping for the straw as if it was precious air. The milkshake was amazing, cool and refreshing. *Stop it.* I tried to tear myself away from the straw, still hopeful I hadn't ingested enough to knock me out. *Stop it,* I kept thinking until the entire cup was empty.

I laid my head back onto the pillow, feeling the familiar, pleasant heaviness spread through my stomach and cursing my weak resolve. Harshit took the cup away and patted my hair. I didn't flinch.

What's the point? There was no escape, not that I could see anymore. The whole world was against me.

Harshit took away his hand and moved about in the darkness. I watched him mindlessly until I saw a quick flash of something in the moonlight.

What's that? He moved again and suddenly I saw a blade. *A knife!*

The little weirdo was interested in sex after all.

An image flashed before my eyes, of him petting that fluffy kitten before skinning it alive. I opened my mouth to scream, but only a pathetic whimper came out.

"No!" I managed, just as he started cutting one of the ropes tying me to the bedposts.

He stopped. "*Nahin?*"

I blinked. It wasn't a knife he was holding. The second strip of shiny metal told me what it was to begin with: just a pair of scissors. The kid was trying to save me, and here I was telling him to stop.

"No, don't stop," I said. "I mean yes, cut, please. Cut!" I could feel my phone between my breasts. All I needed was one free hand and five free minutes.

Harshit started cutting again. It was slow work, not to mention dangerous, but at the time a cut wrist didn't even cross my mind.

After a couple of minutes, I realized that Harshit had no idea how to use scissors. And why would he, living with a grandma who would happily wipe his butt? I tried staying calm and waiting patiently, but it was driving me insane.

It's scissors, not a saw! But how do you explain the proper scissor technique to someone who doesn't speak English, in the dark, with your hands tied?

"Hey, Harshit," I said, and he paused his efforts. "Do you know what an alligator is? The scissors cut like alligator jaws. Like *Jaws*, you know the movie?"

"*Kya?*"

"Scissors, like jaws," I said, snapping my own jaws loudly as an example.

"*Kaatana?*"

Shit. Things were going so well and then I had to butt in and ruin everything. By now he would have already cut through the rope with his peculiar method.

"That's okay," I said. "Just do what you did before. You were doing a great job."

He didn't move.

A new wave of terror enveloped me. What if he'd changed his mind? "Please, cut! I appreciate your help so much." I searched my brain for a Hindi word. "*Bevakoof!*"

"*Bevakoof?*" he said, obviously surprised at my language skills.

"Yes, *bevakoof*! *Bevakoof* very much!"

Harshit jumped off the bed, mumbling fast. It sounded like "something-something-*bevakoof*," repeated over and over. He didn't sound happy.

"What's wrong?" Obviously I'd touched a nerve. Is it inappropriate for a woman to tell a man how to use scissors? Or snap her jaws like an animal? What did I do this time?

He spat a few more words at me and turned to leave.

"Oh, no, no, no!" I cried. "Please come back! I will shut up, I promise!"

My pleas fell on, well, not deaf, but certainly non-English-speaking ears. Harshit muttered something else and left, slipping quietly through the door, past the snoring guards, leaving me to cry myself to sleep.

"What's wrong with you?" I wept, addressing the ceiling. "Divya was right, why don't you just shut up for once? Why are you constantly in your own way? Why?"

The ceiling didn't answer of course, but I could tell what it was thinking.

Idiot.

BEVAKOOF VERY MUCH!

Regret comes in all shapes and sizes, but it always tastes the same—an acrid heartburn of a missed opportunity.

I burped. The faint aftertaste of the milkshake reminded me that last night I messed up the opportunity of a lifetime.

"That is vile," Divya said and waved a dainty hand in front of her nose. We were still in my bedroom-cum-prison cell, but I'd been untied and allowed to shower. Lucky her, 'cause before that I reeked even worse.

It was good to shower, and to drink my fill from the bathroom faucet, but the downfall of having to undress under the watchful eye of Grandma Aadarsha was that my bra bank had been discovered and confiscated, along with the phone and any hope of contacting authorities. My only consolation was that 2ReeL got thrashed for not searching me better. I could still hear Aadarsha screaming from time to time somewhere in the depths of the house.

"Sorry, Divya," I said mechanically, trying to stop the follow-up burp. "They gave us nothing to eat since yesterday. I'm pretty sure even prisoners get rations."

"I would ask for something, but I can't risk you ruining my work," Divya said, returning to lining my eyes with a thick black pencil. She'd been hard at work on my face and hands for at least two hours. My now-brown fingers reminded me of one summer I spent baking in the backyard of my own grandma's house, and I tasted the familiar salty sadness.

Divya didn't notice, even though her face was close to mine. She seemed lost in the moment, like an artist working on a masterpiece. For me, the moment kept dragging on and on, and the more she worked on my face, the more it felt like a mask. "Are we done yet?"

"Almost. And stop talking, I need you to hold still." She leaned back. "Perfect."

"Can I see?"

"Just a minute. Let me touch up the lipstick. Although who am I kidding, this is all for naught. You will just get arrested."

"Don't say that," I muttered without moving my lips.

She sighed. "I don't blame you. I would rather get arrested too, than be here when Aadarsha finds out about it. That will definitely be the end for me and your friend Hardon."

"It's Hard-*en*, and I will come back for him," I said. "I'll get you out too, even though you don't deserve it."

"Thank you kindly," she said with scorn. "Now put these in." She held out a small plastic box with a circle of brown film swimming in a clear liquid.

I didn't expect contacts to hurt like they did. After a couple of attempts to shove pieces of plastic into my eyeballs, I tried suggesting sunglasses instead, but Miss Perfectionist wouldn't hear of it.

"And what would you do if they ask you to take them off? Run out screaming?"

With her mind-reading skills, she should have been a psychic or at least a saleswoman, but when I finally got to look in the mirror, I knew she was born to be a makeup artist. Even through the contacts-induced teary blur, I could see how she'd managed to fool all the bank managers and shop owners before them.

"Wow, I look just like you," I said, surveying my new face. I now had Divya's silky black hair, unblemished latte skin, dark eyes, perfectly arched eyebrows, and delicate pout. She even painted on the cheekbones

I always wished I had. For a moment I felt as if I was Divya, self-assured, bold, and beautiful. It felt … good.

"I can't believe this. *Bevakoof!*"

Divya frowned in the mirror next to me, an identical and suddenly annoyed twin. "Well, that's a bit harsh. I think I did a reasonably good job."

"What do you mean? You did a *brilliant* job. Thank you so much. I can't even see the bruise. It's like I have a completely new face."

"Oh," she said. "Then why did you call me an idiot?"

"What? I didn't."

"You called me *bevakoof*," she said, pouting.

"Yeah—that means 'thank you,' doesn't it?"

She looked at me like I was a moron. "No. It means 'idiot' or 'stupid' in Hindi."

"No, it doesn't."

"Yes, it does."

I still refused to believe what I was hearing. "Is it slang for 'cool' or something?"

"No," she said. "It means 'stupid,' plain and simple."

I sank back in the chair, feeling like the rug was just pulled from under me. "All these people called me an idiot," I said, trying to remember who it was I thought was thanking me. Definitely the old woman who sold me way too much *bhang*. Also Moustache. And Divya herself, too.

I called Harshit an idiot for trying to save me.

"Oh my God," I said, covering my face with my hands. "I want to die."

"Oh, no, you don't," Divya said, slapping my hands away. "You have a job to do. Don't even think about touching your face—it is latex, and it could slip. No crying, or eating, or sweating either. Let's get you dressed."

She was right, of course. My wallowing would have to be done later. I swallowed my sobs as she helped me put on a red skirt and a gold crop top, and then masterfully wrapped me in a new sari. This one looked and felt a hundred times more luxurious and expensive than the one I scored for cheap at the fashion show. It was made of almost see-through silk, in a flame-red shade, with lavish golden embroidery. She draped a matching scarf over my head and pinned it in place with a bejeweled hair clip. She hung more jewelry on my neck and ears, until you could hardly see my sour mug through all the bling.

"That's amazing," I said, with all the enthusiasm of a lobster in a restaurant display tank. "I don't think my mother would recognize me. The only thing, I'm a little bigger than you." In truth, there was a twenty-pound difference between us, not all of which could be attributed to height.

We both stared in the mirror, looking like a pair of those nesting Russian dolls—identical, except for size.

"They will only have a picture of my face for comparison," she said, not sounding convinced herself.

"What if a clerk remembers you and asks me how I managed to grow a foot in two days? What do I do? Run out screaming?"

Divya chuckled. "Still cracking me up. I will miss you, you know."

The truth was I was going to miss her too, in the same messed-up way I fantasized about Hells Apprentice, but before I could put that thought into non-creepy words, her face lit up.

"I have an idea!"

She popped her head out the door and rattled something to the guard outside. He tried to argue, but she just slammed the door shut. Minutes later, the guard was back with a wheelchair.

"Aadarsha uses it sometimes when her arthritis plays up," Divya said, helping me and my cascade of fabric settle into the narrow seat. It was one of those foldable ones that had to be pushed by an assistant.

"Why do I need a wheelchair?" I said, checking it for pee stains. It seemed okay. "I thought I was pretending to be you, not Aadarsha."

"This way nobody will notice how tall you are," Divya said. "Perhaps you've twisted an ankle walking in high heels. That would explain why you need an entourage to come with you to the bank."

She truly was a genius.

YOU'RE VERY PRETTY, YOU KNOW.
WHEN YOUR NOSE IS IN ONE PIECE.

Aadarsha surveyed the final result with an irritable grandeur befitting only Donald Trump. For a moment I thought she was going to refuse risking her wheelchair for the mission, but then she waved her approval.

Nobody bothered to blindfold me as we walked outside, and for the first time, I got to see the exterior of the house. It was just as ancient and formidable as Aadarsha, and perhaps once upon a time, both of them were beautiful. The building was a massive two-story structure, which hugged the arrival court on three sides. The entire facade was covered in intricate mosaic, although most of it had fallen off, revealing the rough stone walls underneath. We waited in the breezeway, which was framed by scalloped archways held up with slim carved posts, and I wondered whether the whole thing was structurally sound. It was surprising to see that someone as rich as Aadarsha would let their house fall into such disrepair, but then again it might be the plague of all old people— somewhere in this old house, there had to be a mattress stuffed full of thousand-rupee bills.

After a few minutes, a black Mercedes pulled up to the door, the one that once belonged to Divya and was now repossessed. There was some fussing, but finally, the wheelchair was folded and placed in the trunk.

2ReeL got into the back seat with me, Hells Apprentice took his place behind the wheel, and we were off.

"Here is your safe key and your passport," 2ReeL said, handing me a small evening purse. It was silver and totally clashed with the gold embroidery on my sari, but I took it and nodded. "When we get there, let me do all the talking. You just look tired and disinterested, understood?"

"What if he asks me something?"

"I will handle it," 2ReeL said and turned away, indicating the conversation was finished.

I was mocking the way he pursed his lips at his maddeningly arrogant back when I noticed the driver's eyes in the rearview mirror. He looked away instantly, but I could swear he was quietly laughing. Maybe humor could transcend language barriers and tough facades.

Maybe I can win him over. As long as I remember not to call him bevakoof.

We pulled up at the front of the bank building, and 2ReeL made a big show of helping me transfer from the car into the wheelchair. There was a bit of a snag when it turned out the building didn't have a wheelchair ramp, but then he and Apprentice just carried me and my chariot up the few front steps, as if I was Cleopatra or something.

A guy in a suit, I assumed the bank manager, was already at the door, alerted by all the commotion. He was mumbling nonstop, clearly apologizing for the state of the access facilities, but I smiled weakly and waved him off. The other staff were staring at us, but I stuck my chin out defiantly, trying to mimic the way Divya ignored everyone on that security tape.

2ReeL took over the conversation, as promised, so all I had to do was look regal and exhausted until the manager weaned the chatter and showed us the way to the back. My heart was bouncing around in my chest, and I laid my hand there to imitate one of Divya's melodramatic gestures, and to monitor my pulse.

We paused in front of a glass sliding door, and the manager said something to me. I could tell from the way 2ReeL's body tensed up that it wasn't good news.

What does he want? I moved my hand to cover my eyes, as if the fluorescent lighting was giving me an impossible headache, hoping the manager would go away.

It never worked with credit card bills or any of my other problems, and this case was no exception. The manager leaned in closer and said something else, bobbing his head apologetically. 2ReeL tried to interrupt, pointing at my legs and my chair, but the manager just stood there, obviously waiting for me to say something.

Shit!

2ReeL was unraveling fast, blabbering and pointing, his already high-pitched voice now resembling a choirboy's. My first thought was to jump up and do a runner, but Hells Apprentice was right behind me, ready to pounce, and my legs were bound by so many layers of silk, it would be a wonder if I managed even a few steps unassisted.

"*Kum* Divya?" The manager asked again.

I lowered my hand for a moment, to give him a tired look from beneath my fake eyelashes. He was sweating profusely, despite the room's temperature approaching all the ambiance of a meat locker. I searched my brain for a Hindi word that would put the man at ease, but it only came up with one.

"*Bevakoof.*" It was out before I could snap my jaw closed.

2ReeL gasped. I closed my eyes and moaned.

We were so close.

The manager and 2ReeL exchanged a few more words, but I didn't listen, waiting for the security guards to pounce on us. There was a small chance they might believe my story, if 2ReeL didn't shoot me first.

Somebody pushed my chair again. I dared to open my eyes just enough to see that we were passing through a sliding security door, the bank manager leading the way. His already stooping shoulders seemed downright deflated.

I twisted around to see who was pushing me. It was now 2ReeL himself. He gave me a murderous look, and I shrank into my fabric cocoon, thankful that my outburst gained us entry into the vaults and not a bullet in my head. We passed another security door and arrived in a small room, its walls completely covered in safe doors.

The manager addressed me again. I touched the fingertips of one hand to my temple. There was no way I'd open my mouth again. There was a brief but tense moment when I once again braced for the security guard's assault, but then 2ReeL jumped in, taking the silver purse from my lap and producing my supposed passport and a large key.

"*Dhanyavaad.*" The manager bowed and took the key's twin from his pocket.

I'd seen a safe-deposit box before, in the movies, but I didn't expect this one to be so large. The bank manager carried it, with visible effort, to the table in a small enclosure off to the side, and bowed out.

I reached for the box, but 2ReeL slapped my hand away.

"I will take it from here."

"Fine," I said, and continued practicing the bored expression. It wasn't easy, considering that my blood adrenaline levels would have caused a horse to be banned from the Kentucky Derby.

2ReeL reached inside the box and started to unload its contents: two large makeup cases and several jewelry boxes. There was also a bubble-wrapped package, which he tore open with shaking fingers. I stared in disbelief at a pair of metal stilettos that were studded with more bling than Lil Jon's grill.

"Son of a bitch," I said. "She was in there for, like, ten minutes, max."

"Shut up," 2ReeL snarled. "You were told to stay quiet. Not another word from you." He was obviously trying to ignore the fact that I saved our asses just a few minutes ago, but he also had a point—it was best not to be overheard babbling in English.

2ReeL opened another box, and I had to concede that House of Borgezie shoes were nothing special compared to the necklace that practically lit up the room. It was roughly the same shape as I remembered from when it weighed down Divya's neck, but it had grown into a beautiful swan since. 2ReeL slammed the lid shut before I even thought to reach out and touch it.

The makeup cases were packed full of hundred-dollar bills, but looked surprisingly small to contain all of the half-million—hardly enough to roll around in, and definitely not enough to dive into. 2ReeL put them in my lap, on top of the briefcase he brought along, which was now full of the jewelry boxes and packages.

It can't be this easy, I thought, waiting for the bank manager to come back and raise the alarm.

This must be where all the world's lost treasures are hidden, in random safe-deposit boxes around the world, under the watchful eyes of bank staff who don't give a damn about what it is they're watching.

The bank manager seemed more concerned with my frown than he was with the loot between my thighs—he couldn't stop chattering and bowing all the way back to the lobby, pausing only to activate the security measures we passed earlier.

Hells Apprentice was waiting for us in one of the guest chairs. He was calm, or perhaps retarded enough not to comprehend the enormity of the situation. For one brief moment, I had the crazy idea of throwing cash in the air, in hopes of inciting a riot, but 2ReeL must have read my mind and snatched the makeup cases from my lap with a venomous smile. After some more bowing and chatting with the bank manager, during which I allowed myself a weak smile and a couple of head bobs, 2ReeL orchestrated another fuss over getting me and my wheelchair down the steps.

I waited to say anything until we were safely in the car and on our way. "I've done my part. Now you have to keep your promise."

"Certainly," 2ReeL said and muttered something to Hells Apprentice. To my surprise, normally quiet Hells Apprentice objected at first, but after another command from the back seat, made a sharp turn. We drove in silence for a few moments, until I was a hundred-percent sure we were driving the wrong way.

"Where are we going?" I dared to ask when the downtown offices gave way to shacks and then to industrial buildings I most certainly had not seen on the way to the bank.

2ReeL barely gave me a look, but said something in Hindi, and the driver pulled over behind a huge weathered-blue shed. As far as the eye could see, there were only dead-grass fields and clumps of struggling trees. A perfect setting for a *Reservoir Dogs* sequel.

"What are we doing here?" I said, not wanting to believe my gut.

2ReeL answered my question by producing a pistol from the depths of his jacket. It looked ridiculous in his delicate hand. "Get out."

My gut was now shouting those exact same words. I fumbled with the door, jumped out, and ran back toward the road, screaming at the top of my lungs.

It was no use. There was nobody around to hear my pleas. Also, the running was over after just a few yards, when my feet got tangled up in the sari and I face-planted, scraping both palms and messing up my perfect hair and makeup. I flipped over on my back. 2ReeL walked closer, unhurried, as if savoring every moment. He still had the gun in one hand, but he didn't even bother pointing it at me as he struck yet another pose. In his head, he must've transformed into a Marvel Comics villain, but he looked ridiculous from up here, sticking out his bony chest like that. Behind him, his beefy minion stepped out of the car.

"I hate you," I spat at him through the tangle of hair and torn latex.

"Pity," he said, tilting his head. "You're very pretty, you know. When your nose is in one piece."

I pulled down my wig and peeled off most of my fake face, taking some of the sunburned skin with it. It hurt like a mofo but I could finally breathe easier, even if it wasn't going to be for much longer.

"You promised. You promised to let us all go. You got the money, and the necklace, and even the stupid shoes. What else do you want?"

He squatted down beside me. I could smell his aftershave, which was way too flowery even for a metrosexual.

"I'd love to play with you," he said, pawing me with the gun barrel like a cat would a half-dead moth. The cold metal brushed one of my raw knees poking through the torn fabric. I winced and saw a smile play at the corner of his mouth. "Unfortunately, I have strict instructions to dispose of you. Just too much risk."

"What about Harden?" I asked, even though I already knew the answer.

"You will see him soon enough," 2ReeL said, taking out his phone. "In the afterlife, I'm afraid."

He looked down at the screen, and I heard the tiny beeps as he pushed the numbers.

One. Two.

I got my feet under me.

Three. Four.

I shifted my weight to the front.

Five. Six.

I clenched my teeth and launched upward like a rocket. I don't know what I was expecting, maybe the crunch of a turkey wishbone. Instead, it was like breaking through that proverbial glass ceiling. A lightning bolt shot from the top of my head, burning through my eyeballs and nearly exploding my molars. I collapsed back down on all fours, blinded with pain, groping around for 2ReeL's gun. There was only dirt.

A strong hand grabbed my shoulder, and it all seemed hopeless for a moment, but just as I was yanked up, my hand found the rubberized grip.

I thrust the gun blindly at my enemy. "Let me go, asshole!"

"Put down your gun!" an unfamiliar voice commanded, and the hand let go of my shoulder.

AGENT ASSHOLE

The line between love and hate is not just thin—it's hypothetical at best. Trust me, it's possible to long for something while wanting to kill it at the same time. I mean, imagine finding out that one of your captors is an undercover FBI agent who spent two days watching you getting kicked and punched with the fake indifference of someone nominated for an Oscar. You too would have a hard time not shooting him in the kneecaps.

"Look, Agent Asshole," I said, pointing 2ReeL's Glock at the beefcake formerly known as Hells Apprentice with one hand and using the other to probe yet another bump on top of my already irregular head. The slightest touch generated throbbing pain aftershocks. "I'm not buying your story. If the FBI is supposed to protect and uphold, or serve, or whatever, then why didn't you protect and serve me, huh?"

"It's Special Agent Nikhil to you. And you're thinking of the police," he said. "The FBI's motto is fidelity, bravery, and integrity."

"Those are also very nice words," I said. "The thing is, I don't care about your motto or your t-shirt logo. All I know is that you're paid by the taxpayer's dollars to protect those same taxpayers. I've paid a ton of tax this year, and what did I get for it? Nada. Some dude, sleeping on the job."

That seemed to strike a chord. "My job," he said with an unnecessary emphasis, "was to infiltrate the Raja, and it was all going smoothly until you came along."

"Who is this Raja?"

He rolled his eyes. "The Raja mafia family. I believe you met its matriarch?"

"Did you just roll your eyes at me?" I motioned at his face with the gun. "Pardon me—I'm not familiar with all the intricate details of the local underworld."

"Take it easy, okay?" He put his hands up. "They're the oldest crime family in Delhi. We believe they might be involved in drug, gun, and even human trafficking—some seriously sick business. This is a joint covert mission involving the FBI, the CIA, the NSA, the DIA, and the DEA. Do you have any idea what it took to plan it? Two years and millions of dollars—and now it's over."

"Don't try to confuse me with your gibberish," I said. "And don't look at me like it's my fault—it's still a pretty shitty excuse to let this psycho shoot me."

"He didn't. I was about to knock him out, but then you beat me to it."

"Yeah, right." Warm goo dripped down from my hair onto my forehead. I wiped it off with my fingers, expecting it to be wig glue, but it was red.

"Jesus! Is this blood?"

"Yes. I think you broke his nose."

"Gross!" I wiped my hand on the sari. "Is he dead?"

"No, just knocked out cold." Nikhil bent down to check.

I panicked. "Hands up where I can see them!"

"Okay, okay," he said, holding up his hands again.

It was miserably hot, to the point I could feel my skin sizzling under the unforgiving sun. I was sweating like mad, my head was threatening to crack like an overripe watermelon, and it all made any attempt to think up a plan utterly useless. I had a gun, which was a great start, but I had no idea where I was, or if I should trust this guy. He spoke with a real

Midwestern accent, but he could also turn out to be another actor, like Divya.

"That was a pretty impressive head-butt," Nikhil said, breaking the silence. "Are you into martial arts?"

"No," I said, slightly flattered. "I did take a kickboxing class once, but I bruised my shin pretty badly, so I never went back."

He nodded.

"So, what do you want to do?" he said after another minute.

"I don't know," I said. "Can you, maybe, call for reinforcements or something?"

"Again, you're thinking police," he said in an overly enunciated tone. "This is a covert operation. There are no reinforcements. If I blow my cover, the FBI will deny any affiliation."

"This sucks," I said. "Why did you take this job? Does it pay well?"

"It's a matter of principle," he said. "And yes, it does."

I bit down on another comment about my taxes. "Okay. Let's call the police then."

Again he spoke to me as if I was a child. "I can't. I'm pretending to be a criminal, remember? In any case, Aadarsha has half the police force on her payroll. Calling the cops will get your friends killed, for sure."

"Shit!" This was worse than the Sunday Sudoku. "Okay, then we have to go get them ourselves."

He lifted an eyebrow. The guy was a first-rate jerk, the kind who has to learn a major lesson by the end of any self-respecting movie. "I told you, it's a covert operation. I can't help you."

"This is just bullshit!" I said. "Stop shooting down my ideas. How about you tell me what you can actually do?"

Now it was his turn to ponder. "I can take you in?"

"Take me in? What, you want to adopt me now? No, thanks, I already got a dad."

Nikhil clenched his teeth. "I can take you to an FBI safe house. From there, we can arrange for you to fly home."

A safe house sounds pretty nice, my gut said. "And what about Harden?"

"You mean the fat guy?"

I jerked up the gun barrel. "Call him fat one more time. I dare you."

"Sorry," he said sarcastically but put his hands higher up. "Okay, Harden. I'll have to ask Central. I'm not sure what we can do—this new development has already compromised the mission."

"Are you serious? People could die, and all you can think about is the damn mission?"

"That's all I can do. C'mon, give me your gun."

"Son of a bitch," I re-laced my fingers on the grip. "You refuse to help me, and now you want my gun, too?"

2ReeL moaned softly at our feet.

"We don't have much time," Nikhil said. "Give me your gun. Right now. I'm the one with authority here."

"I'm the one with a gun," I said.

He looked me up and down. "I have one too. I just don't want to shoot you."

"Thanks for telling me that," I said. "Now give it over."

"I have the authority—"

I shot at the ground, right in front of his feet.

"Fuck!" He jumped back. "Fine—you can have it, just calm down, okay?"

It took a couple more arguments back and forth, but I got him to pull the pistol from a holster inside his jacket and kick it over to me. It was an old one with a polished wooden grip, nice and heavy. I tucked it into the back of my sari skirt.

I looked down at 2ReeL on the ground, sound asleep, looking like a bloodied-up baby.

"I'm gonna go now," I said, circling them in a wide arc back toward the car. "It was nice meeting you, Agent Asshole. All the best with your mission and your career aspirations."

"Wait," he said. "Can you do me a favor?"

"What now? You want the car, too? Sorry, I'm taking it."

"No," he said, and there was clear desperation in his voice. "I need you to shoot me."

I snickered. "With pleasure."

"I'm serious," he said, looking almost terrified. "Think about it. How am I going to explain that you disarmed me and got away, and I don't even have a scratch to show for it?"

That made sense, but still. "I'm not going to shoot you. Are you insane?"

He thought for a second. "Knock me out, then."

"What?"

"Hit me. Please." His eyes were begging me.

Now I was scared. "Look, I would, but I can't hit an unarmed man, it's just not right."

"Pretend I'm armed, then."

I tried to, but my imagination couldn't picture him with a gun. For whatever reason, perhaps as a result of too many blows to the head, it produced a disturbing naked image of him instead. 2ReeL moaned before I had a chance to try again.

"You can do it," Agent Asshole said with a feverish urgency. "I'm a son of a bitch, remember? I hate kittens."

"You do? Why?"

"I don't," he spat. "But just go with it. Hate me! Take the gun by the barrel and hit me with the butt about here." He kneeled down and pointed at the side of his head, above the ear.

"Okay," I said, put the safety on and switched my grip to hold the barrel. It felt weird, like holding a car's tailpipe.

"But not too hard," he said just as I pulled back for a good swing. "Don't crack my skull or anything."

"Jesus!" I said, losing whatever little determination I had. "I don't know how hard is *too hard*. I've never pistol-whipped anyone before."

"Just enough to leave a bruise," he said, tilting his head. "C'mon, hurry up!"

I tried a couple of practice swings. "I can't do it."

"Yes, you can. Do it for your country."

"Don't make me laugh," I said. "It's not helping."

He looked up at me from under the overgrown black bangs. He was almost cute without the usual arrogance. "What if I yelled? Would that help?"

"It might."

Without any warning, he screamed at me with such a maddening force that my hands flew up and down by themselves, the gun just grazing his head. He yelped and fell down on his hands.

"I'm sorry!" I cried, dropping down and patting his shoulder, as if that could make anything better. "You said—"

"Yeah, I know," he said, touching his head and wincing.

"Should I try again?"

"No!" He flinched. "I mean, this will do. God, it hurts."

"There's some blood," I said encouragingly.

We agreed that no more pistol-whipping was necessary, but I went the extra mile, tying both his and 2ReeL's hands with their respective belts. I took both of their phones, and we'd just managed to find Aadarsha's address on Google Maps when 2ReeL muttered something and moved. I sprinted for the car, not looking back.

I dove behind the wheel and drove off, back toward the city, first slow, then picking up confidence and speed as the blood in my ears drummed one word over and over.

Harden.

MY TRIGGER FINGER IS GETTING ALL SWEATY!

I t's a miracle I didn't die driving back. Perhaps the constant panicked screaming helped release the stress, so my brain could work out when to turn, and into which lane. I laid hard into the horn too, to warn other drivers of my erratic moves. It turned out that driving on the wrong side of the road was pretty easy, once I realized all I had to do was listen to my gut and then make the exact opposite move.

I did pull over once, to set up the next stage of my plan, so by the time I made it back to Aadarsha's house it was after noon and stinking hot. The sleepy guard waved the black Mercedes in without asking me to roll down the tinted window. *Someone just lost his job*, I thought, slowly pulling past him and into the wide front courtyard.

The space was deserted, the rest of the inhabitants probably off on siestas somewhere. I grabbed the silver briefcase from the seat next to me and climbed out of the car, gun ready in the other hand.

There was a noise from the house. I ducked behind the car and watched Harshit appear in the front door, a pastry in his hand.

"Hi, Harshit," I said, stepping out from behind the car, my gun pointed straight at his chest. "Sorry, but I have to do this."

There was a flash of recognition, followed with horror, and then he dropped the pastry and started screaming. If I'd seen myself in the mirror just then, covered in blood and latex shreds, I would have screamed too.

"Calm down," I said. "I'm not going to shoot you."

He either didn't understand or didn't believe me, and continued screaming, his hands up, looking from me to the gun, and then over his shoulder.

I ran over to him. "Look, I'm sorry! I didn't mean to scare you, and I didn't mean to call you an idiot. I just want my friends, and then I'll leave, promise."

All I got back was an air-horn wail.

"Can you take me to your grandma?" I said. "Grandma Aadarsha. Do you understand what I'm saying?"

He didn't, of course, but it was no longer necessary. There were other voices now, approaching fast from the dark cavern of the house. I dropped the briefcase, put my free arm around Harshit's neck, and pushed the gun barrel into his side with the steeliest expression I could muster.

A group of men appeared in the doorway, but paused as soon as they saw what my right hand was up to. I moved farther behind Harshit for cover. "Where's Aadarsha? I want to talk to her!"

It only took another moment before Aadarsha appeared from behind her minions, crying Harshit's name. Every bit of her was frazzled, from her normally tidy gray hair to the sari that was threatening to come undone.

"Harshit!" she wailed, clutching her hands to her heart.

At the mere sight of her, Harshit redoubled his efforts to deafen me. I thought about another warning shot, but I had no idea how many bullets I had left.

"Hey!" I screamed, but the two of them just kept howling like two opera singers in the midst of an aria duet. Aadarsha kept inching closer to us, and for all I knew, the old lady could have been armed to the teeth.

"Stop!" I screamed, and she paused her shuffling, but not the crying chants. I kicked the briefcase to her feet. "Here's your money and your jewelry. Take it. I want my friends back."

Aadarsha shut up for a moment and exchanged a few quick, hushed words with one of the guys behind her.

"Don't try anything stupid," I said, feeling pretty stupid myself. For all I knew there were a dozen red dots on my forehead, already bloody. The trouble was, I didn't have any other options. "Where is Harden? Big man?"

Aadarsha bobbed her head slowly. "Yeah, okay. You can have him."

"Whoa!" I said, not believing my ears. "So you do speak English, but only when it suits you? Well, listen to this, Aadarsha, and listen very carefully. You have five minutes to get both Harden and Divya, or Harshit gets it. *Capiche*?"

That last word was Italian, I think, but Aadarsha capiched, all right. There was another quiet exchange, and two of the men left the doorway and went back inside. I didn't have a watch, but it seemed they were gone for an eternity.

"Tell them to hurry up!" I yelled. "My trigger finger is getting all sweaty!"

That was true. The sun was definitely on the Rajas' side that day, determined to burn me alive. I felt the buzzing in my ears that signaled the onset of near-fainting dizziness.

Finally, the two men reappeared with Harden and Divya. Both of them had guns shoved in their necks.

"Harden," I whispered, and almost passed out.

"Isa!" He struggled against the beefcake who was holding him. The beefcake shoved the gun even deeper into the underside of Harden's jaw. For one excruciatingly painful moment, I thought he was going to pull the trigger.

"Stop it!" I moved my gun to Harshit's ear. Aadarsha exhaled a scream so loud that a few more mosaics must've fallen off the walls. She turned around and threw her hands up, chattering so fast there was no way anyone could understand her. The beefcake did, though, and lowered his gun.

"Okay," I said, lowering my gun and trying not to hyperventilate into a coma. At least there wasn't a trace left of the previous sleepy dizziness.

"Let's do an exchange. I gave you the money and the diamonds. Now give me Harden."

"No," Aadarsha said. "Your man for Harshit. Divya for money."

"Love for love and asset for cash," I said. "That's fair enough. Okay—Divya first."

Aadarsha said something, and Divya's guard let go of her, but not before he pushed her so hard, she fell down on all fours.

"Control your dog, or I'm gonna put him down," I growled.

Aadarsha bobbed her head and said something to the guy, who looked ready to explode with rage. That made two of us: I watched his hands, ready to deliver on my promise if he tried anything stupid again.

Divya scrambled up and ran over to us, stepping behind my back. I could hear her teeth chattering.

"There's another gun in the back of my skirt," I said, and instantly felt her hand searching through my backside. I had a moment of anxiety over having a former adversary armed behind my back, but then isn't it better to join forces with unpredictable but similar-minded rebels than face the enemy on your own? Surely, we could come to mutually acceptable terms later.

"Now Harshit," Aadarsha said, waving for the boy to come over.

I locked my elbow around his neck. "Not so fast. Harden first."

"Harshit."

"Harden."

"Harshit."

It was hopeless. The sweat was dripping into my eyes, but I couldn't risk a moment to wipe it away. My face, my body, my whole being felt gross. *As God is my witness, I'll never cross paths with a mafia again.*

"Look, Aadarsha," I said as firmly as I could manage. "I can't trust you not to shoot Harden the moment I let go of your boy. You have a reputation, and I don't even have a passport."

Aadarsha didn't see the humor in that joke. Instead she turned around, grabbed a gun from Divya's disgruntled guard, and shoved it into Harden's neck. Harden groaned and squeezed his eyes shut.

"You are right," Aadarsha said. "I have more reputation, and I have more guns. Give Harshit. Now!"

Fuck!

The cogs in my brain spun madly, trying to analyze my options, but the only two thoughts that kept flashing through were *we are dead,* and *we are dead.* Queen Aadarsha did have more guns and more jacks. It was game over.

Until I remembered the ace up my sleeve.

LET'S NOT GET BOGGED DOWN IN DETAILS.

The key to successful lying is in believable acting. Any magician or teenager can tell you that. You have to believe the lie yourself first, before you can convince anyone else of the same. Of course, props and mood lighting help too, and finally, there's nothing like a good dose of adrenaline to help the brain accept the worst possible scenario.

I moved the gun into my left hand, took Agent Asshole's phone out, and held it up for them to see. "Hey, Aadarsha, there's something you don't know yet."

"What?" she said with disdain. "You called police?" She said something in Hindi and her companions hooted with laughter.

"No," I said and pointed the phone at the silver briefcase between us. I let my hand tremble just a little. "Open the briefcase."

"Why?" There was suspicion in her voice. Old people don't like surprises so much. Maybe because the older you get, the less pleasant those surprises become. She wasn't going to like this one, but she'd remember it for a long time.

"Open it!" I screamed in what I hoped sounded like psychotic desperation. Sweating like a pig added a nice touch to the already convincing show. Aadarsha forgot about Harden entirely. She said something, and one of the men approached the briefcase, hesitant and obviously terrified. He looked up at me before touching the locks.

"Open it," I said, bulging my eyes at him.

ANA SPOKE

He nodded slowly and flicked the two locks. The briefcase was already overstuffed, so the lid flew open, and so did the man's mouth.

"That's right!" I screamed victoriously, pointing at the mess of plastic bits and wires in the briefcase, complete with 2ReeL's cell phone in the middle. "It's a bomb!"

Ah, the element of surprise—I owe you one. Nobody bothered to question the evidence, instead pushing each other out of the way to run back into the house, screaming. I let go of Harshit, he flew into Aadarsha's arms, and then they were both gone, too. In less than a second, Harden, Divya, and I were alone in the courtyard.

"Let's go!" I yelled, running toward the car.

"Is that really a bomb?" Harden said, not moving.

"No! Just trust me for once. Are you coming or not?"

I didn't wait for his counterargument and sprinted for the driver's seat. Divya got into the front, and Harden climbed into the back without another word.

I spun the Mercedes around, gravel flying from under the tires. There was still one more obstacle to overcome before I could waste time on talking or breathing.

"Duck!" I yelled, accelerating straight at the front gate. It was an imposing piece of metal scrollwork, but it snapped off the rusted hinges, barely denting the car. *You do get what you pay for with luxury automobiles.*

"Left!" Divya shouted. I didn't question her judgment. In the rearview mirror I could see someone run out onto the street behind us and winced, ready for fire, but none came. I hit the gas and let Divya navigate, concentrating hard on turning into the correct lane when I had to. That, and taking a breath now and then.

After a while I ventured another look in the rearview mirror, but there were no gangsters chasing us.

"That went off with a bang, y'all!" I said, but they didn't laugh. "Get it? Cause I had a bomb—"

"Was that really a bomb?" Harden said from the back seat.

212

"No." I pointed to the gaping hole in the dashboard. "It was the car radio. I wasn't sure it would work but I had no other ideas."

"Why didn't you call the police?" Harden asked.

"Did you not hear her laugh about it?" I said, defensive. "The old lady practically owns them. If I called the cops, you'd be dead by now and—"

"Watch out!" Divya screamed. I hit the brakes, and we screeched to a stop behind a flock of mopeds. Another one of Delhi's traffic jams. I looked in panic for a black car behind us, prepared to run for it, but thankfully it was just more mopeds, taxis, and the usual old workhorse junkers.

"Let's just all calm down," I said. "There was never a bomb and everyone's alive, so let's not get bogged down in details. Oh yes, and thank you very much, *Isa*, for saving our lives."

"Is this from my safe-deposit box?" Divya said, rummaging through a shopping bag at her feet. "Did you get it all?"

"Yeah." I chuckled. "It was almost fun. I mean, not at the time, but now it's like, wow. Crazy. Way easier than I thought, but tell you what, I wouldn't do it again."

"So you didn't give Aadarsha anything?"

"No," I said, and laughed. "I mean, I had it ready just in case, but I knew we'd be dead as soon as she had what she wanted. 2ReeL spelled it out for me."

"You are right," Divya said thoughtfully. "Aadarsha won't stop until she has what she wants."

"Yep," I said, concentrating on following the cars in front of me as the traffic started moving again. "Now you can have it back. Except for my money. You can thank me later."

"No, I would rather do it now," she said, pointing her gun at me.

I WAS JUST JOKING ABOUT THE BUNNY.

Not every danger in life comes with a warning label, like the deadly hairdryer. Some you might recognize yourself: a spider, maybe, or a snake. But now and then you may find out, usually when it's too late, that the beautiful flower you came to regard as your friend is, in fact, a venomous bitch.

"How can you take my money *again*?" I said, watching Divya gather up the makeup cases and the shopping bag full of jewelry. "I saved your life!"

"Thank you," she said. "You may have my car for that."

"You don't even own it," I said. "I'm pretty sure Aadarsha already reported it as stolen."

"You are probably right," she said, climbing out the door and slamming it shut. She bent down to look at me through the open window, a Manhattan housewife shopping in the afternoon, one arm weighed down by the assortment of bags, barely balanced by the gun in the other. "Sorry, Isa. We could have been friends in another lifetime, but in this one, I have to think of myself first. Aadarsha won't stop until she finds and executes me. I have to disappear without a trace, and it will take every bit of cash I have."

"What do you think Aadarsha's gonna do to me? And by the way, it's my cash!" I yelled after her, but she was already walking away. I watched as she flagged down a taxi fifty yards in front of us. *Poor guy*, I thought, looking at the driver. There was no chance he was getting paid for that fare.

"Thank you," Harden said.

"What? Oh, yeah. You're welcome. Are you gonna leave me now, too?" I laughed bitterly.

"No," he said. "I appreciate what you did, Isa. It was crazy, but I guess you had your reasons. You came back for me. I will never, ever forget that."

I was going to laugh it off, but instead of a clever comeback, a fountain of tears came. I sobbed into my hands, unable to say a word while Harden patted my head through the gap between the front seats. That only made me cry harder. He stopped and opened the car door, and for a moment I did think he was leaving, but he just moved to the front seat, so he could cuddle me until I was spent crying into his shoulder.

"We should probably go," he said after a few minutes. I nodded and turned the car back on.

"Sorry about your money," he said as we pulled into the traffic. "They took my wallet, but I still have my passport in the travel pouch," he patted his belly, "so if we stop by my bank, I have enough in savings to get a pair of tickets to ..."

A travel pouch. Why didn't I think of that?

"Don't worry about it," I said, wiping my nose with the back of my hand. "Look under your seat."

He bent down as far as his bulk allowed and came back up with a bundle of dollars. "What's this?"

"It's cash, silly," I said, taking my eyes off the road for a second. He looked like a huge little kid trying to understand a magic trick.

He spread the banknotes in his hands, like a fan. "But I thought you said ... I mean, I saw ..."

"You saw her take a bag. Abracadabra. Smoke and mirrors. She won't be happy when she opens those makeup cases."

"And the necklace?"

"That was real. A hundred carats of bait. I also lost about fifty grand as camouflage, but the makeup bags are mostly stuffed full of pages from magazines I found in the trunk. She has an unhealthy obsession with celebrities."

"When did you do this?" he said, fishing out wad after wad from under the seat.

"When I manufactured that fake bomb. I have to give credit to Tara for the inspiration. You're right—she was a bad influence, but sometimes a bit of badness is exactly what you need."

"That could've gone so wrong," Harden said, staring at the pile of cash in his lap. "I've never in my life had a gun pointed at me, let alone two."

"I'm so sorry." I searched for his hand, and he took mine. "This is the worst nightmare I've ever been in, and I dragged you into it. I'll make it up to you, I promise."

He squeezed my hand, and I dared another quick look at his face. It was hard to tell what he was thinking, staring at me like that. I wiped at my face, still covered with blood and the remnants of Divya's handiwork.

"Do you hate me? I know, I've been acting crazy, and now I look the part...." I picked a loose piece of latex off my cheek. *Gross.*

"No, not at all," he said. "You're always beautiful, Izz. I'm just so ... I mean, I really thought I was goin' to die, but I didn't, and it's all thanks to you and your ingenuity. I mean, look at you—you're even drivin' on the left."

"Don't remind me, okay?" I said, taking my hand back to the steering wheel and laughing with embarrassment. Harden often said that I'm hot, but it was always "hawt" and always jokey. He'd never called me beautiful before. He'd never implied I was a genius, either.

He looked away. "Okay. What are we gonna do now? My first thought was to call the police, but if you're sure ...."

"I'm sure," I said. "I'll tell you about Moustache, this police officer, later. We have the cash to bribe him now, but I don't know how much Aadarsha's paying him or whomever she has under her thumb. I'd rather stay away from them."

"Okay. Then what?"

"I was thinking we could go to the embassy. They're supposed to hide us from the locals, right? At least they do in the movies."

He chuckled. It was a beautiful sound. "This is real life, Izz."

"Doesn't seem like it at the moment," I said and beamed at him.

"No, it doesn't. Tell you what, the sooner we get on a plane, the better."

"Agreed." I would have walked onto a plane right then and not given a second thought to whether it was an aluminum can or not.

Harden rubbed his neck. "Divya was right. This Aadarsha is an old witch, and now that we've robbed, scared, and pissed her off, she won't stop until she gets her revenge and her money back. She's the kind who would boil the bunny, for sure. Probably alive, too."

"Oh God," I moaned and almost lost control of the car, my body heaving in an effort to puke out my empty stomach.

"Are you okay?" In an instant, Harden's hand was over mine, guiding the steering wheel. "Sorry! I was just jokin' about the bunny."

"It's not that." I could taste bile in the back of my throat, the vile aftertaste of having betrayed someone's trust. Someone just as innocent and sweet as a bunny rabbit. Or Santa Claus. "We have to get Kabir."

"Who's Kabir?"

"The taxi driver I told you about. You were at his house."

"In the slums? You want to go back to the slums?"

"I have to," I said, shaking with fear. "Remember, he put his address on my release form. If you managed to get it off the police, it won't take long for Aadarsha to get it too."

Harden was quiet for a moment. "How do you know she hasn't done it already?"

I moaned in horror. "I don't. But I also don't want to think about what Aadarsha, or worse yet, that psycho 2ReeL will do if they get there first. We have to get him and his wife out of there, now."

"Damn!" Harden punched the dashboard. It was shocking, not just because of the force with which he connected with the hard plastic, but also because I'd never seen him punch anything before. To my knowledge, he'd never even hit a punching bag.

I reeled and almost lost control of the car again. "Sorry," Harden said, his hand back on the steering wheel.

"No, it's me that's sorry," I said, although the punch unsettled me. That was not the Harden I knew for most of my life. I needed him now more than ever, but what if his normally vast patience finally wore thin?

He let go of the wheel. "It's just that when I think this thing's finally over, you throw me another curveball."

"Sorry. I don't know how many times I've said it already, but it just doesn't feel like enough. I'm sorry I got you into this, but I can't stop now. A man's life is at stake."

"Yeah," he said and sighed. "I'll come with you. I'm okay now."

He didn't look okay, but it was something else that gripped my heart in an icy-cold paw, a realization so harrowing, it took me a few moments to get up the courage to say it.

"Harden, I don't even know how to get there. I had the location in my phone, but it's gone now. We have to go back to the police station and bribe them again."

I winced, ready for another dashboard punch, but Harden just covered his eyes with a hand and laid back in his seat.

"Are you okay? I'm so sorry. Look, I can drop you off at the—"

"Give me your phone," he commanded from under his hand. It was a stranger's voice, authoritative and stern.

"Why?" I said but fished out and handed him Nikhil's phone. "The security code is 1-1-1-1. Agent Asshole isn't as smart as he thinks."

Harden didn't laugh. He didn't even ask who Agent Asshole was, instead busying himself with swiping and poking the screen, seemingly oblivious to the world around him.

I dared a look over at the phone. It was a map, although I couldn't tell of what because Harden wouldn't stop zooming in and out.

"What are you ..." I started, but he interrupted me in the same authoritative tone. "Got it."

"Got what?"

"Got his address. Well, not the exact location, but I got the nearest intersection. Take the next left."

I obeyed wordlessly, making a mental note to ask him how he could remember a place after only visiting it once. I myself got lost in the mall all the time, even though I always went to the same one.

We didn't talk the rest of the way, other than for the occasional command from Harden and an acknowledging "yep" from me. Inside my head, though, we were having a full-on argument.

I'm sorry I screwed up, but I don't deserve the silent treatment! I've had enough of this too, you know, but I can't quit. I won't leave a friend behind if he's in danger, or even if she just needs some support at a difficult time in her life, say right after she was kidnapped and then used and abused by her agent. You want to help? Well, then help, but stop being angry with me. Mother Teresa didn't get angry at the people she was helping, and neither did Jesus, from what I understand.

"This is it," Harden said. "That's the metro station, and the house is farther down that way, I'm sure of it."

"Yep." I took a slight right turn down an unpaved street.

It did look familiar, although once you've seen one slum, they all start to look the same. Every other building was a dusty, rusty heap, and my heart leaped more than once, only to fall straight back down again. I was starting to lose hope when the front wheel sent a fan of dirty water out from under the right wheel.

I hit the brakes. "This must be it! I remember the puddle at the front. You're a genius, Harden."

Harden stared out the window. "Yes, I think it is."

I killed the engine and climbed out from behind the wheel, banging the door hard enough to let Harden know what I thought of his attitude, then went to the back and rummaged through the trunk. The reason why Divya didn't have any cash was there, in the form of crumpled-up receipts and shopping bags. I picked the most sturdy-looking bag and slammed the trunk shut.

"What do you wanna do?" Harden said, but I just grabbed wads of money from his lap and threw them in the bag. "Are you okay?"

"Yeah," I said, not looking at him. "Let's just get this over with. Let me get under the seat."

He got out and waited while I searched for loose bills. I had a little time to think when I was down there, mostly about how scared I was just a couple of hours earlier when I was shoving those dollars into the hiding place. All I wanted then was to survive and to get Harden back. It didn't make sense to be pissed off now, when all my prayers had been answered.

Dear God, just one more favor, pretty-please. Let me get Kabir out of here and then let Harden and me get on the plane. Oh, and a safe flight back home. And that's it. That'll be the last request, for like, a very long time.

I straightened out, a pleasantly heavy bag in one arm. Harden searched my face with a worried expression.

"It'll be okay," I said and forced a smile. He only nodded, but I saw his whole body relax.

There was a new display of sheets hanging over the facade of Kabir's shack, but I recognized the corrugated metal siding. The late afternoon sun was beaming down on us, shading the lively composition of assorted surfaces and drying sheets in a way that would make a *National Geographic* photographer cream his pants. All it was missing was some locals, sitting on the front porch with brooding expressions, or maybe cheerful ones, depending on the article's angle. I had a brief thought of snapping that photo myself, but the possibility of the residents inside screaming in horror and pain kicked my ass into gear.

"Let's go," I said, and walked straight into the dark mouth of the front entrance, not knowing what I might find. The worst-case scenario included angry beefcakes with guns, but I was just as unsure of what reception we might get from Mrs. Kabir.

It was going to be a disaster from the moment she saw me, but I managed to pull a stack of dollars from my bag just in time.

"There's more there if you just listen to me."

NOBODY CAN EAT GPS.

True altruism requires no thanks. I mean, if it exists, of course, because I have yet to come across it. Mr. Hue was all about fundraising, but he mostly used it to promote Shizzle, Inc. and make even more money. Then there are all these news stories about charities that do little more than support lawyers' families instead of the intended recipients. Even your average person wants something warm and fuzzy in exchange for their donation, like a photo of the starving child, or a tax deduction.

Still, I didn't expect my beneficiaries to be so mad at me when all I tried to do was to give them a load of cash to start a new life, somewhere far away from Aadarsha and poor infrastructure. Kabir's wife, especially, seemed reluctant to leave the family home. There was so much yelling and hand waving, someone with Auto-Tune skills could easily turn the argument into a Bollywood dramatic solo. She had her reasons, of course, the main one being that perhaps I, inadvertently, made them a target of wrath from a Queen of Delhi mafia. I would have been mad too—I could still remember yelling at Tara for blowing up my car out of supposedly altruistic reasons.

Mrs. Kabir was also not keen on packing up her stuff on such short notice, or leaving behind the dinner, still on the makeshift stove in the courtyard. Kabir, only marginally annoyed, tried his best to translate her monologue, in all likelihood omitting a number of choice words.

"Can you please tell her to hurry up?" I asked him, watching Mrs. Kabir fold sheets and take pictures off the wall. "You have enough money now to buy a house and all that stuff several times over." I gave Mrs. Kabir about half of my shopping bag's contents, which she stuffed into her vast bosom. She would see that we had a lot in common, if she only stopped yelling for a moment.

"Yeah, okay." Kabir tried his best to pacify his wife, but she mostly ignored him, continuing to chant and pile sheets into makeshift bags made with even more sheets. If there was one thing plentiful in their household, it was fabric of all kinds.

"We need to go," Harden said. His face looked ashy in the dim light.

"I know," I said. "Help me load this stuff in the car."

I grabbed one of the fabric parcels, which prompted another bout of grievances. After many assurances that I wasn't about to steal it, dutifully translated by Kabir, we were allowed to take a few packages outside to the car.

It was getting dark quickly, but I could still make out the shapes of various buildings and people in the twilight. The one shape I couldn't see was the black Mercedes.

"Harden," I said, hoping for a miracle, "do you remember where we parked?"

"It was right here," he said.

"Are you sure?" I fought desperately to stay calm. I put down the bags and pulled out the car keys. "Look, I still have the keys."

"Did you lock the doors?"

"Yes," I said, though I couldn't remember doing that. I mean, who can think of such trivial matters when lives are at stake?

"Are you sure?"

"Yes, I'm sure! Don't try to make out like everything's my fault. Did you check that *your* door was locked?"

"It's okay," Harden said.

"Yes, it is," I said, fuming. Good thing I'm much more comfortable with anger than I am with guilt. "Let me just think what to do."

The obvious solution was to pack the stuff into Kabir's sad little automobile. Kabir seemed happy with that, only because he didn't get to see the limousine I intended to use for transporting him and his beloved into the new dimension of safety and comfort. The only problem was, after we were done packing the trunk and the back seat with textile essentials, there was no space left for either Harden or me.

"That's okay," I said and waved my hand bravely, even though I could no longer see it in the dark. "Just go, we'll figure something out."

Harden didn't say anything, and I mentally thanked him for that. It looked like I had a lot more apologizing to do, but that would have to come later. We still had a long flight home, and it was going to be uncomfortable in more ways than one.

Kabir hesitated before getting into the driver's seat. I couldn't see the expression on his face, so I wasn't sure if I should hug him, or stay out of the way. I went with the safer bet.

"Goodbye, American girl," he said finally. "You did good."

"Thank you," I said, trying not to choke on the tears fighting their way up my throat.

He hesitated again, but then his wife yelled something from the passenger seat and he got in to start the usual engine warmup. It sounded hopeless for a few moments, but then the engine sputtered, and they rolled down the street and out of my life.

"What do we do now?" Harden said behind me, and I jumped a little, startled awake from the dream in which Kabir and I crossed paths again, years from now.

"Let's get a taxi," I said, trying to concentrate on the reality. It looked like shit: gloomy and dark, full of pitfalls, both figurative and the literal trip-hazard kind.

"I don't think we can get one here," he said.

I looked up and down the street—he was right. Either the taxi drivers were done for the day, or they knew something I already feared and stayed out of Kabir's neighborhood after dark.

"Okay," I said, trying to sound brave and nonchalant. "Let's walk to the nearest main road. We'll get one there in no time."

Harden didn't argue, and we put our heads together over the dim light of my phone screen. The nearest road that looked wide enough on the map to warrant street lighting was just a few blocks away. We had a false start when it turned out we were going in the wrong direction, but thank God for the GPS, we caught it in time. Or maybe, thank Al Gore—I'm sure he invented it, too.

We walked in the middle of the road, where the moonlight was enough to see the dark shiny puddles before stepping into them. There was little danger of getting run over by a car. The place seemed utterly deserted, a marked change from the daylight hustle and bustle. Occasionally, I could hear the sound of television shows from the houses on both sides, and spotted lights behind the curtains, but not a single soul on the street.

Harden's hand found mine, and I grasped it, grateful for the comfort and support, and for the sign that maybe its owner wasn't all that mad at me after all.

"Look at us. It's like we're Hansel and Gretel," I said, trying to swing his arm.

"Why? Because we're practically brother and sister?" He didn't sound happy.

I chose to ignore his baggage this time. "No, because we're following a trail of breadcrumbs out of the dark and scary forest."

"We didn't leave any breadcrumbs."

I resisted the urge to facepalm. "I'm talking metaphorically. We have GPS."

"If you say so."

There was no humor in his voice and no "Izz" in that sentence. I let go of his hand. "Yes, I say so. And it's a better trail because nobody can eat it."

"No, nobody can eat GPS, that's right."

Maybe he didn't mean to sound sarcastic, but it certainly came out that way.

"Well, then I wish I had breadcrumbs, because at least I could give them to the locals. They could use them. For fried chicken. If they have any around here."

Damn it. I was surrounded by the poor who could use every bit of help they could get, and I didn't even have any breadcrumbs to give them.

Wait a second.

"What are you doin'?" Harden hissed as I dashed to the nearest house.

"What I should've done to begin with," I said, separating several hundred-dollar bills from the mess in my bag and shoving them into a wide gap between the front door and the crumbling brick wall. "Giving my money to the poor."

"I thought you wanted to use it to build an orphanage or something."

"Yeah," I said, scurrying to the next door and repeating the donation process. "That's what I thought to begin with, but after the last couple days, I'm not sure I can. Somebody will either steal it, or confiscate it, or I'll lose it again in yet another unexpected twist. I've had enough of those for the moment."

Harden followed me. "Speakin' of stealing, I'm not comfortable with throwin' money around here. We could get killed for one of those bills, not to mention a whole bag of them."

"Then shut up and help me get rid of 'em," I hissed.

I shoved a bundle into my bra, for emergency expenses, and another bundle into Harden's hands. "Here. You can be Santa Claus."

"Santa Claus? Is it 'cause I'm fat?"

I didn't have time to argue or soothe him. "Just go and do the other side. Leave a couple bills per house. We can empty the bag in minutes."

Math is not my strongest point, but you don't have to be a genius to realize it takes longer than a few minutes to disperse a couple hundred thousand dollars a few banknotes at a time. It took me close to two hours to realize that, after we'd done block after block, but the bag was still half-full. I was kind of proud of myself for having made so much money that it was a drag to get rid of it all, but I was also dead tired. To make matters worse, thunder boomed in the distance, and I felt the first drop of rain land on my cheek.

"Here," I shoved another bundle to Harden when he came back to my side. "Let's start doing five bills at a time. I think it's gonna rain soon."

He snatched it from me, a little too abruptly. I was going to ignore his rudeness, but then he grabbed the handles of my shopping bag and pulled, hard. The rope handles burned my palm.

"What are you doing?" I said, and then I saw that it wasn't Harden at all. The shadowy man was shorter and much smaller, but he had the survival drive of a hungry wolf. I could smell the desperation on him, a mix of sweat and stale bread.

I screamed, and then Harden was there, throwing the man off me with one swipe of a paw.

"Who is that?" I cried, but Harden just grabbed my hand and pulled. "Run!"

We raced down the street, Harden plowing the way like a tank, me and my bag in tow. A few more raindrops landed on my face and arms, and then the sky opened up, enveloping us in a warm shower and turning the already treacherous road into a Slip'N Slide.

I held onto Harden's hand, trying not to fall on my face. I dared a look back, hopeful we might have lost our tail, but the hungry wolf-man wasn't far behind, and he wasn't alone, either. I was pretty sure I was sober, but I could swear he kept multiplying as more shadows joined him on the quest for my cash.

"Wait," I yelled over the noise of a million, maybe even a billion droplets hitting the dirt, and when Harden didn't respond, I jerked my wet hand out of his.

It took him a few skidding steps to overcome the inertia. "What are you doin'?" he shouted, trying to skate his way back and grab my hand again.

I had just a moment to swing the bag up high, letting go of the handles and a spectacular spray of banknotes. The rain knocked them right down, but they still shimmered in the mud like a flock of seagulls on a murky sea. Our pursuers saw them too—as Harden pulled me away, I could still hear them shouting and fighting for the loot.

I ran blindly through the rain with only Harden's hand for reference. We turned corners, and I could no longer tell if we were going the right way, not that I knew which way that was from the beginning. I just ran, the survival instinct screaming in my ears, demanding to put as much distance as possible between me and the men behind us.

No matter how strong, the survival instinct can only carry you for so long. You still need nutrition and training to make it as an athlete. A stitch in my side reminded me I'd had neither.

"Wait," I begged, trying to catch my breath and squeeze the pain out of my liver, or whatever else went into failure mode halfway between my pelvis and belly button. "I can't. Go. On."

"You have to." Harden tried pulling me along.

I half-collapsed, hanging onto his hand. "Save yourself."

"No." Harden grabbed me and heaved me over his shoulder as if I was made of feathers.

In hindsight that was romantic as hell, but at the time I almost threw up from fear and from banging my diaphragm against his shoulder. "Let me down!"

He did. We both panted, looking around. There was nobody behind us, only the constant, steady flow of the monsoon.

"I think we lost them," I said, and then a new sound pierced the monotonous drizzling of the rain.

The unmistakable sound of a gun being cocked.

An unfamiliar man, who had to be one of Aadarsha's beefcake minions, stepped out from the dark. I didn't get to see his gun, but I could smell it. Spent gunpowder, which used to be one of my favorites.

I heard someone calling my name from far away.

Then the last of the moonlight went out.

WHAT EXACTLY IS MY SITUATION?

It was dark, except for the light seeping through the cracks in the ground. It wasn't just the light—I could feel the heat from the invisible lava below. The ground groaned, giving way to whatever force was tearing through to get to the surface.

To get me.

The heat took hold of my legs, spreading upward and setting my insides on fire. I took a step back, turned, and bolted into the darkness, not caring if I was about to fall off the cliff or impale myself on a fencepost or something—whatever was behind me had to be worse than death. It uttered an unholy shriek, so loud my head felt like it was about to explode into a million pieces.

"Isabella!" the creature commanded. I didn't turn, but it got ahold of me, bringing me down to my knees.

"No," I begged, and then a bright light burst into my eyes, flash frying my corneas.

Someone was shaking my shoulder.

"Ms. Maxwell."

"Leave me alone," I mumbled, trying to get a grip on reality. An ugly creature towered over me, but it wasn't a demon after all. I was still alive. The thought was oddly depressing.

"Am I dead?" I said, trying to focus my eyes. I was lying on a worn-out couch, and its wooden ribs were stabbing my back through the thin upholstery.

"No," the creature said and moved in closer. It was a man, the kind that would scare small children with his bald head and thin lips pressed together into a minus sign. A high school principal by design.

"Who the hell are you?" I tried to sit up, but my various body parts rallied together against malnutrition and sleep deprivation. I willed my right hand to push me up so I could at least get a decent look at my inquisitor. We were alone in a small room, but I could hear men's voices outside the door.

He sat down on the opposite end of the couch. I pulled my feet away from him and hugged my body into a ball. I wasn't scared of him, because he didn't look like any of Aadarsha's men: too old, white, and skinny. It was my stomach that was giving me grief, twisting itself into a fiery knot of pain.

"Where's Harden?" I asked.

"He's here. There's nothing to worry about, Ms. Maxwell." His voice had no warmth in it, but no threat, either.

"Right. And now you're gonna ask me to trust you, too?"

Principal didn't even crack a smile. "I completely understand your concern, Ms. Maxwell. Anybody in your situation would have the right to be suspicious."

"Situation? What exactly is my *situation*?"

"Perhaps you should have something to eat before we have a little chat." He motioned to the coffee table in front of me, to a plateful of rice and curry.

My stomach screamed, but I couldn't tell if it was in excitement or fear. "Do you think I'm that big of an idiot? What's in this stuff? Hallucinogen? Or poison?"

"Chicken, I think."

"No, thanks," I said and vomited all over the floor.

WHAT'S THERE TO INVESTIGATE?

True friends are known in times of trouble, and while I couldn't imagine Principal and me hanging out at the mall, I certainly appreciated his reaction to my revolting display. He didn't run out the door screaming—in fact, he hardly moved at all, except to call out for someone. The next thing I knew, there was a sick bucket next to me, someone cleaning up my barf, and someone else checking my temperature and shoving pills into my mouth. Principal didn't even move an eyebrow when I cried out for the bathroom, right before my body betrayed me in more ways than one.

"Looks like you've picked up a bit of Delhi belly," he said when I was back on the couch and everyone else cleared out of the room.

"A what?" I felt a whole lot better after the purge, but a lot weaker, too. Things didn't compute all that well. If Principal wanted information, all he had to do was show me another plate of curry.

"A stomach virus. Or it could be bacteria. In any case, it's common amongst first-time visitors. Did you drink tap water or eat from a street vendor?"

"No." I remembered drinking from the tap in Aadarsha's bathroom. "Maybe. It was desperate times."

"Could happen to anyone. I've had more than a fair share of this in my travels."

I had to remind myself that we weren't socializing at a brunch. "So who the hell are you? And where the hell am I?"

"You're in an FBI safe house, and I'm Special Agent in Charge Morris." He didn't offer his hand, and I didn't blame him, considering I'd just introduced him to the contents of my stomach.

"The FBI? Well, nice of you to finally show up."

"Actually, Ms. Maxwell, we've had an eye on you for a little while now."

"You have?" I didn't like how he said it. Or maybe it was the way he was looking at me that made me want to run for it.

"The consul general advised us of the bank heist in which, I believe, you've lost a considerable sum of money?"

I let out a relieved breath. "Yes, of course. He was a really nice man, the consul. I was going to contact you myself, but then so many things happened...."

"Yes, about that." Agent Morris took a notepad from his pocket and leafed through its contents. "Perhaps you could explain how your fingerprints ended up on the dashboard of a stolen vehicle?"

I dry-heaved as each word punched me in the diaphragm.

"It was stolen from Taj Palace Hotel, along with a pair of valuable designer shoes. Ridiculously valuable, from memory."

"I didn't take the shoes!" I found my voice. "It was ... somebody else." For some reason, I couldn't say Divya's name. At least not yet—as I'd discovered recently, it pays to have an ace saved for later.

Morris scribbled something on his pad. "What about the stolen car and the fingerprints? We also have the description of the thief, which matches you perfectly."

"Oh, that." I swallowed back the bile that was rising in my throat. "It was just a mix-up with the valet. I thought it was my rental ... you know how all new cars look the same?"

"You've rented an Aston Martin?"

Shit. "No—I rented a Civic, but it looked almost the same."

He raised an eyebrow.

"Yeah, especially when you're in the hurry," I said, feeling a strike of inspiration. "Of course, once I drove off, I realized it was the wrong car!" I chuckled and shook my head at my silliness.

Morris just watched me, still as a statue.

"So of course, I immediately turned around and returned it. I have no idea what happened to it afterward."

Morris scribbled something else. "Do you know how we found you, Ms. Maxwell?"

"No," I said, wondering if it had something to do with Divya. Perhaps she was an undercover agent herself and slipped a tracking device into the many layers of my sari.

"We had a couple of agents in the area, investigating reports that someone was distributing hundred-dollar bills to the residents of Vivekananda Camp. A lot of hundred-dollar bills."

I shrugged. "Well, that was nice of them, whomever they were. What's there to investigate?"

"Whether or not that money belonged to them in the first place."

I opened my mouth to object that it was my money and that I could do whatever I wanted with it, when he added, "The serial numbers of the bills we've managed to recover match those that were reported stolen from your bank, Ms. Maxwell."

My lips formed a surprised "Wow!" just in time. I couldn't follow his allegations fast enough to understand if admitting my Robin Hood pranks would get me a medal or five years behind bars.

"What were you doing in the Vivekananda slums in the middle of the night, Ms. Maxwell?"

I took a moment to clear my throat. Inspiration kicked in again, just as unwilling to go back to jail as I was. "I was visiting a friend who bailed me out of jail. With Harden. We were on our way back and got lost—you know how dark it is there." Lying is easy when it's true.

"Oh, yes, you were incarcerated." Morris consulted his pad again. "Public intoxication with illegal substances, I believe?"

"Yes, but the charges were dropped," I said with a new attitude. In the past forty-eight hours I'd survived bigger challenges than getting questioned by a bureaucrat. "You can ask the consul general about that."

"Certainly, but I'd like to ask you another question."

"Sure." I folded my arms.

He reached out, and I thought the creep was going to pat my cheek. I reeled back and he took away a small shred of my latex skin. "What's this?"

For a second, I was about to spill the beans about everything. Divya, the breaking and entering, the kidnapping, and the other bank heist. Then I remembered driving on the wrong side of the road. Everything about this conversation was going the wrong way. It was time to do the opposite of what my gut was telling me, no matter how much I wanted this to be over.

"Makeup."

He rubbed the bit between his fingers. "It doesn't feel like it."

"How would you know? Do you wear it often?"

He chuckled. "No, but my wife does. I've never seen it peel like that."

"I can't imagine your wife going through what I've experienced in the last couple of days," I said, remembering just in time not to say too much. "You know, the rain and stuff."

Morris tapped the pen on his pad, deep in thought.

"If you don't mind, I'd like to get some rest now," I said, trying to get comfortable between the wooden ribs of the couch. "If you have any further questions …"

Morris put the pad down and leaned closer toward me. "Perhaps everything you said is true."

I tensed, waiting for the "but" to follow.

"However, should we get a different story from your friend Harden, who is under interrogation in the next room, things could change very quickly."

I jumped up, almost breaking a hip against the wooden frame. "What do you mean, 'interrogation'? What are your charges?"

Morris put a hand up. "I meant questioning."

"What right do you have to question him? And where is his lawyer? Speaking of which, where's my lawyer?"

"You won't need one."

"Oh, I've heard that before." I tried to get up from the couch.

Morris put his hand on my leg. "Please stay, Ms. Maxwell."

"Get off me!" I kicked off his hand. "Help! Rape!"

There was a commotion outside, and a new guy burst through the door. He was wearing a pair of jeans and a baggy t-shirt, but his crew haircut alone would have betrayed him in any covert mission.

"It's okay," Morris said. "Everything's under control."

"It's not okay!" I shouted. "Now I have witnesses! Help!"

The guy hesitated, but then closed the door behind him.

Morris put his hands up in a conciliatory gesture. "I apologize, Ms. Maxwell. We started off on the wrong foot. Truth is, we're working for the same cause."

"Which is?"

"Righting the wrongs. Helping the weak. Isn't that why you came to India?"

How would he know that? "Maybe. So then why are you giving me the third degree?"

"Just fact-checking, that's all." He threw the pad onto the coffee table. "No more questions. Although there's something else I need to ask you. A favor."

Here we go. My stomach lurched.

"Nikhil!" Morris yelled, loud enough to make me jump.

A moment later, Agent Asshole poked his head through the door.

WHAT IF HE HAS AN STD?

B eware the wolf, even if he wears a sheepskin, or a pair of unnecessarily tight blue jeans and an even tighter t-shirt.

"I believe you've met Special Agent Nikhil?" Morris said.

I looked Nikhil up and down. "Yes, now that you've mentioned it, I remember this asshole."

"Sir," Nikhil ignored me, although I could see his jaw stiffen. "As I was saying, it would never work."

"What? What wouldn't work?" I felt strange—both angry and about to throw up again. I pulled the bucket closer, just in case.

Morris put his hand up to silence Nikhil. I would've kissed him for that right there if I had any strength left or wasn't worried he'd start throwing up himself. Nikhil tightened his jaw to about a thousand pounds psi, filling my heart with effervescent joy.

"Ms. Maxwell," Morris said. "I have a proposition for you."

I snorted. "Do you have a ring, too?"

He didn't acknowledge my zinger. "The FBI would like your assistance on a very important mission."

"Mission? What mission?"

"I'm afraid I can't disclose any details of this matter until you agree to help us, Ms. Maxwell, and even then, the information will be available to you only on a need-to-know basis. The mission is classified Top Secret, and you simply won't have the appropriate level of clearance."

"Let me get this right," I said, squeezing my head between my hands, as if that was going to help my overheated brain process the puzzle. "You want me to agree to something, but you won't tell me what it is? Sorry, but it's a no-can-do."

Morris and Nikhil exchanged a look.

"Unfortunately, this is the reality of covert missions," Morris said. "Sometimes it's best not to know all the details, for your own protection. In this case, we simply can't tell you about the assignment unless we know you will agree to undertake it and to consent to a nondisclosure agreement. Since you've already written one tell-all book, you can understand how complicated that could get."

"It was not tell-all," I said. "I mean, it told a lot, but some of that was made up. I might still sue my agent, once I get my paperwork sorted and get my money back. For the lawyers, I mean."

"The FBI can help you recover your money," Morris said. "In addition, there will be a generous payment for your services."

I deliberated with my gut for a moment. "Out of interest, how generous?"

"It's classified."

"Of course it is." I chuckled and laid back down. It was too much for any brain, let alone one engaged in fighting off a virus. "In any case, I don't care about your carrot."

"A what?" Nikhil said, and Morris silenced him again. I was starting to develop warm and fuzzy feelings for the old man, in a way someone with a gangrene might fall in love with penicillin.

"Your dangling money carrot. It won't work," I said. "I can always write another bestseller and not worry about whatever mess you're trying to drag me into. And in any case, shouldn't I have some training first?"

"As I was saying," Morris droned in a tired voice, "you're not eligible to become an FBI agent, at least not yet. You're too young, you don't have a qualifying degree, and frankly, I doubt you would pass the psych test."

"Way to go with the reverse psychology, sir," I said hotly. "It won't work either."

He still wouldn't take the bait. "We were, however, quite impressed with Agent Nikhil's report on your ingenuity, quick thinking, and courage. The fake bomb was truly a stroke of genius. How did you come up with that idea?"

"It's not that original," I said, feeling a delightfully warm blush creep up my neck. "Wait, how do you know about that?"

"Let's just say we've questioned a few of the Raja family members," Morris said.

"The head-butt was impressive, too," Nikhil chimed in.

Morris nodded. "The fact that an untrained civilian disarmed a mafioso and then a *Special Agent*, is unparalleled."

Nikhil looked down at his hands.

"I'm not just any civilian," I said, trying to shake off that warm and fuzzy feeling. "I've been shooting guns for a few years now, mostly to impress my boyfriend. I mean, an ex-boyfriend, but we've been together since high school, so I've had years of practice. Anyway, you just said I'm not qualified to be an agent, so why do you want me? Besides the fact that I'm obviously a natural at this."

They exchanged another look. "I can't tell you all the details," Morris said, "but I guess I could let it slip that your celebrity status is the key to the success of this mission. You, Ms. Maxwell, are our only chance at infiltrating a particularly tight criminal circle."

"Me?" The blush turned uncomfortably hot. "Why me?"

Morris got up from the couch and began to pace the tiny room. "We have definite knowledge that the target is a massive fan of yours, Ms. Maxwell."

"A fan?" My ego could hardly take all the stroking. I tried to remember the names on some of the fan emails I'd gotten over the last few months. "Who is he?"

"I can't tell you that, not yet. All I can say is this individual is obsessed with you, your connection to Mr. Hue, and your sudden rise to fame.

Once you're introduced, we're hoping this obsessive interest will enable you to establish a close relationship with the target, thus allowing us to gather key intelligence needed to bring down a drug-trafficking network."

"Oh my God," I said, incredulous. "I barely got away from one mafia and you want me to get in bed with another one? Do you really think I'm that stupid?"

"Not at all, Ms. Maxwell. In fact, based on how you've handled yourself over the last couple of days, we believe you're a gifted young lady. And while there would be certain risks, we would not expect you to sleep with the target."

Gifted young lady. I told my ego to shut up.

"But that wouldn't hurt the mission, right? No, thanks, that's just gross. Not to mention dangerous. What if he has an STD?"

"I can assure you, there would be no danger of that," Nikhil said. "I will be there with you every step of the way, as your new boyfriend."

Boyfriend? The nerve of this guy! I glared at him. One thing was for sure, he had really muscular arms. And chest. He was kind of thick all around.

I was thinking how to articulate his fat chances in the most condescending way possible when Morris spoke again. "You and Special Agent Nikhil would be working together, as a team."

"I thought he's already working undercover?" I nodded in Nikhil's direction, still too pissed off to address him directly. "On a mission that's a lot more important than my life or well-being."

"We had to bring him in," Principal said. "It was too dangerous to continue, now that his cover might have been compromised. We had no choice but to terminate the mission."

"Yeah, thanks for that." Nikhil gave me a cynical smile.

"Sorry about that, sir," I said, ignoring the sarcasm. "Of course, if I were aware I was in the tender loving care of Agent A— Nikhil, I would've opted for a lot less *radical* method." I gave Nikhil a suitably mocking smile back.

"That's understandable," Morris said. "Not all has been lost. We've managed to arrest several key individuals and will be certain to extract all relevant information from them. Unfortunately, we haven't been able to locate one Divya Sharma, also known as Vivien Sircar, Advika Prasad, and Riya Johar. I believe you were the last one to see her?"

"Yes, her and her gun. And my money," I said with righteous anger.

"So we've heard," Principal said, looking straight into my eyes. I looked straight back into his, trying to concentrate on his right pupil and not on the vision of the FBI in hot pursuit of a sad and rusty little car, carrying an elderly couple in possession of stolen and re-stolen cash.

Morris either believed me, or didn't care about what happened to the money. "The new mission is even more important to national security than bringing down the house of Raja, although Nikhil's experience working with mafia will be invaluable."

"Oh yeah, the new mission," I said with seething sarcasm. "So what is it you want me to do, become BFFs with a stalker and pump him for information?"

Morris chuckled. "Not at all, Ms. Maxwell. We don't expect you to pump anyone, as you've put it. Your role will be simply to attract the target's attention."

"You mean you'll be using me as a decoy?"

"Hardly," Morris said. "Okay, yes."

"Thanks, but no thanks," I said, trying to stand up. It was a lot harder than I remembered. "If you don't mind, I want to check on Harden. Where is he?"

"In a moment, Ms. Maxwell," Morris said, and there was enough steel in his voice to stop my feeble attempts at escape. "You're free to go, of course, but before you do, I want to give you this." He pulled an envelope from his pocket.

"You can't buy me."

"It's not money, Ms. Maxwell. It's something far more precious."

He opened an envelope, pulled out a stack of photographs, and laid them in my lap. The top one was of a mountain range set off by a seemingly endless field of white flowers.

"That's very pretty," I said, shoving the photos away, "but *precious* might be a slight exaggeration."

Morris didn't move. "That's a poppy field in Afghanistan. Have a look through the rest of the photos, Ms. Maxwell."

There was a new note in his voice, a barely contained passion. I couldn't tell if it was love or hate, but it made me pick up the photo stack. The next shot was of a pretty young girl with dark hair, maybe eight or ten years old at the most. She was looking straight into the camera with huge, doe-like eyes. "Who is this?"

"She's a slave, Ms. Maxwell," Morris said slowly. "Taken hostage by an opium gang so her father would agree to work in those poppy fields."

That didn't compute. "A slave? Is she okay?"

"We don't know. Have a look at the others."

I thumbed through the rest of the pictures. They were all of children, mostly very young girls. "Why are you telling me this?"

"Because we need your help to fight for them, Ms. Maxwell. You can help us win the war on drugs, in this particular case heroin. Did you know that heroin is made from poppy plants? If we can stop it from being exported and sold in the States, therefore eliminating the demand for poppy plants in Afghanistan, there would be no opium gangs, no poppy fields, and no child slaves."

I dropped the photos back into my lap and tried to blink away the dark-haired girl, but her huge, terrified eyes wouldn't leave my field of vision.

"I can't," I said finally. "This is too much. You're asking too much of me. I want to help, but I can't fight a war. Can't I do something less violent, like humanitarian aid or something?"

"Unfortunately, humanitarian aid is not what we do. If that's what interests you, perhaps you should join the Peace Corps." Morris stood and motioned for Nikhil to join him. "This mission is dangerous, and it is also completely voluntary. Even Nikhil could choose to decline. We cannot and will not pressure you into participating."

I held out the photos for him, but he waved them away. "Keep them, Ms. Maxwell, in case you change your mind later. My phone number is on the back of the envelope."

He turned, and they left before I had a chance to explain that I did want to help them, but that I was simply too young and inexperienced for a mission of such magnitude. That I was still a child myself, and that my parents too would be devastated if anything happened to me.

A moment later, Harden poked his head into the room. "Are you okay? I heard—"

"Oh, God, Harden," I held out my hands, and then he was next to me on the couch, cradling my head and patting my back. "It was horrible!"

"Yeah, they told me. I wanted to take you to the hospital, but they said you're likely to pick up something worse there."

"No, I didn't mean *that*. The old guy asked me to do something I didn't want to…."

I had to grab his shirt to keep him from charging out of the room. "Let me go, Isa," he said, trying to pry my fingers off with the gentleness reserved for babies. "I swear, I'm gonna show that prick—"

"No, wait, it was nothing like that. I mean, I don't think so—they said there would be no sex."

He paused his efforts at seizing my fingers. "Who the hell do they think they are?"

"The FBI. Although I think that's classified. Everything is classified with them. I'm surprised they even told me where the toilet is in this place."

He chuckled. "I guess you're not that sick."

"I was feeling better until I found out about the heroin slaves."

"What?"

I told him. He didn't say anything else and just sat there, dumbfounded, while I explained about the mission, the poppy fields, and the slaves.

"So they think I'm the only one who can help them get access to this drug lord," I said finally.

"That's bullshit," he said, shaking his head. "They have all the resources possible, and somehow it has to be you, or millions of children die? Sounds like emotional blackmail to me, Izz."

"Yeah," I said. "It couldn't be millions, could it? Of children?"

"No." He stroked my arm, in almost exact spot where Harshit touched me just a day or so earlier when I was tied up and fearing for our lives. I closed my eyes and wept while he kept patting me and telling me how nothing was my fault.

IT'S ALL OVER, KIDDO.

I startled awake, not from a dream, but from a place so deep and dark, it felt like coming up for air from the bottom of a well. Somehow, I'd been transported to a bed, which was a lot more comfortable than the skeletal couch. I was drenched in sweat, and my stomach still hurt, but my head felt a lot better. Morris and his proposal seemed a distant memory, no more concrete than one of my usual weird dreams. I closed my eyes again, pulled the comforter over my head, and savored the certainty that this particular nightmare was nearly over.

Half an hour later, when thirst and hunger drove me out of my down-filled fortress, the house was nearly empty. Harden was in the kitchen, in the company of a meat pie and a guy I didn't remember seeing before. He, too, turned out to be a special agent, and I had to suppress the urge to ask him what made all FBI agents so special, and if some were not, what were they called. I obviously had low blood sugar, or maybe issues with a particular not-so-special agent. I decided to eliminate one of those possibilities by accepting a plate of food.

There were a few moments of silence as we collectively poked at our pie slices. Mine was generously stuffed with spicy chicken and vegetables and promised to pile on whatever weight I might have lost during the last few days. I didn't care. Being alive and feeling full were now firmly at the top of my priority list.

The FBI guy got a call and left the room, muttering some gibberish code into his cellphone. Harden watched him close the door, then fished an envelope from his pocket. "Your friend left somethin' for us."

"What friend? Kabir?"

"No, the good-lookin' FBI agent," Harden said. "Nikita or somethin'."

"Oh. Nikhil. He's not that good-looking." I picked up the envelope. "What's this?"

"Your passport and credit cards. They found them at Aadarsha's. The FBI also bought us a couple of tickets home."

"Well, isn't that nice of them. I mean, they could have recovered my money from the bank, so I could buy the tickets myself, but …"

Harden returned to mindlessly poking at his plate. "Technically, we're gettin' deported, Izz."

"Fine." I didn't care what the technical term was, as long as it meant I got to go home. I also no longer cared about the Taj Mahal, or any other wonders of the world, other than the one that could fly me to Los Angeles.

"I asked the agent if we could exchange them for tickets to Cambodia," Harden said, not looking at me. "He said it didn't matter where we went, as long as we left the country. Somethin' about security measures."

I was so certain he was coming back home with me, the idea that he might have some other plan never even crossed my mind. "Cambodia? So you're going back to the Peace Corps?"

"I have to. I mean, I want to. And I was hopin' that, maybe, you'd want to come along?"

I felt feverish again. "I don't know … this is so sudden. I don't even have any luggage. I mean, I need some clothes and maybe a toothbrush. Don't I need a visa or something?"

He kept looking at his plate. "You can buy a one-month tourist visa at the airport. And your friend Nikhil brought a bag of supplies for you."

"He's not my friend," I said.

We sat in silence for a few moments.

"I don't know, Harden," I said finally. "What would I do there?"

"Help people," he said, looking up at me. "That's what you want to do, right?"

I hesitated for a moment. Of all the people I knew, I was the one in need of most help. My stomach rumbled in agreement. "I'm not sure I can, Harden. I don't have any more money to give."

He didn't take his eyes off mine. Something in them hypnotized me—it was hunger and sadness, and hope, all at once. "You don't need to have money to be appreciated, Izz. Give 'em your time."

I nodded, feeling my body's defenses crumble.

"Maybe you could give me some of your time, too," he said and put his hand over mine. It was big and warm, and the next thing I knew, I agreed to follow it to yet another country I wasn't even sure existed.

~

When the Special Agent Babysitter came back, Harden borrowed his phone to call the airline, and I excused myself from the table and went to the bathroom to scrub off the gunk and memories of the last twenty-four hours. I should've called my parents, but the thought of trying to explain to them what had happened made me nauseated again. I stood under the shower, being careful not to swallow any more water. My skin was creeping with that feeling you get right before the flu cuts you at the knees. *Another adventure*, I thought, but for some reason, it was hard to breathe.

I dried myself off and put on the clothes Nikhil left for me—white cotton panties, a generic pair of jeans, and a black t-shirt, all brand new and still in plastic packaging, but way too large. I finally cracked it when I unfolded the bra, which looked like a pair of parachutes attached to a safety harness. I felt an aching need to see Agent Asshole again, if only to gift him a package of undersized condoms.

I put the clothes on, except for the bra, opting to keep my sweat-stained one. The jeans were threatening to fall off my hips, but the feeling of clean fabric against my skin did wonders for my well-being. I brushed my teeth and hair, and looked at myself in the mirror.

It's all over, kiddo. You did good.

The kid in the mirror didn't smile back. It hurt too much to move my peeling cheeks, plus I couldn't believe it was all over, or that what I did was any good. At least Harden forgave me.

I tiptoed past the kitchen, where he was still on the phone, into the bedroom. The envelope Morris gave me was on the bed. I lay down next to it, flipped it over, and looked at the back. There was no name there, just a long number in big rounded handwriting. I had a feeling that if I ever had the nerve to call it, there would be no need to explain whom I was trying to reach.

I opened the envelope and looked again at the dark-haired girl with terrified eyes.

There will be plenty of girls like that in Cambodia, equally deserving of help and a chance at happiness.

"What about me? I deserve a chance at happiness too," I said out loud. There was nobody around to contradict me.

I put the photos back in the envelope. There was a knock on the door and Harden stuck his head in. "Are you okay?"

"Not really." I put my head down next to the envelope, feeling the girl's eyes staring at me through the thick paper.

"We have two seats on a plane to Phnom Penh in three hours." Harden sat down next to me.

"Try to say that three times fast."

He didn't laugh. "Are you sure you're okay? Maybe we should go to the hospital first?"

"No. I mean, I'm okay. Just so … sad, you know?"

He sat on the bed next to me and stroked my shoulder. "That's okay. Any normal person would be sad after what you've been through. You probably have post-traumatic stress disorder."

"I feel disordered," I said, and he chuckled. I closed my eyes and let him pat me into oblivion.

GIRL LOST, NO NAME.

"Are you excited?"

I looked over at Harden. There was no doubt he was thrilled to be on the way to the airport, judging by the way he was bouncing in his seat. We were huddled together in the back of a nondescript car driven by Special Agent Babysitter. I wondered if the guy was going to personally make sure we got on that plane. Either that, or the FBI didn't want to splurge on a taxi.

"Yeah," I said and bit my lip on the "but" that almost came after. There were not going to be any more "buts," and there was not going to be any more trouble. Harden beamed at me, took my hand, and went back to looking out his window, like a kid who can't wait to get to Disney World.

I leaned my head against my window, grateful for the cool glass. Yesterday's rain was still going strong, shrouding the buildings, cars, and people in a murky haze. It didn't seem to have any impact on the traffic, which hugged our car on all sides and carried it along like a leaf caught in a current. The sea of mopeds no longer bothered me, although it was strange to see that their defiantly helmetless drivers were more afraid of the rain than death—each one of them was now wrapped in a billowing plastic sheet.

We passed a huge weird circle intersection with a market building in the middle, which I recognized from my first taxi trip just a few days ago.

India was passing me by as if the last few days were being rewound back to the beginning, but I felt little regret at not discovering all of its hidden charms. I might not have found what I was looking for, but I found something else, something I thought I'd lost forever. I squeezed Harden's hand and he beamed at me again.

We unloaded from the car in the same spot where I'd wrestled with illegal taxi drivers and met Kabir in what now seemed like a dream. Deja vu was so strong, I almost expected an electrical shock to hit me when I passed through the sliding door again, but nothing happened. Nothing continued to happen as Babysitter left us alone and I let Harden take charge, mindlessly following him through check-in, security, and finally to our gate.

"Just about an hour left," Harden said.

"Yeah," I said and nodded, carefully lowering myself into a plastic chair.

"Are you okay, Izz?"

"Yeah, why? I'm fine."

"You don't look fine," he said. "You look like you might throw up again."

"I'm not gonna throw up," I said, but then the lobby did a quick spin. "Maybe I'll go to the bathroom, just in case."

Harden wanted to come with me, but agreed not to, after I painted a picture of him being arrested in the ladies room. I shuffled off to the bathroom, which was only a couple of hundred yards away, feeling his eyes on my back.

It turned out that puking into a toilet bowl is about as pleasant as it is into a hole in the floor, which was what I found inside one of the bathroom stalls. I didn't get a chance to consider the technicalities of how one might use it to relieve themselves before the meat pie lunged out of my throat. I used a conveniently provided hose to wash off the overspray, thinking that the bars back home could benefit from this setup.

Back in the common area, with more conventional sinks and hand dryers, I scrubbed my hands with soap and washed my face. I resisted the urge to gulp the water to extinguish the fire in my throat. The kid in the mirror now looked like a zombie in desperate need of a soda.

I was shuffling back to the waiting area, sipping from a cold can and feeling marginally better, when I saw a little girl running through the middle of the wide aisle. I thought she was playing tag with someone, until she face-planted a few steps in front of me, bawling into the carpet. Nobody rushed to help her.

"Hey," I said, kneeling. "Are you okay? Did you hurt your head?"

The girl pushed up to look at me with huge dark eyes, framed with tear-soaked eyelashes.

Well, someone's going to grow up to be a model. To think of it, I was sure I'd seen her in a commercial or maybe in a magazine already.

Whatever the poor thing saw made her cry even harder. I tried my best not to get offended.

"It's okay, I'm just sunburned," I said, helping her up. "Where's your mommy?"

The girl let out another heartbreaking wail. I looked around. Everyone was going about their business, and no one looked as if they were missing an heir.

"Are you lost, honey?" I said. "That's okay. We're gonna fix it."

I took her hand, and she held onto my pinkie and ring finger. She was no more than five years old, and her tiny hand was lost in mine, the same way my hand got lost in Harden's.

"Let's find somebody to help us." I looked around. Next to the vending machines, where I'd acquired the caramelized life elixir, was a small island with an information sign over it. I started walking toward it, not sure if the little girl would follow, but she stopped crying and walked alongside me as if she'd known me her whole life. Nobody had ever trusted me so completely and so quickly. I winced as some forgotten instinct kicked into a rusty gear.

"Excuse me," I said to the man reading a paper behind the desk. "This little girl is lost. Can you please make an announcement for her parents?"

The man, dressed in a security guard's uniform, looked me over with such contempt, for one enormously long, terrifying moment I thought he was about to accuse me of child abduction. That would have been a strange, but not an entirely surprising addition to my already rather long rap sheet. Instead, he put down his paper and said something to the girl in Hindi. She gripped my hand even harder and hid behind my back.

"She won't say anything to me either," I said in my most appeasing voice. The guard ignored me, came out from behind the desk, and tried to take the girl's hand, but she clutched onto my leg for dear life.

"Hey!" I said, blocking him. "Take it easy. Just announce that she's lost, okay?"

"I need child's name," he said with an arrogance unbefitting a public servant. "What I announce? Girl lost, no name?"

"That would be a good start," I said with a matching attitude. "How often do little girls get lost in this airport?"

We exchanged another look of mutual loathing, and he finally backed off and spoke into a microphone. I listened to his voice reverberate through the great hall, first in Hindi, then in English, asking for parents of a girl aged about five to meet her at the information desk.

Nothing left to do but wait. The girl kept her face buried in my baggy jeans, and I kept patting her silky hair, thinking I would rather adopt her myself than leave her alone with this brute. What could be a better way to help an orphan than to give them a home and a doting mother, even if she's still a bit young and maybe not all that mature? Angelina adopted three children, so I should be able to adopt this one, especially since she practically chose me.

I was in the middle of a fantasy of introducing my parents to their new grandchild, right at the part where my dad has a massive coronary, when a heavy hand landed on my shoulder.

"Harden! Jesus, you almost gave me a heart attack."

Harden's face was as red as if he was having a heart attack himself. He had both our bags over one shoulder, and he looked all sweaty, like he'd just run a mile. "I've been lookin' for you everywhere. It's the last boardin' call, and we gotta go. Right now."

"Already? But I thought—"

"Isa, please, let's just go." He grabbed my hand.

"Sorry, Harden. I can't. I found this girl." I jerked out of his grip to point out the kid, still playing hide-and-seek in my mom jeans. "She's lost, and I have to wait until her parents come and get her." I decided not to divulge my plans for assembling an international brood.

That derailed him for less than a second. "Can't you leave her with the security guard?" He nodded to the guy behind the desk.

"No," I said in a guttural growl, giving the guard a foul look for good measure. He didn't look up from his paper.

"Why not?"

"Because. How do I know they'll find her parents and not just send her off to some orphanage?"

"C'mon, Isa. We're in a tightly secure airport. You don't think her parents left without her, do you? I'm sure they're nearby."

"Where?" I swept my arm around the place. "We've been waiting here forever. Like, at least five minutes. Maybe even six."

A woman's voice overhead said something in Hindi. I wasn't paying attention until my name jarred my ears. She confirmed in English that Isa-bela Max-vel and Har-don Kala-gun better get their asses on the plane before it left without them.

"I can't leave her," I said. The girl, as if sensing we were talking about her, pulled away from my butt and looked up at me with those huge dark eyes.

That's why she looks so familiar. The little girl wasn't a model—but she could have been a little sister of the one whose photo was still in my travel bag.

"She'll be fine," Harden assured me and pulled on my elbow.

"You don't know that," I said, and shrugged his arm away. "How can you be so callous, Harden? Of all people, I expected better from you."

"I'm not callous," he said, wounded. "It's just there are authorities in charge of this kind of thing. Like child protection services, or somethin'."

"Sure, but I've met a few authorities in my short time here, and I'm doubting how good they are at what they're supposed to do." I gave the security guard another evil look. He demonstratively flipped a page and buried his face in it.

"*Maamii!*" The girl let go of my hand and darted off.

I spun around, ready to run after her, but she was already in the hands of another woman. The woman was dark-haired and pretty enough to be the girl's mother, although she was not much older than me. For a split second, I wanted to question her relationship with the kid, and maybe ask for some proof of identity, but they were so wrapped up in each other, it seemed pointless.

"Thank God," Harden said behind me. "Let's go."

I turned to face him. "I can't, Harden. I'm sorry."

"Why not? She's fine now." I looked over my shoulder, hoping the girl would at least wave goodbye, but she just kept wailing into her mother's chest. The guard continued to closely examine his paper. There wasn't going to be any acknowledgment of my heroics.

"She's fine," I said, "but that other girl is not."

"What girl?"

I slipped my bag off his shoulder and took the envelope from the front pocket.

"You can't be serious," Harden said. "You're not still talkin' about that hostage story the FBI concocted to lure you in."

"They were not luring! And keep your voice down, it's classified."

He puffed. "Is this about Nikhil?"

"What?"

"Nikhil. You know exactly who I'm talkin' about."

"You mean Agent Asshole? What about him? What are you trying to say?" I knew what he was suggesting, but it was so ridiculous I simply couldn't say it out loud.

"I don't know. I thought … I mean, he bought you gifts and the next thing I know, you start actin' weird. Am I wrong? I saw the looks you gave him."

"What looks? I hate that dude! I told you, I pistol-whipped him, and

I'd do it again, easy. And anyway, since when am I forbidden to look at others? Who are you, my dad?"

"No," he said. "But I hoped I was somethin' to you."

I searched his face for a sign that he was kidding again, but there was nothing, except for the pressed-lip seriousness. "You are, Harden. You're my best friend in the whole world."

"Then forget Nikhil and come with me to Cambodia."

Oh my God, are you jealous? I bit my lip. "I want to, Harden. I'd love nothing more than to travel the world with you and not worry about getting shot."

"Then why won't you do that? Just enjoy your life, without constantly tryin' to prove yourself, or sacrifice yourself to a cause."

Why can't I just enjoy my life? I didn't have the ready answer for that question. Someone smart, with more than an associate degree, would have connected it to my overbearing father, or that time Tiffany made fun of my sweater in front of the whole class. All I knew was that I couldn't afford to be content with what I had, which at that point was a whole lot of nothing.

"I don't know, Harden. It's just that … what if this is my one chance to do something important? I'm talking international-scale history-in-the-making big. What if I pass this up, and nothing like this ever comes along again? I don't want to be an old woman regretting this decision till the day I die."

He grimaced as if I'd punched him. "I had no idea you felt like this."

"It didn't come out right," I said. "I didn't mean I'd regret spending time with you, I meant I'd regret not doing the right thing. You understand that, don't you?"

He looked into my eyes, and I could see him laboring over his answer. "Oh, I understand all right," he said after a moment. "I won't stand in your way, Isa—and I sure as hell don't wanna be your biggest regret."

"You're not," I said, but he just turned around and walked away.

I wanted to run after him, grab his arm, and tell him I would never regret *him*. That he was the most important person in my life. I wanted to explain the pain I felt from the pressure of being the chosen one. I couldn't.

I had a phone call to make.

Dear Reader,

Thank you for reading my book—I'd love to hear about your thoughts and reactions. Please leave an Amazon review, or if you want to be notified about the release of the next installment in Isa Maxwell Escapades series, sign up for my newsletter at anaspoke.com.

Until next time,

Ana Spoke

www.ingramcontent.com/pod-product-compliance
Lightning Source LLC
Chambersburg PA
CBHW031620040426
42452CB00007B/594